Mastering Swift 3 - Linux

Learn to build fast and robust applications on the Linux platform with Swift

Jon Hoffman

BIRMINGHAM - MUMBAI

Mastering Swift 3 - Linux

First published: January 2017

Production reference: 1281216

Published by Packt Publishing Ltd.
Livery Place
35 Livery Street
Birmingham
B3 2PB, UK.
ISBN 978-1-78646-141-4

www.packtpub.com

Credits

Author

Jon Hoffman

Reviewers

Andrea Prearo
Doug Sparling

Commissioning Editor

Ashwin Nair

Acquisition Editor

Smeet Thakkar

Content Development Editor

Sumeet Sawant

Technical Editor

Egan Lobo

Copy Editor

Safis Editing

Project Coordinator

Shweta H Birwatkar

Proofreader

Safis Editing

Indexer

Aishwarya Gangawane

Graphics

Disha Haria

Production Coordinator

Nilesh Mohite

About the Author

Jon Hoffman has over 20 years of experience in the field of information technology. Over these 20 years, Jon has worked in the areas of system administration, network administration, network security, application development, and architecture. Currently, Jon works as a senior software engineer for Syn-Tech Systems.

Jon has developed extensively for the iOS platform since 2008. This includes several apps that he has published in the App Store, apps that he has written for third parties, and numerous enterprise applications. What really drives Jon is the challenges that the field of information technology provides and there is nothing more exhilarating to him than overcoming a challenge.

You can follow Jon on his blogs: `http://masteringswift.blogspot.com` and `http://myro boticadventure.blogspot.com`.

Some of Jon's other interests are watching baseball (Go Sox) and basketball (Go Celtics). Jon also really enjoys Tae Kwon Do where he and his oldest daughter Kailey earned their black belts together early in 2014, Kim (his wife) earned her black belt in December 2014, and his youngest daughter is currently working towards her black belt.

I would like to thank my wonderful wife, Kim, without whose support, encouragement, patience, and understanding, this book would have never been written. I would also like to thank my two wonderful daughters, Kailey and Kara, who have both been my inspiration and driving force since the days they were born.

About the Reviewers

Andrea Prearo is a software engineer with over 15 years of experience.

He is originally from Italy, and after a decade of writing software in C/C++ and C#, he moved to the Bay Area in 2011 to start developing mobile apps.

In the last few years, he has been focusing on Swift, Objective-C, iOS, and microservices, with some short explorations of the Android platform.

Currently, he is a member of the iOS development team at Capital One, working on the company's flagship mobile banking app.

His interests include reading books, watching movies, and hiking. From time to time, he also blogs about tech on Medium: https://medium.com/@andrea.prearo.

> *I would like to thank my wonderful wife, Nicole, for her never-ending support in all my endeavors.*

Doug Sparling works as a technical architect and software developer for Andrews McMeel Universal, a publishing and syndication company in Kansas City, MO. At AMU, he uses Go for web services, Python for backend services, and Ruby on Rails and WordPress for website development, and Objective-C, Swift, and Java for native iOS and Android development. AMU's sites include www.gocomics.com, www.uexpress.com, www.puzzlesociety.com, and dilbert.com.

He also was the co-author of a Perl book, Instant Perl Modules for McGraw-Hill and a reviewer for other Packt Publishing books, including Swift Data Structure and Algorithms, jQuery 2.0 Animation Techniques: Beginner's Guide, and WordPress Web Application Development. Doug has also played various roles for Manning Publications as a reviewer, technical development editor, and proofer, working on books such as Go in Action, The Well-Grounded Rubyist 2nd Edition, iOS Development with Swift, and Programming for Musicians and Digital Artists.

www.PacktPub.com

For support files and downloads related to your book, please visit www.PacktPub.com.

Did you know that Packt offers eBook versions of every book published, with PDF and ePub files available? You can upgrade to the eBook version at www.PacktPub.com and as a print book customer, you are entitled to a discount on the eBook copy. Get in touch with us at service@packtpub.com for more details.

At www.PacktPub.com, you can also read a collection of free technical articles, sign up for a range of free newsletters and receive exclusive discounts and offers on Packt books and eBooks.

https://www.packtpub.com/mapt

Get the most in-demand software skills with Mapt. Mapt gives you full access to all Packt books and video courses, as well as industry-leading tools to help you plan your personal development and advance your career.

Why subscribe?

- Fully searchable across every book published by Packt
- Copy and paste, print, and bookmark content
- On demand and accessible via a web browser

Table of Contents

Preface

In December 2015, Apple released Swift as an open source project on its GitHub page. With this release, Apple also released a version of Swift for Linux. Swift is a general-purpose programming language that takes a modern approach to development.

What this book covers

Chapter 1, *Taking the First Steps with Swift*, gives a brief introduction to the Swift language. We will also cover the basic Swift language syntax and discuss proper language styles.

Chapter 2, *Learning About Variables, Constants, Strings, and Operators*, shows how to use variables and constants in Swift. We will also look at the various data types and how to use operators in Swift.

Chapter 3, *Using Swift Collections and the Tuple Type*, looks at how we can use the Swift collection types to store related data. These collection types are the dictionary, array and set types.

Chapter 4, *Control Flow and Functions*, covers control flow and functions in Swift. It is essential to understand the concepts in this chapter before going on. Every application that we write, beyond the simple Hello World applications, will rely very heavily on the control flow statements and functions.

Chapter 5, *Classes and Structures*, dedicates itself to Swift's classes and structures. We'll look at what makes them similar and what makes them different. We'll also look at access controls and object-oriented design. We'll close this chapter out by looking at memory management in Swift.

Chapter 6, *Using Protocols and Protocol Extensions*, covers both protocols and protocol extensions in detail since protocols are very important to the Swift language. Having a solid understanding of them will help us write flexible and reusable code.

Chapter 7, *Protocol-Oriented Design*, covers the best practices of protocol-oriented Design with Swift. It will be a brief overview of what is covered in my *Swift 3 Protocol-Oriented Programming* book.

Chapter 8, *Writing Safer Code with Error Handling*, looks at Swift's error-handling features. This feature is really important for writing safe code. While we are not required to use this feature in our custom types however it does give us a uniform manner to handle and respond to the error. Apple has also started to use this error handling in their frameworks. It is recommended that we use error handling in our code.

Chapter 9, *Custom Subscripting,* discusses how we can use custom subscripts in our classes, structures, and enumerations. Subscripts in Swift can be used to access elements in a collection. We can also define custom subscripts for our classes, structures, and enumerations.

Chapter 10, *Using Optional Types,* explains what optional types really are, what the various ways to unwrap them are, and optional chaining. For a developer who is just learning Swift, optional types can be one of the most confusing items to learn.

Chapter 11, *Working with Generics,* explains how Swift implements generics. Generics allow us to write very flexible and reusable code that avoids duplication.

Chapter 12, *Working with Closures,* teaches us how to define and use closures in our code. Closures in Swift are similar to blocks in Objective-C except that they have a much cleaner and easier to use syntax. We will conclude this chapter with a section on how to avoid strong reference cycles with closures.

Chapter 13, *Using C Libraries with Swift,* explains how we can link and use standard C libraries with our Swift applications. This gives Swift developers access to all of the same libraries that Linux C developers have access to.

Chapter 14, *Concurrency and Parallelism in Swift,* shows how to use **Grand Central Dispatch (GCD)** to add concurrency and parallelism to our applications. Understanding and knowing how to add concurrency and parallelism to our apps can significantly enhance the user experience.

Chapter 15, *Swift's Core Libraries,* explains how to use the Swift core libraries, including reading/writing files, network primitives, and JSON parsing.

Chapter 16, *Swift on Single Board Computers,* shows how we can use Swift to develop IoT devices and robots using a single board computer.

Chapter 17, *Swift Formatting and Style Guide,* defines a style guide for the Swift language that can be used as a template for enterprise developers who need to create a style guide, since most enterprises have style guides for the various languages that they develop in.

Chapter 18, *Adopting Design Patterns in Swift,* shows you how to implement some of the more common design patterns in Swift. A design pattern identifies a common software development problem and provides a strategy for dealing with it.

What you need for this book

To follow along with the samples in this book, the reader will need a computer that has Ubuntu 14.04, 15.10, 16.04, or 16.10 installed. To follow along with the samples in Chapter 16, *Swift on Single Board Computers*, the reader will need a BeagleBone Black or Green single board computer and the additional components mentioned in the chapter.

Who this book is for

Swift is a modern, fast, and safe open source language created by Apple. This book is for Linux developers who are interested in learning how to use Swift to quickly create exciting applications for the desktop, server, and embedded Linux platforms. This book will be written for developers who learn best by working with code, as every topic discussed will be reinforced with code samples.

Conventions

In this book, you will find a number of text styles that distinguish between different kinds of information. Here are some examples of these styles and an explanation of their meaning.

Code words in text, database table names, folder names, filenames, file extensions, pathnames, dummy URLs, user input, and Twitter handles are shown as follows: "We can change the value of the `highTemperture` variable without an error because it is a variable"

A block of code is set as follows:

```
var x = 3.14      // Double type
var y = "Hello"   // String type
var z = true      // Boolean type
```

When we wish to draw your attention to a particular part of a code block, the relevant lines or items are set in bold:

```
<head>
<script src="d3.js" charset="utf-8"></script>
  <meta charset="utf-8">
  <meta name="viewport" content="width=device-width">
  <title>JS Bin</title>
</head>
```

Any command-line input or output is written as follows:

```
sudo mkdir swift
```

New terms and **important words** are shown in bold. Words that you see on the screen, for example, in menus or dialog boxes, appear in the text like this: "In order to download new modules, we will go to **Files** | **Settings** | **Project Name** | **Project Interpreter**."

Warnings or important notes appear in a box like this.

Tips and tricks appear like this.

Reader feedback

Feedback from our readers is always welcome. Let us know what you think about this book-what you liked or disliked. Reader feedback is important for us as it helps us develop titles that you will really get the most out of. To send us general feedback, simply e-mail feedback@packtpub.com, and mention the book's title in the subject of your message. If there is a topic that you have expertise in and you are interested in either writing or contributing to a book, see our author guide at www.packtpub.com/authors.

Customer support

Now that you are the proud owner of a Packt book, we have a number of things to help you to get the most from your purchase.

Downloading the example code

You can download the example code files for this book from your account at http://www.packtpub.com. If you purchased this book elsewhere, you can visit http://www.packtpub.com/support and register to have the files e-mailed directly to you.

You can download the code files by following these steps:

1. Log in or register to our website using your e-mail address and password.
2. Hover the mouse pointer on the **SUPPORT** tab at the top.
3. Click on **Code Downloads & Errata**.
4. Enter the name of the book in the **Search** box.

5. Select the book for which you're looking to download the code files.
6. Choose from the drop-down menu where you purchased this book from.
7. Click on **Code Download**.

Once the file is downloaded, please make sure that you unzip or extract the folder using the latest version of:

- WinRAR / 7-Zip for Windows
- Zipeg / iZip / UnRarX for Mac
- 7-Zip / PeaZip for Linux

The code bundle for the book is also hosted on GitHub at `https://github.com/PacktPublishing/Mastering-Swift-3-Linux`. We also have other code bundles from our rich catalog of books and videos available at `https://github.com/PacktPublishing/`. Check them out!

Downloading the color images of this book

We also provide you with a PDF file that has color images of the screenshots/diagrams used in this book. The color images will help you better understand the changes in the output. You can download this file from `https://www.packtpub.com/sites/default/files/downloads/MasteringSwift3Linux_ColorImages.pdf`.

Errata

Although we have taken every care to ensure the accuracy of our content, mistakes do happen. If you find a mistake in one of our books-maybe a mistake in the text or the code- we would be grateful if you could report this to us. By doing so, you can save other readers from frustration and help us improve subsequent versions of this book. If you find any errata, please report them by visiting `http://www.packtpub.com/submit-errata`, selecting your book, clicking on the **Errata Submission Form** link, and entering the details of your errata. Once your errata are verified, your submission will be accepted and the errata will be uploaded to our website or added to any list of existing errata under the Errata section of that title.

To view the previously submitted errata, go to `https://www.packtpub.com/books/content/support` and enter the name of the book in the search field. The required information will appear under the **Errata** section.

Piracy

Piracy of copyrighted material on the Internet is an ongoing problem across all media. At Packt, we take the protection of our copyright and licenses very seriously. If you come across any illegal copies of our works in any form on the Internet, please provide us with the location address or website name immediately so that we can pursue a remedy.

Please contact us at `copyright@packtpub.com` with a link to the suspected pirated material.

We appreciate your help in protecting our authors and our ability to bring you valuable content.

Questions

If you have a problem with any aspect of this book, you can contact us at `questions@packtpub.com`, and we will do our best to address the problem.

1

Taking the First Steps with Swift

Ever since I was 12 years old and wrote my first program in the BASIC language, programming has been a passion for me. Even as programming became my career, it always remained more of a passion than a job, but over the past few years, that passion has waned. I was unsure why I was losing that passion. I attempted to recapture it with some of my side projects, but nothing really brought back the excitement that I used to have. Then, something wonderful happened! Apple announced Swift, which is an exciting and progressive language that has brought a lot of that passion back and made programming fun for me again. Now that Apple has released Swift for Linux, I can use it for most of my projects.

In this chapter, you will learn the following topics:

- What is Swift?
- Some of the features of Swift
- How to get started with Swift
- What are the basic syntaxes of the Swift language?

What is Swift?

Swift is Apple's new programming language that was introduced at the **Worldwide Developers Conference** (**WWDC**) in 2014, alongside the integrated development environment Xcode 6 and iOS 8. Swift was arguably the most significant announcement at WWDC 2014, and very few people, including Apple insiders, were aware of the project's existence prior to it being announced. In this initial release of Swift it could only be used to develop applications for the Apple platforms.

It was amazing, even by Apple's standards, that they were able to keep Swift a secret for as long as they did, and no one suspected that they were going to announce a new development language. At WWDC 2015, Apple made another big splash when they announced Xcode 7 and Swift 2. Swift 2 was a major enhancement to the language. During that conference, *Chris Lattner* said that a lot of enhancements were based directly on feedback that Apple received from the development community. It was also announced at WWDC 2015 that Apple would be releasing Swift as open source, and they would be offering a port for Linux.

In December 2015, Apple officially released Swift as an open source project with the `swift.org` site dedicated to the open source Swift community. The Swift repository is located on Apple's github page (`http://github.com/apple`). The Swift evolution repository (`https://github.com/apple/swift-evolution`) tracks the evolution of the Swift language by documenting all of the proposed changes. You can also find a list of proposals that were accepted and rejected in this repository. If you are interested in understanding where Swift is heading, then you should check out this repository. It is interesting to note that Swift 3 contains several enhancements that were proposed by the community.

Swift 3 is a major enhancement to the language and is **NOT** source-compatible with previous releases. It contains fundamental changes to the language itself and to the Swift standard library. One of the main goals of Swift 3 is to be source-compatible across all platforms, so the code that we write for one platform will be compatible with all other platforms that Swift supports. This means that the code we develop for Mac OS will also work on Linux.

Development on Swift was started in 2010 by *Chris Lattner*. He implemented much of the basic language structure with only a few people being aware of its existence. It wasn't until late 2011 that other developers began to really contribute to Swift, and in July 2013, it became a major focus of the Apple Developer Tools group.

There are a lot of similarities between Swift and Objective-C. Swift adopts the readability of Objective-C's named parameters and its dynamic object model. When we refer to Swift as having a dynamic object model, we are referring to its ability to change at runtime. This includes adding new (custom) types and changing/extending the existing types.

While there are a lot of similarities between Swift and Objective-C, there are also significant differences between them as well. Swift's syntax and formatting are a lot closer to Python than Objective-C, but Apple did keep the curly braces. I know that Python people would disagree with me, and that is all right because we all have different opinions, but I like the curly braces. Swift actually makes the curly braces required for control statements such as `if` and `while`, which eliminates bugs, such as the `goto fail` in Apple's SSL library, which Apple patched in 2014.

Swift's features

When Apple said that Swift is Objective-C without the C, they were really only telling us half the story. Objective-C is a superset of C and provides object-oriented capabilities and a dynamic runtime to the C language. This means that, with Objective-C, Apple needed to maintain compatibility with C, which limited the enhancements it could make to the Objective-C language. As an example, Apple could not change how the `switch` statement functioned and still maintains the C compatibility.

Since Swift does not need to maintain the same C compatibility as Objective-C, Apple was free to add any feature/enhancement to the language. This allowed Apple to include the best features from many of today's most popular and modern languages, such as Objective-C, Python, Java, Ruby, C#, and Haskell.

The following chart shows a list of some of the most exciting enhancements that Swift includes:

Swift feature	Description
Type inference	Swift can automatically deduce the type of the variable or constant, based on the initial value.
Generics	Generics allow us to write the code only once to perform identical tasks for different types of objects.
Collection mutability	Swift does not have separate objects for mutable or nonmutable containers. Instead, you define mutability by defining the container as a constant or variable.
Closure syntax	Closures are self-contained blocks of functionality that can be passed around and used in our code.
Optionals	Optionals define a variable that might not have a value.
Switch statement	The Switch statement has been drastically improved. This is one of my favorite improvements.

Multiple return types	Functions can have multiple return types using tuples.
Operator overloading	Classes can provide their own implementation of existing operators.
Enumerations with Associated values	In Swift, we can do a lot more than just defining a group of related values with enumerations.

Before we can look at the Swift language itself, we need to download and install it. Let's look at how we can install Swift.

Installing Swift 3 for Linux

The following instructions were current when this book was written and works for both Ubuntu 15.10 and Ubuntu 16.04 LTS. The most up-to-date installation instructions can be found on the `swift.org` installation page: `https://swift.org/getting-started/#instal ling-swift`.

The first step in installing Swift is to install `clang` and configure it. The following are the commands:

```
sudo apt-get update
sudo apt-get install clang-3.6
sudo update-alternatives -install /usr/bin/clang clang
/usr/bin/clang-3.6 100
sudo update-alternatives -install /usr/bin/clang++ clang++
/usr/bin/clang++-3.6 100
```

If you forget to do the `update-alternatives` commands, you will receive an `error: invalid inferred toolchain` error when you try to build a package. Forgetting to run the `update-alternatives` commands is a very common error.

Now that we have the correct clang installed, we need to download Swift. You can download the latest version from the `swift.org` download page. The link for this page is: `https://swift.org/download/`.

Once you have downloaded Swift, you can install it in the location of your choice; however, you will want to avoid installing it off the root directory because that may overwrite the /usr directory. As a personal preference, I like to install Swift in the /opt directory. The following instructions will show how I install Swift.

 Anytime you see {swift version}, substitute it for the version information of the Swift you are installing.

1. Go to the /opt directory:

```
cd /opt
```

2. Create a directory to hold this and all future Swift versions:

```
sudo mkdir swift
```

3. Change to the swift directory, and copy the downloaded swift file to this location:

```
cd swift
sudo cp -R ~/Downloads/swift-{swift version}.tar.gz ./
```

4. Gunzip and untar the swift file:

```
tar -zxvf  swift-{swift version}.tar.gz
```

5. The last command should have created a new directory that contains the Swift files. We will now want to create a symbolic link to this directory indicating that it is our current version of Swift:

```
sudo ln -s /opt/swift-{swift version} swift-current
```

6. All of the files in the swift directory are owned by the root user. If you attempt to build a Swift package with the package manager, while all of the files are owned by root, you will receive a permission denied error. The easiest way to fix this is to change the ownership of the Swift files to your user. If you want to give permission for multiple users to use Swift, you can add write permissions for all users. Instructions for both options are listed here and you only need to follow one of them:

```
//Change ownership of the Swift files
sudo chown -R {username}:{username} swift-{swift version}
//Alternatively change write permission
sudo chmod -R +x swift-{swift-version}
```

7. Now, we need to add Swift to our path. To do this you will have to edit your `~/.profile` file and add the following line to it:

```
PATH=/opt/swift/swift-current/usr/bin:$PATH
```

8. You can either start a new terminal session to pick up the changes or run the following command in your current session:

```
. ~/.profile
```

To verify everything is good, run the `swift -version` command, which should output your new version of Swift. When a new version of Swift is released, install it to the `/opt/swift` directory and then change the swift-current symbolic link to point to this new version.

Swift language syntax

The Swift language uses modern concepts and syntax to create very concise and readable code. There is also a heavy emphasis on eliminating many common programming mistakes. Before we look at the Swift language itself, let's take a look at some of the basic syntax of the language.

Comments

When we write comments for Swift code, we can use the traditional double slash `//` for single-line comments and the `/*` and `*/` for multi-line comments. If we want to use the comments to also document our code, we need to use the triple slash `///`.

When we write our code on a Linux computer, we do not have access to the Xcode IDE. However, since the code we write for Linux can be compatible with Apple's platforms it is a good habit to comment our code in such a manner that it will be recognized in the Xcode IDE.

 This book is about using Swift for Linux, therefore we try to avoid any functionality that requires an Apple computer or an iPad. We do however use Playgrounds and Xcode in this section to illustrate how comments can be used for documentation on the Apple platform so we will understand why the format is important.

To document our code, we can use the following specific fields that Xcode recognizes:

- **Parameter**: When we start a line with `- parameter {param name}`, Xcode recognizes this as the description for a parameter
- **Return**: When we start a line with `- return:`, Xcode recognizes this as the description for the return value
- **Throws**: When we start a line with `- throws:`, Xcode recognizes this as the description for the errors that this method may throw

This example shows both single-line and multi-line comments and how to use the comment fields:

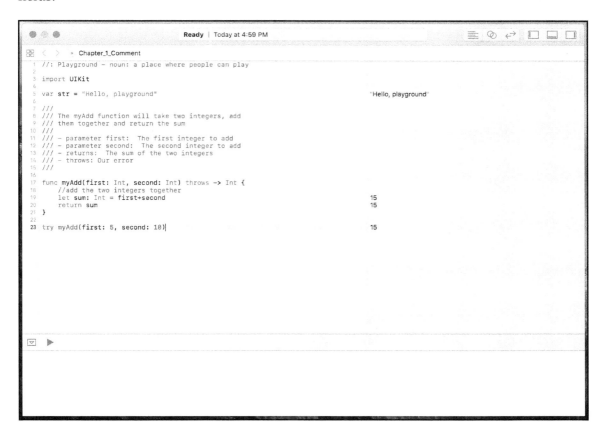

To write good comments, I would recommend using single-line comments within a function to give quick one-line explanations of your code. We will then use multi-line comments outside functions and classes to explain what the function and types do. The preceding Playground shows a good use of comments. When we use proper code comments, as we did in the preceding screenshot, we can take advantage of the documentation feature within Xcode. If we hold down the *option* key and then click on the function name anywhere in our code, Xcode will display a popup with a description of the function.

The next screenshot shows what that popup looks like:

```
 6
 7  ///
 8  /// The myAdd function will take two integers, add
 9  /// them together and return the sum
10  ///
11  /// - parameter first:  The first integer to add
12  /// - parameter second:  The second integer to add
13  /// - returns:  The sum of the two integers
14  /// - throws: Our error
15  ///
16
17  func myAdd(first: Int, second: Int) throws -> Int {
18      //add the two integers together
```

Declaration	func myAdd(first: Int, second: Int) throws -> Int
Description	The myAdd function will take two integers, add them together and return the sum
Parameters	first The first integer to add
	second The second integer to add
Throws	Our error
Returns	The sum of the two integers
Declared In	Chapter_1_Comment.playground

This screenshot shows the documentation feature of Xcode if we hold down the *option* key and then click on the `myAdd()` method. We can see that the documentation contains six fields. These fields are as follows:

- **Declaration**: This is the function's declaration (that is, its signature)
- **Description**: This is the description of the function as it appears in the comments

- **Parameters**: The parameter descriptions are prefixed with the – `Parameters:` tag in the comment section
- **Throws**: The throws description is prefixed with the – `throws:` tag and describes what errors are thrown by the methods
- **Returns**: The return description is prefixed with the – `returns:` tag in the comment section
- **Declared In**: This is the file that the function is declared in, so that we can easily find it

Semicolons

You may have noticed, from the code samples so far, that we are not using semicolons at the end of lines. Semicolons are optional in Swift; therefore, both lines in the following code are valid in Swift:

```
print("Hello from Swift")
print("Hello from Swift");
```

For style purposes, it is strongly recommended that you do not use semicolons in your Swift code. If you are really set on using semicolons in your code, then be consistent and use them in every line of the code; however, Swift will not warn you if you forget them. I will stress again that it is recommended that you do not use semicolons in Swift.

Parentheses

In Swift, parentheses around conditional statements are optional; for example, both `if` statements in the following code are valid:

```
var x = 1

if x == 1 {
    print("x == 1")
}

if (x == 1) {
    print("x == 1")
}
```

For style purposes, it is recommended that you do not include the parentheses in your code unless you have multiple conditional statements on the same line. For readability purposes, it is a good practice to put parentheses around the individual conditional statements that are on the same line.

Curly brackets

In Swift, unlike most other languages, curly brackets are required after conditional or loop statements. This is one of the safety features that is built into Swift. Arguably, there have been numerous security bugs that might have been prevented if the developer had used curly braces. These bugs could also have been prevented by other means, such as unit testing and code reviews, but requiring developers to use curly braces, in my opinion, is a good security standard.

The following code shows how to use curly brackets:

```
let x = 1

//Valid
if x == 1 {
    print("x == 1")
}

//Not Valid
if x == 1
    print("x == 1")
```

Assignment operators do not return a value

In most other languages, the following line of code is valid, but it is probably not what the developer meant to do:

```
if (x = 1) {}
```

You can download the example code files from your account at http://www.packtpub.com for all the Packt Publishing books you purchased. If you purchased this book from elsewhere, you can visit http://www.packtpub.com/support and register to have the files e-mailed directly to you.

In Swift, this statement is invalid. Using an assignment operator (=) in a conditional statement (if and while) will throw an error. This is another safety feature built into Swift. It prevents the developer from forgetting the second equal to sign (=) in a comparison statement.

Spaces are optional in conditional and assignment statements

For both conditional (if and while) and assignment (=) statements, white spaces are optional. Therefore, in the following code, both The i block and The j block code blocks are valid:

```
//The i block
var i=1
if i==1 {
    print("HI")
}

//The j block
var j = 1
if j == 1 {
    print("HI")
}
```

 For style purposes, I would recommend adding the white spaces (such as The j block) for readability, but as long as you pick one style and are consistent, either style should be acceptable.

Hello World

All good computer books that are written to teach a programming language have a section that shows a user how to write a Hello World application. This book is no exception. In this section, we will show you how to write a Hello World application with Swift.

Let's begin by creating a new file named main.swift. The main.swift file is a special file in Swift and is the entry point for our application. It is the only file that can contain top-level code. Top-level code is the code that is not part of a function or type (enumeration, class, or structure). All of the code for our Hello World application is considered top-level code.

In Swift, to print a message to the console, we use the `print()` function. In its most basic form, we would use the print function to print out a single message as shown in the following code:

```
print("Hello World")
```

Usually, when we use the `print()` function, we want to print more than just static text. We can include the value of variables and/or constants using a special sequence of characters, \( ), or by separating the values within the `print()` function with commas. The following code shows how to do this:

```
var name = "Jon"
var language = "Swift"

var message1 = "Welcome to the wonderful world of "
var message2 = "\(name) Welcome to the wonderful world of \(language)!"

print(name, message1, language, "!")
print(message2)
```

In order to compile this code, it will need to be in a file name `main.swift`. You can use any text editor, like emacs or VI, to create this file. Once the `main.swift` file is created, we will need to build our Hello World application. Type the following line in the same directory where the `main.swift` file is located:

swiftc main.swift

Once the swift compiler finishes building the application, we will have an executable file named `main` in our directory. We can run the file using the following command:

./main

If all goes well, you can see the following output:

```
Jon Welcome to the wonderful world of Swift!
Jon Welcome to the wonderful world of Swift!
```

We will look at the `swift` and `swiftc` commands later in this chapter.

We can also define two parameters in the `print` function that change how the message is displayed in the console. These parameters are the `separator` and `terminator` parameters. The `separator` parameter defines a string that is used to separate the values of the variable/constant in the `print()` function. By default, the `print()` function separates each variable/constant with a space. The `terminator` parameter defines which character is inserted at the end of the line. By default, the newline character is added at the end of the line.

The following code shows how we could create a comma-separated list that does not have a newline character at the end:

```
var name1 = "Jon"
var name2 = "Kim"
var name3 = "Kailey"
var name4 = "Kara"

print(name1, name2, name3, name4, separator:", ", terminator:"")
```

There is one other parameter that we can add to our `print()` function. This is the `toStream` parameter. This parameter will let us redirect the output of the `print()` function. In the following example, we redirect the output to a variable named `line`:

```
var name1 = "Jon"
var name2 = "Kim"
var name3 = "Kailey"
var name4 = "Kara"

var line = ""

print(name1, name2, name3, name4, separator:", ",  terminator:"", to:&line)
```

The `print()` function was simply a useful tool for basic debugging, but now we can use the new enhanced `print()` function a lot more.

Executing Swift code

In the next couple of sections, we will look at the various ways in which we can execute our Swift code. We could easily write a complete book on these tools; however, in this section, we will give a brief overview of each tool, so you will be aware of how to use them to execute your code or build your applications. After reading these sections, you should be able to build and execute the examples in this book, as well as your own applications.

Swift and the Swift REPL

There are a couple of ways in which you can quickly experiment with Swift code. The first is the Swift interactive **Read Evaluate Print Loop** (**REPL**). The REPL is a command line tool that evaluates our code as we write it. Developers who are used to interpreting languages will be comfortable using this tool.

To start the REPL, you will need to open a terminal prompt and enter the following command:

```
swift
```

You will be greeted with a prompt similar to the following:

```
Welcome to Swift version 3.0 ({your-swift-version}). Type :help for
assistance
1>
```

From here, we can type in any Swift statement and hit *Enter*. The REPL will immediately execute our code. The following is an example:

```
1>  var x = 10
x: Int = 10
2>  x += 5
3>  print(x)
15
```

To exit the REPL, type the following command:

```
:quit
```

We can also quickly test a Swift source file using the swift command. To try this out, create a file named Hello.swift, and put the following code in it:

```
print("Hello")
```

Now let's run the following command to execute this source file:

```
swift Hello.swift
```

You should see the message Hello printed to the console. The REPL and Swift commands are extremely powerful tools, and you can do a lot more than just prototyping new code. If you find these tools useful, I would recommend spending time learning about the various advanced features.

Swift compiler

When we run our code using the swift command, or the Swift REPL tool, we are running the code as we would run a typical interpreted script such as a **Bourne Again SHell** (**BASH**) or Python script. This is really nice if we want to use Swift as a scripting language but if we want to build applications with Swift, we will need to compile our code into an executable form. To do this, we can use the Swift compiler.

Let's see how we would use the Swift compiler to build the Hello World example that we created earlier. If you recall from that example, we had to create a main.swift file. While using a main.swift file is not required for an application that only contains a single source file, it is required for applications that contain multiple source files. The Swift compiler will look for the main.swift and use it as the entry point for the application, similar to how a C compiler uses the main() function.

> It is a good habit, when all of our code is contained in one file, to name that file main.swift.

To build the Hello World application that we created earlier, we would need to run the following command in the same directory that the main.swift file is in:

```
swiftc main.swift
```

This command should only take a second or so to run. Once it is completed, we should have an executable file named main. If your application contains multiple files, you can list them one by one as follows:

```
swiftc main.swift file1.swift file2.swift file3.swift
```

If you want to change the name of the output file, you can use the -o option as follows:

```
swiftc main.swift file1.swift file2.swift -o myexecutable
```

There are a number of command line options that you can use with the swift compiler. However, if you find that you are using a lot of command line options and making a complex compiler statement, you may want to look at the Swift Package Manager.

Using the Swift Package Manger

According to Apple, the Swift Package Manager is defined as:

> *A tool for managing the distribution of Swift code. It's integrated with the Swift build system to automate the process of downloading, compiling, and linking dependencies.*

The first part of the previous statement means that the Swift Package Manager can be used to manage the distribution of modules. Some applications may have all their code organized into a single module. More complex applications may separate their code into different modules. As an example, if you were developing an application that communicates with another device over Bluetooth, you may want to put the Bluetooth code into a separate module, so you can reuse it in other applications.

The Swift Package Manager will manage module or application dependencies and will automate the process of downloading, compiling, and linking these dependencies. This allows us to concentrate on our code rather than figuring out how to write complex build scripts to compile our applications or modules.

A package consists of the Swift source files and a manifest file called `Package.swift`. The manifest file defines the package's name and contains instructions on how to build the package. We can customize the manifest file to declare build targets or dependencies, include or exclude source files, and specify build configurations for the module or application.

Let's look at how we can use the Package Manager to create a simple application. Firstly, we need to decide how we will name the application. For our example, we will use the name `PMExample`. Let's create a directory with that name and then change to that directory:

```
mkdir PMExample
cd PMExample
```

Now, we need to build the framework that the Package Manager needs. To do this, we will run the following command:

```
swift package init
```

This command will create both the `Sources` and `Tests` directory. It will also create a number of files including the `Package.swift` manifest file and also a file in the `Sources` directory with the same name as your application. If you look at the `Package.swift` manifest file, it should look as follows:

```
import PackageDescription
let package = Package( name: "PMExample" )
```

This is the most basic manifest file, and it simply defines the name for the package. We will look at this manifest file in greater depth in Chapter 13, *Using C Libraries with Swift*.

Now, let's look at the `PMExample.swift` that was created for us in the `Sources` directory. It should contain code similar to the following code:

```
struct PMExample {
    var text = "Hello, World!"
}
```

Let's add some code to this file, so it contains the following code:

```
struct PMExample {
    var text = "Hello, World!"
    func sayHello() {
        print(text)
    }
}
```

All we did in this example was add a method that prints `Hello, World!` to the console.

 Don't worry if you do not understand this code yet. We are looking to get you familiar with the Package Manager and the compiler, so you feel comfortable compiling the code examples in this book.

Now let's add the `main.swift` file to the `Sources` directory. This will be the entry point to our application. Add the following code to this file:

```
let example = PMExample()
example.sayHello()
```

Now, go back to the `PMExample` directory, and run the following command to build the PMExample application.

```
swift build
```

This will build the application. If all is well, we will have an executable application in the `PMExample/.build/debug` directory named `PMExample`.

Note that, in the `PMExample.swift` file, all of the code was contained in the `PMExample` structure, whereas the code in the `main.swift` file was top-level code. Remember what we noted earlier: the `main.swift` file is the only file that can contain top-level code.

We only scratched the surface of what the Package Manager can do in this section. We will look at it further in Chapter 13, *Using C Libraries with Swift*.

When all of the source code is in one file, it will be much easier to use the swift compiler to build your executable code; however, once your application grows past that single source file, I would recommend looking at the Package Manager to manage your dependencies and your builds.

Editors for Swift

You can use pretty much any text editor such as VI, Emacs, or gedit to write your Swift code. It can be pretty painful at times to use these text editors to write code, especially when you are accustomed to using standard IDEs, which come with code completion. If you want to spend a little money, you could get an IDE (such as CLion) that comes with a Swift plugin, but there is one free code editor that works really well with Swift. That editor is Visual Studio Code from Microsoft.

Yes, Microsoft makes a free code editor that can run on Linux and can edit Swift files (are you as surprised as I was?). I was pretty skeptical at first, but once I started using it, I realized that it was the best Swift editor for Linux that I could find at the time I wrote this book. To download Visual Studio Code, you can go to `https://code.visualstudio.com`, and select the download link. Keep in mind that, when we use Visual Studio Code to write applications in Swift, it is nothing more than a code editor. We cannot run or debug our code from within Visual Studio Code.

Hopefully, as more developers use Swift on Linux, we will begin to see some good developer tools emerge.

Summary

In this chapter, we showed you how to start and use Playgrounds to experiment with Swift programming. We also covered the basic Swift language syntax and discussed proper language styles. The chapter concluded with two Hello World examples.

In the next chapter, we will see how to use variables and constants in Swift. We will also look at the various data types, and how to use operators in Swift.

2
Learning About Variables, Constants, Strings, and Operators

The first program that I ever wrote was written in the BASIC programming language, and it was the typical Hello World application. This application was pretty exciting at first, but the excitement of printing static text wore off pretty quickly. For my second application, I used BASIC's input command to prompt the user for a name and then printed out a custom hello message to the user with their name in it. At the age of 12, it was pretty cool to display Hello Han Solo. This application led me to create numerous Mad Lib style applications that prompted the user for various words and then put those words into a story that was displayed after the user had entered all the required words. These applications introduced me to, and taught me, the importance of variables. Every useful application that I created since then has used variables.

In this chapter, we will cover the following topics:

- What variables and constants are
- The difference between explicit and inferred typing
- Explaining numeric, string, and boolean types
- Defining optional types
- Explaining how enumerations work in Swift
- Explaining how Swift's operators work

Constants and variables

Constants and variables associate an identifier (such as `myName` or `currentTemperature`) with a value of a particular type (such as `String` or `Int`), where the identifier can be used to retrieve and set the value. The difference between a constant and variable is that a variable can be updated or changed, whereas a constant cannot be changed once a value is assigned to it.

Constants are good for defining values that you know will never change, such as the freezing temperature of water or the speed of light. Constants are also good for defining a value that we use many times throughout our application, such as a standard font size or a character limit in a buffer. There will be numerous examples of constants throughout this book.

Variables tend to be more common in software development than constants; however, this is mainly because developers tend to prefer variables to constants. In Swift, we receive a warning if we declare a variable that is never changed. We can make useful applications without using constants (although it is a good practice to use them); however, it is almost impossible to create a useful application without variables.

 The use of constants is encouraged in Swift. If we do not expect or want the value to change, we should declare it as a constant. This adds a very important safety constraint to our code, thus ensuring that the value never changes.

You can use almost any character in the identifier of a variable or constant (even Unicode characters); however, there are a few rules that you must follow:

- An identifier must not contain any whitespace
- An identifier must not contain any mathematical symbols
- An identifier must not contain any arrows
- An identifier must not contain private use or invalid Unicode characters
- An identifier must not contain line- or box-drawing characters
- An identifier must not start with a number, but it can contain numbers
- If you use a Swift keyword as an identifier, surround it with back ticks

 Keywords are words that are used by the Swift programming language. Some examples of keywords that you will see in this chapter are `var` and `let`. You should avoid using Swift keywords as identifiers to avoid confusion while reading your code.

Defining constants and variables

Constants and variables must be defined prior to using them. To define a constant, you use the keyword, `let`; to define a variable, you use the keyword, `var`. The following code shows how to define both constants and variables:

```
// Constants
let freezingTemperatureOfWaterCelsius = 0
let speedOfLightKmSec = 300000

// Variables
var currentTemperature = 22
var currentSpeed = 55
```

We can declare multiple constants or variables in a single line by separating them with a comma. For example, we could shrink the preceding four lines of a code down to two lines, as shown here:

```
// Constants
let freezingTempertureOfWaterCelsius = 0, speedOfLightKmSec = 300000

// Variables
var currentTemperture = 22, currentSpeed = 55
```

We can change the value of a variable to another value of a compatible type; however, as we noted earlier, we cannot change the value of a constant. Let's look at the following code. Can you tell what is wrong with the code?

```
let speedOfLightKmSec = 300000
var highTemperture = 93

highTemperture = 95
speedOfLightKmSec = 29999
```

Did you figure out what was wrong with the code? Any physicist can tell you that we cannot change the speed of light, and in our code, the `speedOfLightKmSec` variable is a constant, so we cannot change it here either. When we try to change the `speedOfLightKmSec` constant, an error is reported. We can change the value of the `highTemperture` variable without an error because it is a variable. We mentioned the difference between variables and constants a couple of times because it is a very important concept to grasp, especially when we define mutable and immutable collection types later in `Chapter 3`, *Using Swift Collections and the Tuple Type*.

Type safety

Swift is a type-safe language. In a type-safe language, we must be clear about the types of values we store in a variable. We will get an error if we attempt to assign a value to a variable that is of a wrong type. The following code attempts to put a string value into a variable that expects integer values; note that we will discuss the most popular types a little later in this chapter:

```
var integerVar = 10
integerVar = "My String"
```

Swift performs a type check when it compiles the code; therefore, it will flag any mismatched types with an error. So, the question is, How does Swift know that `integerVar` is of the `Int` type? Swift uses type inference to figure out the appropriate type. Let's take a look at what type inference is.

Type inference

Type inference allows us to omit the variable type when we define it. The compiler infers the type based on the initial value. For example, in the C language, we would define an integer as follows:

```
int myInt = 1
```

This tells the compiler that the `myInt` variable is of the `Int` type, and the initial value is the number 1. In Swift, we would define the same integer as follows:

```
var myInt = 1
```

Swift infers that the variable type is an integer because the initial value is an integer. Let's take a look at a couple of additional examples:

```
var x = 3.14       // Double type
var y = "Hello"    // String type
var z = true       // Boolean type
```

In the preceding example, the compiler will correctly infer that variable x is `Double`, variable y is `String`, and variable z is `Boolean` based on the initial values.

We can always check the variable type at runtime by using the `type(of:)` function. For our example, we could print out the variable types to the console as follows:

```
print(type(of: x))
print(type(of: y))
print(type(of: z))
```

This would show the following output, which confirms our expectations about the inferred variable types:

```
Double
String
Bool
```

Explicit types

Type inference is a very nice feature in Swift and is one that you will probably get used to very quickly. However, there are times when we would like to explicitly define a variable's type. For example, in the preceding example, the variable is inferred to be `Double`, but what if we wanted the variable type to be `Float`? We can explicitly define a variable type as follows:

```
var pi : Float = 3.14
```

Notice the `Float` declaration (colon and the word `Float`) after the variable identifier. This tells the compiler to define this variable to be of the `Float` type and gives it an initial value of `3.14`. When we define a variable in this manner, we need to ensure that the initial value is of the same type as the variable itself. If we try to give a variable an initial value that is of a different type than what we are defining it as, we will receive an error.

We will also need to explicitly define the variable type if we are not setting an initial value. For example, the following line of code is invalid, because the compiler does not know what type the x variable should be set to:

```
var x
```

If we use this code in our application, we will receive a `Type annotation missing in pattern` error. If we are not setting an initial value for a variable, we are required to define the type as follows:

```
var x: Int
```

Now that we have seen how to explicitly define a variable type, let's take a look at some of the most commonly used types.

Numeric types

Swift contains many of the standard numeric types that are suitable for storing various integer and floating-point values.

Integers

An integer is a whole number and can be either signed (positive, negative, or zero) or unsigned (positive or zero). Swift provides several integer types of different sizes. The following chart shows the value ranges for the different integer types:

Type	Minimum	Maximum
Int8	−128	127
Int16	−32,768	32,767
Int32	−2,147,483,648	2,147,483,647
Int64	−9,223,372,036,854,775,808	9,223,372,036,854,775,807
Int	−9,223,372,036,854,775,808	9,223,372,036,854,775,807
UInt8	0	255
UInt16	0	65,535
UInt32	0	4,294,967,295
UInt64	0	18,446,744,073,709,551,615
UInt	0	18,446,744,073,709,551,615

 Unless there is a specific reason to define the size of an integer, I would recommend using the standard `Int` or `UInt` type. This will save you from the need to convert between different types of integers.

In Swift, integers (as well as other numerical types) are actually named types and are implemented in Swift's standard library using structures. This gives us a consistent mechanism for memory management for all data types as well as properties that we can access. The following code will retrieve the min and max values for numerous Int and UInt types:

```
print("UInt8 max \(UInt8.max)")
print("UInt8 min \(UInt8.min)")

print("UInt16 max \(UInt16.max)")
print("UInt16 min \(UInt16.min)")

print("UInt32 max \(UInt32.max)")
print("UInt32 min \(UInt32.min)")

print("UInt64 max \(UInt64.max)")
print("UInt64 min \(UInt64.min)")

print("UInt max \(UInt.max)")
print("UInt min \(UInt.min)")

print("Int8 max \(Int8.max)")
print("Int8 min\(Int8.min)")

print("Int16 max \(Int16.max)")
print("Int16 min \(Int16.min)")

print("Int32 max \(Int32.max)")
print("Int32 min \(Int32.min)")

print("Int64 max \(Int64.max)")
print("Int64 min \(Int64.min)")

print("Int max \(Int.max)")
print("Int min \(Int.min)")
```

If you run the preceding code, you will get the following output:

```
UInt8 max 255
UInt8 min 0
UInt16 max 65535
UInt16 min 0
UInt32 max 4294967295
UInt32 min 0
UInt64 max 18446744073709551615
UInt64 min 0
UInt max 18446744073709551615
```

```
UInt  min  0
Int8  max  127
Int8  min-128
Int16  max  32767
Int16  min  -32768
Int32  max  2147483647
Int32  min  -2147483648
Int64  max  9223372036854775807
Int64  min  -9223372036854775808
Int  max  9223372036854775807
Int  min  -9223372036854775808
```

Integers can also be represented as binary, octal, and hexadecimal numbers. We just need to add a prefix to the number to tell the compiler which base the number should be in. The following chart shows the prefix for each numerical base:

Base	Prefix
Decimal	None
Binary	0b
Octal	0o
Hexadecimal	0x

The following code shows how the number 95 can be represented in each of the numerical bases:

```
var a = 95
var b = 0b1011111
var c = 0o137
var d = 0x5f
```

Swift also allows us to insert arbitrary underscores in our numeric literals. This can improve the readability of our code. As an example, if we are defining the speed of light, which is constant, we can define it as follows:

```
let speedOfLightKmSec = 300_000
```

Swift will ignore these underscores; therefore, they do not affect the value of the numeric literals in any way.

Floating point

A floating-point number is a number with a decimal component. There are two standard floating-point types in Swift: `Float` and `Double`. `Float` represents a 32-bit floating-point number, whereas `Double` represents a 64-bit floating-point number. Swift also supports an extended floating-point type, that is, Float80. The **Float80** type is an 80-bit floating-point number.

It is recommended that you use the `Double` type over the `Float` type unless there is a specific reason to use the latter. The `Double` type has a precision of at least 15 decimal digits, whereas the `Float` type can be as small as six decimal digits. Let's look at an example of how this can affect our application without us knowing about it. The following code adds two floating point numbers and sets the results into both a float and double constant:

```
let f: Float = 0.111_111_111 + 0.222_222_222
let d: Double = 0.111_111_111 + 0.222_222_222
```

If we ran this code and printed out the results, the `f` constant would contain `0.333_333_3`, while the `d` constant would contain `0.333_333_333`. The two decimal numbers that we are adding together contain nine digits past the decimal point; however, the results in the `Float` type only contain seven digits, while the results in the `Double` type contain all nine digits.

The loss of precision can cause issues if we are working with currency or other numbers that need accurate calculations. The floating-point accuracy is not an issue confined to Swift; all languages that implement the IEEE 754 floating-point standard have similar issues. The best practice is to use `Double` types for floating-point numbers, unless there is a specific reason not to.

What if we have two variables, one an `Int` and the other a `Double`? Do you think we can add them together as the following code depicts:

```
var a : Int = 3
var b : Double = 0.14
var c = a + b
```

If we put the preceding code into a Playground, we would receive the following error: `binary operator '+' cannot be applied to operands of type 'Int' and 'String'`.

This error lets us know that we are trying to add two different types of number, which is not allowed. To add an `Int` and a `Double` together, we need to convert the `Int` value into a `Double` value. The following code shows how to this:

```
var a : Int = 3
var b : Double = 0.14
var c = Double(a) + b
```

Note how we use the `Double()` function to convert the `Int` value to a `Double` value. All the numeric types in Swift have a conversion convenience initializer, similar to the `Double()` function shown in the preceding code sample. For example, the following code shows how you can convert an `Int` variable to `Float` and `UInt16` variables:

```
var intVar = 32
var floatVar = Float(intVar)
var uint16Var = UInt16(intVar)
```

The Boolean type

Boolean values are often referred to as logical values because they can be either `true` or `false`. Swift has a built-in Boolean type that accepts one of the two built-in Boolean constants: `true` or `false`.

Boolean constants and variables can be defined as follows:

```
let swiftIsCool = true
let swiftIsHard = false

var itIsWarm = false
var itIsRaining = true
```

Boolean values are especially useful while working with conditional statements, such as `if` and `while`. For example, what do you think this code would do?

```
let isSwiftCool = true
let isItRaining = false
if isSwiftCool {
    print("YEA, I cannot wait to learn it")
}
if isItRaining {
    print("Get a rain coat")
}
```

If you answered that this code would print out YEA, I cannot wait to learn it, then you are correct. Since isSwiftCool is set to true, the YEA, I cannot wait to learn it message is printed out, but isItRaining is false; therefore, the Get a rain coat message is not.

The String type

A string is an ordered collection of characters, such as Hello or Swift. In Swift, the String type represents a string. We have seen several examples of strings already in this book, so the following code should look familiar. This code shows how to define two strings:

```
var stringOne = "Hello"
var stringTwo = " World"
```

Since a string is an ordered collection of characters, we can iterate through each character of a string. The following code shows how to do this:

```
var stringOne = "Hello"
for char in stringOne.characters {
    print(char)
}
```

There are two ways to add one string to another string. We can concatenate them or include them inline. To concatenate two strings, we use the + or += operator. The following code shows how to concatenate two strings. The first example appends stringB to the end of stringA, and the results are put into a new stringC variable. The second example appends stringB directly to the end of stringA, without creating a new string:

```
var stringC = stringA + stringB
stringA += stringB
```

To include a string inline with another string, we use a special sequence of characters \ ( ). The following code shows how to include a string inline with another string:

```
var stringA = "Jon"
var stringB = "Hello \(stringA)"
```

In the previous example, stringB contained the message Hello Jon because Swift replaced the \(stringA) sequence of characters with the value of stringA.

In Swift, we define the mutability of variables and collections using the `var` and `let` keywords. If we define a string as a variable using `var`, the string is mutable, meaning that we can change and edit the value of the string. If we define a string as a constant using `let`, the string is immutable, meaning that we cannot change or edit the value once it is set. The following code shows the difference between a mutable and an immutable string:

```
var x = "Hello"
let y = "HI"
var z = "World"

//This is valid, x is mutable
x += z

//This is invalid, y is not mutable.
y += z
```

Strings in Swift have two methods that can convert the case of the string. These methods are called `lowercased()` and `uppercased()`. The following example shows these methods:

```
var stringOne = "hElLo"
print("Lowercase String:  " + stringOne.lowercased())
print("Uppercase String:  " + stringOne.uppercased())
```

If we run this code, the results will be as follows:

```
Lowercase String:   hello
Uppercase String:   HELLO
```

Swift provides four ways to compare a string; these are string equality, prefix equality, suffix equality, and `isEmpty`. The following example shows these methods:

```
var stringOne = "Hello Swift"
var stringTwo = ""
stringOne.isEmpty  //false
stringTwo.isEmpty  //true
stringOne == "hello swift"  //false
stringOne == "Hello Swift"  //true
stringOne.hasPrefix("Hello")  //true
stringOne.hasSuffix("Hello")  //false
```

We can replace all the occurrences of a target string with another string using the `stringByReplacingOccurrencesOfString()` method. The following code shows this:

```
var stringOne = "one,to,three,four"
print(stringOne.replacingOccurrences(of: "to", with: "two"))
```

The preceding example will print one,two,three,four on the screen because we are replacing all the occurrences of to with two.

We can also retrieve substrings and individual characters from our strings. The following shows how to do this:

```
var stringOne = "one,two,three,four"
print(stringOne.replacingOccurrences(of: "to", with: "two"))

var path = "/one/two/three/four"
//Create start and end indexes
let startIndex = path.index(path.startIndex, offsetBy: 4)
let endIndex = path.index(path.startIndex, offsetBy: 14)

let myRange = startIndex..<endIndex

path.substring(with: myRange)    //returns the String /two/three

path.substring(to:startIndex)    //returns the String /one
path.substring(from:endIndex)    //returns the String /four

path.characters.last
path.characters.first
```

In the preceding example, we used the substring(with:) function to retrieve the substring between a start and end indexes. The indexes are created with the index(_: offsetBy:) function. The first property in the index(_: offsetBy:) function gives the index of where we wish to start, and the offsetBy property tells us by how much we should increase the index.

The substring(to:) function creates a substring from the beginning of the string till the index. The substring(from:) function creates a substring from the index to the end of the string. We then use the last property to get the last character of the string and the first property to get the first character.

We can retrieve the number of characters in a string using the count property. The following example shows how you can use this function:

```
var path = "/one/two/three/four"
var length = path.characters.count
```

This completes our whirlwind tour of strings. I know that we went through these properties and functions very quickly, but we will be using strings extensively throughout this book and so we will have a lot of time to get used to them.

Optional variables

All of the variables we have looked at so far are considered to be non-optional variables. This means that the variables are required to have a non-nil value; however, there are times when we want or need our variables to contain `nil` values. This can occur if we return a `nil` from a function whose operation has failed or if a value is not found.

In Swift, an optional variable is a variable to which we are able to assign `nil` (no value). Optional variables and constants are defined using a question mark (?). The following code shows how to define both an optional string variable and a non-optional string variable:

```
var optionalString: String?
var nonoptionalString: String
```

If we attempt to assign a nil to the `nonoptionalString` variable, we will receive an error.

Optional variables were added to the Swift language as a safety feature. They provide a compile time check of our variables to check whether they contain a valid value. Unless our code specifically defines a variable as optional, we can assume that the variable contains a valid value, and we do not have to check for `nil` values. Since we are able to define a variable before initiating it, this can give us a `nil` value in a non-optional variable; however, the compiler checks for this and will give us a `Variable'{name}' used before being initialized` error. To check whether an optional variable or a constant contains a valid (non-nil) value, our first thought might be to use the `!=` (not equals to) operator to check whether the variable is not equal to `nil`, but there are also other ways. These other ways are optional binding and optional chaining. Before we cover optional binding and optional chaining, let's see how to use the not equals to (`!=`) operator and what force unwrapping is.

To use force unwrapping, we must first make sure that the optional has a non-nil value and then we can use the exclamation point to access that value. The following example shows how we can do this:

```
var name: String?
name = "Jon"

if name != nil {
    var newString = "Hello " + name!
}
```

In this example, we create an optional variable named name and assign it a value of Jon. We then use the != operator to verify that this optional variable is not equal to nil. If it is not equal to nil, we use the exclamation point to access its value. While this is a perfectly viable option, it is recommended that we use the optional binding method discussed next instead of force unwrapping.

Optional binding is used to check whether an optional variable or a constant has a non-nil value, and if so, assign that value to a temporary variable. For optional binding, we use the if let or if var keywords together. If we use if let, the temporary value is a constant and cannot be changed, whereas the if var keywords puts the temporary value into a variable that allows us to change the value. The following code illustrates how optional binding is used:

```
var myOptional: String?
if let temp = myOptional {
    print(temp)
    print("Can not use temp outside of the if bracket")
} else {
    print("myOptional was nil")
}
```

In the preceding example, we use the if let keywords to check whether the myOptional variable is nil. If it is not nil, we assign the value to the temp variable and execute the code between the brackets. If the myOptional variable is nil, we execute the code in the else bracket, which prints out the message, myOptional was nil. One thing to note is that the temp variable is scoped only for the conditional block and cannot be used outside of the conditional block.

It is perfectly acceptable with optional binding to assign the value to a variable of the same name. The following code illustrates this:

```
if let myOptional = myOptional {
    print(myOptional)
} else {
    print("myOptional was nil")
}
```

To illustrate the scope of the temporary variable, let's take a look at this code:

```
var myOptional: String?

myOptional = "Jon"
print("Outside: \(myOptional)")

if var myOptional = myOptional {
    myOptional = "test"
    print("Inside: \(myOptional)")
}

print("Outside: \(myOptional)")
```

In this example, the first line that is printed to the console is `Outside: Optional(Jon)` because we are outside of the scope of the `if var` statement where the `myOptional` variable is set to `Jon`. The second line that is printed to the console would be `Inside: test` because we are within the scope of the `if var` statement where we assign the value of `test` to the `myOptional` variable. Inside the inner scope, `myOptional` is unwrapped, because of the optional binding, and, hence, not an optional anymore. The third printed line is `Outside: Optional(Jon)`, like the first one, because we are again outside of the scope of `if var`, where the value of the is `myOptional = "test"` assignment is not visible.

We can also test multiple optional variables in one line by separating each optional check with a comma. The following is an example:

```
if let myOptional1 = myOptional1, let myOptional2 = myOptional2, let
myOptional3 = myOptional3 {
  // only reach this if all three optionals
  // have non-nil values
}
```

Optional chaining allows us to call properties, methods, and subscripts on an optional that might be `nil`. If any of the chained values return `nil`, the return value will be `nil`. The following code gives an example of optional chaining using a fictitious `car` object. In this example, if either `car` or `tires` are `nil`, the variable will be `nil`; otherwise, `s` will be equal to the `tireSize` property:

```
var s = car?.tires?.tireSize
```

The following code illustrates three ways to verify whether an optional contains a valid value prior to using them:

```
//Optional Variable
var stringOne : String?
//--------stringOne is nil --------------//
//Explicitly check for nil
if stringOne != nil {
    print(stringOne)
} else {
    print("Explicit Check:  stringOne is nil")
}
//option binding
if let tmp = stringOne {
    print(tmp)
} else {
    print("Optional Binding: stringOne is nil")
}
//Optional chainging
var charCount1 = stringOne?.characters.count

//--------adding value to stringONe --------------//
stringOne = "http://www.packtpub.com/all"

//--------stringOne is nil --------------//
//Explicitly check for nil
if stringOne != nil {
    print(stringOne)
} else {
    print("Explicit Check:  stringOne is nil")
}
//option binding
if let tmp = stringOne {
    print(tmp)
} else {
    print("Optional Binding: stringOne is nil")
}

//Optional chainging
var charCount2 = stringOne?.characters.count
```

In the preceding code, we begin by defining the optional string variable, stringOne. We then explicitly check for nil using the != operator. If stringOne is not equal to nil, we print the value of stringOne to the console. If stringOne is nil, we print the Explicit Check: stringOne is nil message to the console. As we can see in the results console, Explicit Check: stringOne is nil is printed to the console because we have not assigned a value to stringOne yet.

We then use optional binding to check whether `stringOne` is not `nil`. If `stringOne` is not `nil`, the value of `stringOne` is put into the `tmp` temporary variable, and we print the value of `tmp` to the console. If `stringOne` is `nil`, we print the `Optional Binding: stringOne is nil` message to the console. As we can see in the results console, `Optional Binding: stringOneisnil` is printed to the console because we have not assigned a value to `stringOne` yet.

We use optional chaining to assign the value of the `characters.count` property of the `stringOne` variable to the `charCount1` variable if `stringOne` is not `nil`. As we can see, the `charCount1` variable is `nil` because we have not assigned a value to `stringOne` yet.

We then assign a value of `http://www.packtpub.com/all`to the `stringOne` variable and rerun all three tests again. This time, `stringOne` has a non-nil value; therefore, the value of `charCount2` is printed to the console.

 It would be tempting to say that I might need to set this variable to `nil`, so let me define it as optional; however, that would be a mistake. The mindset for optionals should be to only use them if there is a specific reason for the variable to have a `nil` value.

We will discuss optionals further in Chapter 10, *Using Optional Types*.

Enumerations

Enumerations (otherwise known as enums) are a special data type that enables us to group related types together and use them in a type-safe manner. Enumerations in Swift are not tied to integer values as they are in other languages such as C or Java. In Swift, we are able to define an enumeration with a type (string, character, integer, or floating-point) and then define its actual value (known as the raw value). Enumerations also support features that are traditionally supported only by classes such as computed properties and instance methods. We will discuss these advanced features in depth in Chapter 5, *Classes and Structures*. In this section, we will look at the traditional features of enumerations.

We will define an enumeration that contains a list of `Planets` as follows:

```
enum Planets {
    case Mercury
    case Venus
    case Earth
    case Mars
    case Jupiter
    case Saturn
    case Uranus
    case Neptune
}
```

The values defined in an enumeration are considered to be the *member* values (or simply the members) of the enumeration. In most cases, you will see the member values defined in the preceding example, because they are easy to read; however, there is a shorter version. This shorter version lets us define multiple members in a single line, separated by commas, as the following example shows:

```
enum Planets {
    case Mercury, Venus, Earth, Mars, Jupiter
    case Saturn, Uranus, Neptune
}
```

We can then use the `Planets` enumeration, like this:

```
var planetWeLiveOn = Planets.Earth
var furthestPlanet = Planets.Neptune
```

The types for the `planetWeLiveOn` and `furthestPlanet` variables are inferred when we initialize the variable with one of the member values of the `Planets` enumeration. Once the variable type is inferred, we can then assign a new value without the `Planets` prefix as shown here:

```
planetWeLiveOn = .Mars
```

We can compare an enumeration value using the traditional equals (`==`) operator or a `switch` statement. The following example shows how to use the `equals` operator and the `switch` statement with an enum:

```
// Using the traditional == operator
if planetWeLiveOn == .Earth {
    print("Earth it is")
}
// Using the switch statement
switch planetWeLiveOn {
case .Mercury:
```

```
    print("We live on Mercury, it is very hot!")
case .Venus:
    print("We live on Venus, it is very hot!")
case .Earth:
    print("We live on Earth, just right")
case .Mars:
    print("We live on Mars, a little cold")
default:
    print("Where do we live?")
}
```

Enumerations can come prepopulated with raw values, which are required to be of the same type. The following example shows how to define an enumeration with string values:

```
enum Devices: String {
    case MusicPlayer = "iPod"
    case Phone = "iPhone"
    case Tablet = "iPad"
}
print("We are using an " + Devices.Tablet.rawValue)
```

The preceding example creates an enumeration with three types of device. We then use the rawValue property to retrieve the raw value for the Tablet member of the Devices enumeration. This example will print a message saying We are using an iPad.

Let's create another Planets enumeration but, this time, assign numbers to the members as follows:

```
enum Planets: Int   {
    case Mercury = 1
    case Venus
    case Earth
    case Mars
    case Jupiter
    case Saturn
    case Uranus
    case Neptune
}
print("Earth is planet number \(Planets.Earth.rawValue)")
```

The big difference between these last two enumeration examples is that in the second example, we only assign a value to the first member (Mercury). If integers are used for the raw values of an enumeration, we do not have to assign a value to each member. If no value is present, the raw values will be auto-incremented.

In Swift, enumeration can also have associated values. Associated values allow us to store additional information along with member values. This additional information can vary each time we use the member. It can also be of any type, and the types can be different for each member. Let's take a look at how we might use associated types by defining a `Product` enumeration, which contains two types of products:

```
enum Product {
    case Book(Double, Int, Int)
    case Puzzle(Double, Int)
}
var masterSwift = Product.Book(49.99, 2016, 310)
var worldPuzzle = Product.Puzzle(9.99, 200)

switch masterSwift {
case .Book(let price, let year, let pages):
    print("Mastering Swift was published in \(year) for the price of
        \(price) and has \(pages) pages")
case .Puzzle(let price, let pieces):
    print("Master Swift is a puzze with \(pieces) and sells for
        \(price)")
}

switch worldPuzzle {
case .Book(let price, let year, let pages):
    print("World Puzzle was published in \(year) for the price of
        \(price) and has \(pages) pages")
case .Puzzle(let price, let pieces):
    print("World Puzzle is a puzze with \(pieces) and sells for
        \(price)")
}
```

In the preceding example, we begin by defining a `Product` enumeration with two members–`Book` and `Puzzle`. The `Book` member has an associated value of `Double`, `Int`, and `Int`, and the `Puzzle` member has an associated value of `Double`, `Int`. We then create two products: `masterSwift` and `worldPuzzle`. We assign the `masterSwift` variable a value of `Product.Book` with the associated values of `49.99, 2016, 310`. We then assign the `worldPuzzle` variable a value of `Product.Puzzle` with the associated values of `9.99, 200`.

We can then check the `Products` enumeration using a `switch` statement, as we did in an earlier example. We extract the associated values within the `switch` statement. In this example, we extracted the associated values as constants with the `let` keyword, but you can also extract the associated values as variables with the `var` keyword.

If you put the previous code into a Playground, the following results will be displayed:

```
Master Swift was published in 2016 for the price of 49.99 and has
310 pages
World Puzzle is a puzzle with 200 and sells for 9.99
```

We have only scratched the surface of what enumerations can do in Swift. In Chapter 5, *Classes and Structures*, we will look at some additional features on enumerations with Swift and see why they are so powerful.

Operators

An **operator** is a symbol or combination of symbols that we can use to check, change, or combine values. We have used operators in most of the examples so far in this book; however, we did not specifically call them operators. In this section, we will show how to use most of the basic operators that Swift supports.

Swift supports most standard C operators and also improves them to eliminate several common coding errors. For example, the assignment operator does not return a value, which prevents it from being used where we meant to use the equality operator (==).

Let's look at the operators in Swift.

The assignment operator

The assignment operator initializes or updates a variable.

Prototype:

```
varA = varB
```

Example:

```
let x = 1
var y = "Hello"
a = b
```

Comparison operators

The comparison operator returns the `true` Boolean if the statement is true or the Boolean `false` if the statement is not true.

Prototypes:

```
Equality:  varA == varB
Not equal:  varA != varB
Greater than:  varA > varB
Less than:  varA < varB
Greater than or equal to:  varA >= varB
Less than or equal to:  varA <= varB
```

Example:

```
2 == 1 //false, 2 does not equal 1
2 != 1 //true, 2 does not equal 1
2 > 1  //true, 2 is greater than 1
2 < 1  //false, 2 is not less than 1
2 >= 1 //true, 2 is greater or equal to 1
2 <= 1 //false, 2 is not less or equal to 1
```

Arithmetic operators

Arithmetic operators perform the four basic mathematical operations.

Prototypes:

```
Addition:  varA + varB
Subtraction:  varA - varB
Multiplication:  varA * varB
Division:  varA / varB
```

Example:

```
var x = 4 + 2  //x will equal 6
var x = 4 - 2  //x will equal 2
var x = 4 * 2  //x will equal 8
var x = 4 / 2  //x will equal 2
var x = "Hello " + "world"  //x will equal "Hello World"
```

The remainder operator

The remainder operator calculates the remainder if the first operand is divided by the second operand.

Prototype:

```
varA % varB
```

Example:

```
var x = 10 % 3   //x will equal 1
var x = 10 % 2.6  //x will equal 2.2
```

Compound assignment operators

Compound assignment operators combine an arithmetic operator with an assignment operator.

Prototypes:

```
varA += varB
varA -= varB
varA *= varB
varA /= varB
```

Example:

```
var x = 6
x += 2  //x is equal to 8
x -= 2  //x is equal to 4
x *= 2  //x is equal to 12
x /= 2  //x is equal to 3
```

The ternary conditional operator

The ternary conditional operator assigns a value to a variable based on the evaluation of a comparison operator or Boolean value.

Prototype:

```
(boolValue ? valueA : valueB)
```

Example:

```
var x = 2
var y = 3
var z = (y > x ? "Y is greater" : "X is greater")  //z equals   "Y is
greater"
```

The logical NOT operator

The logical NOT operator inverts a Boolean value.

Prototype:

```
varA = !varB
```

Example:

```
var x = true
var y = !x  //y equals false
```

The logical AND operator

The logical AND operator returns `true` if both operands are true. Otherwise, it returns `false`.

Prototype:

```
varA && varB
```

Example:

```
var x = true
var y = false
var z = x && y  //z equals false
```

The logical OR operator

The logical OR operator returns `true` if either of the operands is true.

Prototype:

```
varA || varB
```

Example:

```
var x = true
var y = false
var z = x || y  //z equals true
```

For those who are familiar with the C language or similar languages, these operators should look pretty familiar. For those who aren't that familiar with the C operators, rest assured that you will use them enough and they will become second nature.

Summary

In this chapter, we covered a lot of different topics ranging from variables and constants to data types and operators. The items in this chapter will be the foundation of every application that you write; therefore, it is important to understand the concepts discussed here.

In the next chapter, we will look at how we can use Swift collection types to store related data. These collection types are the dictionary and array types. We will also look at how we can use the Cocoa and Foundation data types in Swift.

3
Using Swift Collections and the Tuple Type

Once I got past the basic Hello World beginner applications, I quickly began to realize the shortcomings of variables, especially with the Mad Libs style applications that I was starting to write. These applications requested that the user enter in numerous strings, and I was creating a separate variable for each input field that the user entered. Having all of these separate variables quickly became very cumbersome. I remember talking to a friend about this and he asked me why I was not using arrays. At that time, I was not familiar with arrays, so I asked him to show me what they were. Even though he had a TI-99/4A and I had a Commodore Vic-20, the concept of arrays was the same. Even today, the arrays found in modern development languages have the same basic concepts as the arrays I used on my Commodore Vic-20. While it is definitely possible to create a useful application without using collections, when used correctly, collections do make application development significantly easier.

In this chapter, we will cover the following topics:

- What an array is in Swift and how to use it
- What a dictionary is in Swift and how we can use it
- What a set is in Swift and how we can use it
- What a tuple is in Swift and how we can use it

Swift collection types

A collection groups multiple items into a single unit. Swift provides three native collection types. These collection types are arrays, sets, and dictionaries. An array stores the data in an ordered list, sets are an unordered collection of unique data, and dictionaries are an unordered collection of key-value pairs. In an array, we access the data by the location (index) in the array; in a set, we tend to iterate over the set; and dictionaries are usually accessed using a unique key.

The data stored in a Swift collection is required to be of the same type. This means, as an example, that we are unable to store a string value in an array of integers. Since Swift does not allow us to mismatch data types in a collection, we can be certain of the data type when we retrieve an element from a collection. This is another feature that on the surface might seem like a shortcoming, but is actually a design feature that helps eliminate common programming mistakes. We will see how to work around this feature using the `AnyObject` and `Any` aliases in this chapter.

Mutability

For those who are familiar with Objective-C, you will know that there are different classes for mutable and immutable collections. For example, to define a mutable array, we use the `NSMutableArray` class, and to define an immutable array, we use the `NSArray` class. Swift is a little different because it does not contain separate classes for mutable and immutable collections. Instead, we define whether a collection is a constant (immutable) or a variable (mutable) using the `let` and `var` keywords. This should seem familiar since, in Swift, we define constants with the `let` keyword and variables with the `var` keyword.

 It is good practice to create immutable collections unless there is a specific need to change the objects within the collection. This allows the compiler to optimize performance.

Let's begin our tour of collections by looking at the most common collection type–the array type.

Arrays

Arrays are a very common component of modern programming languages and can be found in virtually all of them. In Swift, arrays are an ordered list of objects of the same type.

When an array is created, we must declare the type of data to be stored in it by explicit type declaration or through type inference. Typically, we only explicitly declare the data type of an array when we are creating an empty array. If we initialize an array with data, we should let the compiler use type inference to infer the most appropriate data type for the array.

Each object in an array is called an **element**. Each of these elements is stored in a set order and can be accessed by its location (index) in the array.

Creating and initializing arrays

We can initialize an array with an array literal. An array literal is a set of values that prepopulates the array. The following example shows how to define an immutable array of integers using the `let` keyword:

```
let arrayOne = [1,2,3]
```

As we mentioned, if we need to create a mutable array, we will use the `var` keyword to define the array. The following example shows how to define a mutable array:

```
var arrayTwo = [4,5,6]
```

In the preceding two examples, the compiler inferred the types of value stored in the array by looking at the type of values stored in the array literal. If we need to create an empty array, we will need to explicitly declare the type of values to store in the array. The following example shows how to declare an empty mutable array that can be used to store integers:

```
var arrayThree = [Int]()
```

In the preceding examples, we created arrays with integer values, and the majority of the array examples in this chapter will also use integer values; however, we can create arrays in Swift with any type. The only rule is that, once an array is defined as containing a particular type, all the elements in the array must be of that type. The following example shows how we would create arrays of various data types:

```
var arrayOne = [String]()
var arrayTwo = [Double]()
var arrayThree = [MyObject]()
```

Swift does provide special type aliases for working with nonspecific types. These aliases are AnyObject and Any. We can use these aliases to define arrays whose elements are of different types, such as this:

```
var myArray: [Any] = [1,"Two"]
```

The AnyObject aliases can represent an instance of any class type while the Any aliases can represent an instance of any type. We should use the Any and AnyObject aliases only when there is an explicit need for this behavior. It is always better to be specific about the types of data our collections contain.

We can also initialize an array to a certain size with all the elements of the array set to a predefined value. This can be very useful if we want to create an array and prepopulate it with the default values. The following example defines an array with seven elements, and each element contains the number 3:

```
var arrayFour = [Int](repeating: 3, count: 7)
```

While the most common array is a one-dimensional array, we can also create multidimensional arrays. A multidimensional array is really nothing more than an array of arrays. For example, a two-dimensional array is an array of arrays, while a three-dimensional array is an array of arrays of arrays. The following examples show the two ways to create a two-dimensional array in Swift:

```
var multiArrayOne = [[1,2],[3,4],[5,6]]
var multiArrayTwo = [[Int]]()
```

Accessing the array elements

We use the subscript syntax to retrieve values from an array. The subscript syntax for an array is where a number appears between two square brackets and that number specifies the location (index), within the array, of the element we wish to retrieve. The following example shows how to retrieve elements from an array using the subscript syntax:

```
let arrayOne = [1,2,3,4,5,6]
print(arrayOne[0])   //Displays '1'
print(arrayOne[3])   //Displays '4'
```

In the preceding code, we begin by creating an array of integers that contains six numbers. We then print out the value at index 0 and 3.

If we want to retrieve an individual value within a multidimensional array, we will need to provide a subscript for each dimension of the array. If we do not provide a subscript for each dimension, we will return an array rather than an individual value within the array. The following example shows how we can define a two-dimensional array and retrieve an individual value within the two dimensions:

```
var multiArray = [[1,2],[3,4],[5,6]]
var arr = multiArray[0] //arr contains the array [1,2]
var value = multiArray[0][1] //value contains 2
```

In the preceding code, we begin by defining a two-dimensional array. When we retrieve the value at index 0 of the first dimension (`multiArray[0]`), we retrieve the array, `[1,2]`. When we retrieve the value at index 0 of the first dimension and index 1 of the second dimension (`multiArray[0][1]`), we retrieve the integer, 2.

We can retrieve the first and last elements of an array using the `first` and `last` properties. The `first` and `last` properties return an optional value since the values may be nil if the array is empty. The following example shows how to use the `first` and `last` properties to retrieve the first and last elements of both single-dimensional and multidimensional arrays:

```
let arrayOne = [1,2,3,4,5,6]
var first = arrayOne.first  //first contains 1
var last = arrayOne.last  //last contains 6

let multiArray = [[1,2],[3,4],[5,6]]
var arrFirst1 = multiArray[0].first //arrFirst1 contains 1
var arrFirst2 = multiArray.first //arrFirst2 contains[1,2]
var arrLast1 = multiArray[0].last //arrLast1 contains 2
var arrLast2 = multiArray.last  //arrLast2 contains [5,6]
```

Counting the elements of an array

At times, it is essential to know the number of elements in an array. To retrieve the number of elements in an array, we use the read-only `count` property. The following example shows how to use this property to retrieve the number of elements in both single-dimensional and multidimensional arrays:

```
let arrayOne = [1,2,3]
let multiArrayOne = [[3,4],[5,6],[7,8]]
print(arrayOne.count)  //Displays 3
print(multiArrayOne.count)  //Displays 3 for the three arrays
print(multiArrayOne[0].count)  //Displays 2 for the two elements
```

The value that is returned by the `count` property is the number of elements in the array and not the largest valid index of the array. For non-empty arrays, the largest valid index is the number of elements in the array minus one. This is because the first element of the array has an index number of zero. As an example, if an array has two elements, the valid indexes are 0 and 1, while the count property would return 2. The following code illustrates this:

```
let arrayOne = [0,1]
print(arrayOne[0])  //Displays 0
print(arrayOne[1])  //Displays 1
print(arrayOne.count) //Displays 2
```

If we attempt to retrieve an element from an array, using the subscript syntax, the application will throw an `Array index out of range` error. Therefore, if we are unsure of the size of an array, it is good practice to verify that the index is not outside the range of the array. The following examples illustrate this concept:

```
//This example will throw an array index out of range error
var arrayTwo = [1,2,3,4]
print(arrayTwo[6])

//This example will not throw an array index out of range error
var arrayOne = [1,2,3,4]
if (arrayOne.count > 6) {
    print(arrayOne[6])
}
```

In the preceding code, the first block of code would throw an `array index out of range` error exception because we are attempting to access the value from the array `arrayTwo` at index 6; however, there are only four elements in the array. The second example would not throw the error because we are checking whether the `arrayOne` array contains more than six elements before trying to access the element at the sixth index.

Is the array empty?

To check whether an array is empty (does not contain any elements), we use the `isEmpty` property. This property will return `true` if the array is empty, or `false` if it is not. The following example shows how to check whether an array is empty or not:

```
var arrayOne = [1,2]
var arrayTwo = [Int]()
arrayOne.isEmpty  //Returns false because the array is not empty
arrayTwo.isEmpty  //Returns true because the array is empty
```

Appending to an array

A static array is somewhat useful, but having the ability to add elements dynamically is what makes arrays really useful. To add an item to the end of an array, we can use the `append` method. The following example shows how to append an item to the end of an array:

```
var arrayOne = [1,2]
arrayOne.append(3)  //arrayOne will now contain 1, 2, and 3
```

Swift also allows us to use the addition assignment operator (+=) to append an array to another array. The following example shows how to use the addition assignment operator to append an array to the end of another array:

```
var arrayOne = [1,2]
arrayOne += [3,4]  //arrayOne will now contain 1, 2, 3, and 4
```

The way you append an element to the end of an array is really up to you. Personally, I prefer the assignment operator because, to me, it is a bit easier to read, but we will be using both in this book.

Inserting a value into an array

We can insert a value into an array using the `insert` method. The `insert` method will move all the items, starting at the specified index, up one spot to make room for the new element and then inserts the value into the specified index. The following example shows how to use the `insert` method to insert a new value into an array:

```
var arrayOne = [1,2,3,4,5]
arrayOne.insert(10, at: 3) //arrayOne now contains 1, 2, 3, 10, 4, and 5
```

You cannot insert a value that is outside the current range of the array. Attempting to do so will throw an `Index out of range` exception. For example, in the preceding code, if we attempt to insert a new integer at index `10`, we will receive an `Index out of range` exception error because `arrayOne` only contains five elements. The exception to this is that we are able to insert an item directly after the last element; therefore, we can insert an item at index 6. However, it is recommended that we use the `append` function to append an item to avoid errors.

Replacing elements in an array

We use the subscript syntax to replace elements in an array. Using the subscript, we pick the element of the array we wish to update and then use the assignment operator to assign a new value. The following example shows how we will replace a value in an array:

```
var arrayOne = [1,2,3]
arrayOne[1] = 10  //arrayOne now contains 1, 10, 3
```

 You cannot update a value that is outside the current range of the array. Attempting to do so will throw the same `Index out of range` exception that was thrown when we tried to insert a value outside the range of the array.

Removing elements from an array

There are three methods that we can use to remove one or all of the elements in an array. These methods are `removeLast()`, `remove(at:)`, and `removeAll()`. The following example shows how to use the three methods to remove elements from the array:

```
var arrayOne = [1,2,3,4,5]
arrayOne.removeLast()  //arrayOne now contains 1, 2, 3, and 4
arrayOne.remove(at:2)  //arrayOne now contains 1, 2, and 4
arrayOne.removeAll()  //arrayOne is now empty
```

The `removeLast()` and `remove(at:)` methods will also return the value of the element that it is removing. Therefore, if we want to know the value of the item that was removed, we can rewrite the `remove(at:)` and `removedLast()` lines to capture the value, as shown in the following example:

```
var arrayOne = [1,2,3,4,5]
var removed1 = arrayOne.removeLast()  //removed1 contains the value 5
var removed = arrayOne.remove(at:2)  //removed contains the value 3
```

Adding two arrays

To create a new array by adding two arrays together, we use the addition (+) operator. The following example shows how to use the addition (+) operator to create a new array that contains all the elements of two other arrays:

```
let arrayOne = [1,2]
let arrayTwo = [3,4]
var combine = arrayOne + arrayTwo //combine contains 1, 2, 3, and 4
```

In the preceding code, `arrayOne` and `arrayTwo` are left unchanged, while the `combine` array contains the elements from `arrayOne`, followed by the elements from `arrayTwo`.

Reversing an array

We can create a new array from the original array with the elements in reverse order using the `reverse()` method. The original array will remain unchanged by the `reverse` method. The following example shows how to use the `reverse()` method:

```
var arrayOne = [1,2,3]
var reverse = arrayOne.reversed() //reverse contains 3, 2, and 1
```

In the preceding code, the elements of `arrayOne` are left unchanged, while the `reverse` array will contain all the elements from `arrayOne`, but in the reverse order.

Retrieving a subarray from an array

We can retrieve a `subarray` from an existing array by using the subscript syntax with a range operator. The following example shows how to retrieve a range of elements from an existing array:

```
let arrayOne = [1,2,3,4,5]
var subArray = arrayOne[2...4] //subArray contains 3, 4, and 5
```

The . . . operator (three periods) is known as a **range** operator. The range operator, in the preceding code, says I want all the elements, 2 to 4, inclusively (including elements 2 and 4 as well as what is between them). There is another range operator, . . <, which is the same as the . . . range operator, but it excludes the last element. The following example shows how to use the . . < operator:

```
let arrayOne = [1,2,3,4,5]
var subArray = arrayOne[2..<4] //subArray contains 3 and 4
```

In the preceding example, `subArray` will contain two elements 3 and 4.

Making bulk changes to an array

We can use the subscript syntax with a range operator to change the values of multiple elements. The following example shows how to use the subscript syntax to change a range of elements:

```
var arrayOne = [1,2,3,4,5]
arrayOne[1...2] = [12,13]//arrayOne contains 1, 12, 13, 4, and 5
```

In the preceding code, the elements at index 1 and 2 will be changed to number 12 and 13. After this, when the code runs, `arrayOne` will contain 1, 12, 13, 4, and 5.

The number of elements that you are changing in the range operator does not need to match the number of values that you are passing in. Swift makes bulk changes by first removing the elements defined by the range operator and then inserting the new values. The following example demonstrates this concept:

```
var arrayOne = [1,2,3,4,5]
arrayOne[1...3] = [12,13]
//arrayOne now contains 1, 12, 13 and 5 (four elements)
```

In the preceding code, `arrayOne` starts with five elements. We then say that we want to replace the range of elements 1 to 3 inclusively. This causes elements 1 through 3 (three elements) to be removed from the array. We then add two elements (12 and 13) to the array, starting at index 1. After this is complete, `arrayOne` will contain these four elements: 1, 12, 13, and 5. Let's see what happens if we try to add more elements than we remove:

```
var arrayOne = [1,2,3,4,5]
arrayOne[1...3] = [12,13,14,15]
//arrayOne now contains 1, 12, 13, 14, 15 and 5 (six elements)
```

In the preceding code, `arrayOne` starts with five elements. We then say that we want to replace the range of elements 1 through 3 inclusively. This causes elements 1 to 3 (three elements) to be removed from the array. We then add four elements (12, 13, 14, and 15) to the array, starting at index 1. After this is complete, `arrayOne` will contain these six elements: 1, 12, 13, 14, 15, and 5.

Algorithms for arrays

Swift arrays have several methods that take a closure as the argument. These methods transform the array in a way defined by the code in the closure. Closures are self-contained blocks of code that can be passed around, and are similar to blocks in Objective-C and lambdas in other languages. We will discuss closures in depth in Chapter 12, *Working with Closures*. For now, we just want to get familiar with how the algorithms work in Swift.

Sort

The sort() algorithm sorts the array in place. This means that, when the sort() method is used, the original array is replaced by the sorted one. The closure takes two arguments (represented by $0 and $1), and should return a Boolean value that indicates whether the first element should be placed before the second element. The following code shows how to use the sort algorithm:

```
var arrayOne = [9,3,6,2,8,5]
arrayOne.sort(){ $0 < $1 }
//arrayOne contains 2, 3, 5, 6, 8, and 9
```

The preceding code will sort the array in increasing order. We can tell this because our rule will return true if the first number ($0) is less than the second number ($1). Therefore, when the sort algorithm begins, it compares the first two numbers (9 and 3) and returns true if the first number (9) is less than the second number (3). In our case, the rule returns false, so the numbers are reversed. The algorithm continues sorting, in this manner, until all of the numbers are sorted in the correct order.

The preceding example sorted the array in numerically increasing order; if we wanted to reverse the order, we would reverse the arguments in the closure. The following code shows how to reverse the sort order:

```
var arrayOne = [9,3,6,2,8,5]
arrayOne.sort(){ $1 < $0 }
//arrayOne contains 9,8,6,5,3 and 2
```

When we run this code, arrayOne will contain the elements 9, 8, 6, 5, 3, and 2.

Sorted

While the sort algorithm sorts the array in place (replaces the original array), the sorted algorithm does not change the original array, it instead creates a new array with the sorted elements from the original array. The following example shows how to use the sorted algorithm:

```
var arrayOne = [9,3,6,2,8,5]
let sorted = arrayOne.sorted(){ $0 < $1 }
//sorted contains 2,3,5,6,8 and 9
//arrayOne contains 9,3,6,2,8 and 5
```

When we run this code, `arrayOne` will contain the original unsorted array (9, 3, 6, 2, 8, and 5) and the sorted array will contain the new sorted array (2, 3, 5, 6, 8, and 9).

Filter

The filter algorithm will return a new array by filtering the original array. This is one of the most powerful array algorithms and may end up being the one we use the most. If we need to retrieve a subset of an array, based on a set of rules, I recommend using this algorithm rather than trying to write your own method to filter the array. The closure takes one argument and it should return a Boolean `true` if the element should be included in the new array, as shown in the following code:

```
var arrayOne = [1,2,3,4,5,6,7,8,9]
let filtered = arrayOne.filter{$0 > 3 && $0 < 7}
//filtered contains 4, 5, and 6
```

In the preceding code, the rule that we are passing to the algorithm returns `true` if the number is greater than 3 or less than 7; therefore, any number that is greater than 3 or less than 7 is included in the new filtered array.

Let's take a look at another example; this one shows how we can retrieve a subset of cities that contain the letter o in their name from an array of cities:

```
var city = ["Boston", "London", "Chicago", "Atlanta"]
let filtered = city.filter{$0.range(of:"o") != nil}
//filtered contains "Boston", "London" and "Chicago"
```

In the preceding code, we use the `range(of:)` method to return `true` if the string contains the letter o. If the method returns `true`, the string is included in the filtered array.

Map

The map algorithm returns a new array that contains the results of applying the rules in the closure to each element of the array. The following example shows how to use the map algorithm to divide each number by `10`:

```
var arrayOne = [10, 20, 30, 40]
let applied = arrayOne.map{ $0 / 10}
//applied contains 1,2,3 and 4
```

In the preceding code, the new array contains the numbers 1, 2, 3, and 4, which is the result of dividing each element of the original array by `10`.

The new array created by the map algorithm is not required to contain the same element types as the original array; however, all the elements in the new array must be of the same type. In the following example, the original array contains integer values, but the new array created by the map algorithm contains string elements:

```
var arrayOne = [1, 2, 3, 4]
let applied = arrayOne.map{ "num:\($0)"}
//applied contains "num:1", "num:2", "num:3" and "num:4"
```

In the preceding code, we created an array of strings that appends the numbers from the original array to the `num:` string.

forEach

We can use `forEach` to iterate over a sequence. The following example shows how we would do this:

```
var arrayOne = [10, 20, 30, 40]
arrayOne.forEach{ print($0) }
```

This example will print the following results to the console:

```
10
20
30
40
```

While using the `forEach` method is very easy, it does have some limitations. The recommended way to iterate over an array is to use the `for-in` loop, which we will see in the next section.

Iterating over an array

We can iterate over all elements of an array, in order, with a `for-in` loop. We will discuss the `for-in` loop in greater detail in Chapter 4, *Control Flow and Functions*. The `for-in` loop will execute one or more statements for each element of the array. The following example shows how we would iterate over the elements of an array:

```
var arr = ["one", "two", "three"]
for item in arr {
    print(item)
}
```

In the preceding example, the `for-in` loop iterates over the `arr` array and executes the `print(item)` line for each element in the array. If we run this code, it will display the following results in the console:

```
one
two
three
```

There are times when we would like to iterate over an array, as we did in the preceding example, but we would also like to know the index as well as the value of the element. To do this, we can use the `enumerated` method, which returns a tuple (see the *Tuples* section later in this chapter) for each item in the array that contains both `index` and `value` of the element. The following example shows how to use the `enumerate` function:

```
var arr = ["one", "two", "three"]
for (index,value) in arr.enumerated() {
    print("\(index) \(value)")
}
```

The preceding code will display the following results in the console:

```
0 one
1 two
2 three
```

Now that we have introduced arrays in Swift, let's take a look at what a dictionary is.

Dictionaries

While dictionaries are not as commonly used as arrays, they have an additional functionality that makes them incredibly powerful. A dictionary is a container that stores multiple key-value pairs, where all the keys are of the same type, and all the values are of the same type. The key is used as a unique identifier for the value. A dictionary does not guarantee the order in which the key-value pairs are stored since we look up the values by the key, rather than by the index of the value.

Dictionaries are good for storing items that map to unique identifiers, where the unique identifier should be used to retrieve the item. As an example, countries with their abbreviations are a good example of items that can be stored in a dictionary. In the following chart, we show countries with their abbreviations as key-value pairs:

Key	Value
US	United States
IN	India
UK	United Kingdom

Creating and initializing dictionaries

We can initialize a dictionary using a dictionary literal, similarly to how we initialized an array with the array literal. The following example shows how to create a dictionary using the key-value pairs in the preceding chart:

```
let countries = ["US":"UnitedStates","IN":"India","UK":"United Kingdom"]
```

The preceding code creates an immutable dictionary that contains each of the key-value pairs in the preceding chart. Just like the array, to create a mutable dictionary we will use the `var` keyword rather than `let`. The following example shows how to create a mutable dictionary containing the countries:

```
var countries = ["US":"UnitedStates","IN":"India","UK":"United Kingdom"]
```

In the preceding two examples, we created a dictionary where the key and value were both strings. The compiler inferred that the key and value were strings because that was the type of the keys and values used to imitate the dictionary. If we wanted to create an empty dictionary, we would need to tell the compiler what the key and value types are. The following examples create various dictionaries with different key-value types:

```
var dic1 = [String:String]()
var dic2 = [Int:String]()
var dic3 = [String:MyObject]()
```

 If we want to use a custom object as the key in a dictionary, we will need to make our custom object conform to the Hashable protocol from Swift's standard library. We will discuss protocols and classes in Chapter 5, *Classes and Structures*, but, for now, just understand that it is possible to use custom objects as a key in a dictionary.

Accessing dictionary values

We use the subscript syntax to retrieve the value for a particular key. If the dictionary does not contain the key we are looking for, the dictionary will return nil; therefore, the variable returned from this lookup is an optional variable. The following example shows how to retrieve a value from a dictionary using its key in the subscript syntax:

```
let countries = ["US":"United States", "IN":"India","UK":"United Kingdom"]
var name = countries["US"]
```

In the preceding code, the variable name will contain the string, United States.

Counting key or values in a dictionary

We use the count property of the dictionary to get the number of key-value pairs in the dictionary. The following example shows how to use the count property to retrieve the number of key-value pairs in the dictionary:

```
let countries = ["US":"United States", "IN":"India","UK":"United Kingdom"];
var cnt = countries.count  //cnt contains 3
```

In the preceding code, the cnt variable will contain the number 3 since there are three key-value pairs in the countries dictionary.

Is the dictionary empty?

To test whether the dictionary contains any key-value pairs at all, we can use the isEmpty property. The isEmpty property will return false if the dictionary contains one or more key-value pairs and true if it is empty. The following example shows how to use the isEmpty property to determine whether our dictionary contains any key-value pairs:

```
let countries = ["US":"United States", "IN":"India","UK":"United Kingdom"]
var empty = countries.isEmpty
```

In the preceding code, the isEmpty property is false as there are three key-value pairs in the countries dictionary.

Updating the value of a key

To update the value of a key in a dictionary, we can use either the subscript syntax or the updateValue(_ forKey:) method. The updateValue(_:, forKey:) method has an additional feature that the subscript syntax doesn't–it returns the original value associated with the key prior to changing the value. The following example shows how to use both the subscript syntax and the updateValue(_:, forKey:) method to update the value of a key:

```
var countries = ["US":"United States", "IN":"India","UK":"United Kingdom"]

countries["UK"] = "Great Britain"
//The value of UK is now set to "Great Britain"

var orig = countries.updateValue("Britain", forKey: "UK")
//The value of UK is now set to "Britain" and orig now contains "Great Britain"
```

In the preceding code, we use the subscript syntax to change the value associated with the key UK from United Kingdom to Great Britain. The original value of United Kingdom was not saved prior to replacing it, so we are unable to see what the original value was. We then used the updateValue(_:, forKey:) method to change the value associated with the key UK from Great Britain to Britain. With the updateValue(_:, forKey:) method, the original value of Great Britain is assigned to the orig variable, prior to changing the value in the dictionary.

Adding a key-value pair

To add a new key-value pair to a dictionary, we can use the subscript syntax or the same `updateValue(_:, forKey:)` method that we used to update the value of a key. If we use the `updateValue(_:, forKey:)` method and the key is not currently present in the dictionary, the `updateValue(_:, forKey:)` method will add a new key-value pair and return nil. The following example shows how to use the subscript syntax and also the `updateValue(+:, forKey:)` method to add a new key-value pair to a dictionary:

```
var countries = ["US":"United States", "IN":"India","UK":"United Kingdom"]

countries["FR"] = "France" //The value of "FR" is set to "France"

var orig = countries.updateValue("Germany", forKey: "DE")
//The value of "DE" is set to "Germany" and orig is nil
```

In the preceding code, the countries dictionary starts with three key-value pairs and we then add a fourth key-value pair (`FR`/`France`) to the dictionary using the subscript syntax. We use the `updateValue(_:, forKey:)` method to add a fifth key-value pair (`DE`/`Germany`) to the dictionary. The `orig` variable is set to nil because the countries dictionary did not contain a value associated with the `DE` key.

Removing a key-value pair

There may be times when we need to remove values from a dictionary. We can do this with the subscript syntax, the `removeValue(forKey:)` method, or the `removeAll()` method. The `removeValue(forKey:)` method returns the value of the key prior to removing it. The `removeAll()` method removes all the elements from the dictionary. The following example shows how to use the subscript syntax, the `removeValue(forKey:)` method, and the `removeAll()` method to remove key-value pairs from a dictionary:

```
var countries = ["US":"United States", "IN":"India","UK":"United Kingdom"];

countries["IN"] = nil //The "IN" key/value pair is removed

var orig = countries.removeValue(forKey:"UK")
//The "UK" key value pair is removed and orig contains "United Kingdom"

countries.removeAll() //Removes all key/value pairs from the countries
dictionary
```

In the preceding code, the `countries` dictionary starts off with three key-value pairs. We then set the value associated with the key `IN` to `nil`, which removes the key-value pair from the dictionary. We use the `removeValue(forKey:)` method to remove the key associated with the `UK` key. Prior to removing the value associated with the `UK` key, the `removeValue(forKey:)` method saves the value in the `orig` variable. Finally, we use the `removeAll()` method to remove all the remaining key-value pairs in the countries dictionary.

Now let's look at the set type.

Set

The set type is a generic collection that is similar to the array type. While the array type is an ordered collection that may contain duplicate items, the set type is an unordered collection where each item must be unique.

Similar to the key in a dictionary, the type stored in an array must conform to the `Hashable` protocol. This means that the type must provide a way to compute a hash value for itself. All of Swift's basic types, such as `String`, `Double`, `Int`, and `Bool`, conform to the `Hashable` protocol and can be used in a set by default.

Let's look at how we would use the set type.

Initializing a set

There are a couple of ways in which we can initialize a set. Just like the array and dictionary types, Swift needs to know what type of data is going to be stored in it. This means that we must either tell Swift the type of data to store in the set or initialize it with some data so that it can infer the data type.

Just like the array and dictionary types, we use the `var` and `let` keywords to declare whether the set is mutable or not:

```
//Initializes an empty Set of the String type
var mySet = Set<String>()

//Initializes a mutable set of the String type with initial values
var mySet = Set(["one", "two", "three"])

//Creates aimmutable set of the String type.
let mySet = Set(["one", "two", "three"])
```

Inserting items into a set

We use the `insert` method to insert an item into a set. If we attempt to insert an item that is already in the set, the item will be ignored and no error will be thrown. Here are some examples on how to insert items into a set:

```
var mySet = Set<String>()
mySet.insert("One")
mySet.insert("Two")
mySet.insert("Three")
```

The number of items in a set

We can use the `count` property to determine the number of items in a Swift set. Here is an example on how to use the `count` method:

```
var mySet = Set<String>()
mySet.insert("One")
mySet.insert("Two")
mySet.insert("Three")
print("\(mySet.count) items")
```

When executed, this code will print the message `Three items` to the console because the set contains three items.

Checking whether a set contains an item

We can very easily check to see whether a set contains an item by using the `contains()` method, as shown here:

```
var mySet = Set<String>()
mySet.insert("One")
mySet.insert("Two")
mySet.insert("Three")
var contain = mySet.contains("Two")
```

In the preceding example, the `contain` variable is set to true because the set does contain the string `"Two"`.

Iterating over a set

We can use the `for` statement to iterate over the items in a set. The following example shows how we would iterate through the items in a set:

```
for item in mySet {
    print(item)
}
```

The preceding example would print out each item in the set to the console.

Removing items in a set

We can remove a single item or all the items in a set. To remove a single item, we would use the `remove()` method; to remove all the items, use the `removeAll()` method. The following example shows how to remove items from a set:

```
//The remove method will return and remove an item from a set
var item = mySet.remove("Two")

//The removeAll method will remove all items from a set
mySet.removeAll()
```

Set operations

Apple has provided four methods that we can use to construct a set from two other sets. These operations can either be performed in place, on one of the sets, or used to create a new set. These operations are:

- `union` and `fromUnion`: These create a set with all the unique values from both sets
- `subtracting` and `subtract`: These create a set with values from the first set that are not in the second set
- `intersection` and `fromIntersection`: These create a set with values that are common to both sets
- `symmetricDifference` and `fromSymmetricDifference`: These create a new set with values that are in either set but not in both sets

Let's look at some examples and see the results we get from each of these operations. For all the set operations examples, we will be using the following two sets:

```
var mySet1 = Set(["One", "Two", "Three", "abc"])
var mySet2 = Set(["abc","def","ghi", "One"])
```

The first example that we will look at uses union method. This method will take unique values from both sets to make another set:

```
var newSetUnion = mySet1.union(mySet2)
```

The newSetUnion variable would contain the following values: "One", "Two", "Three", "abc", "def", and "ghi". We can use the fromUnion method to perform the union function in place without creating a new set:

```
mySet1.fromUnion(mySet2)
```

In this example, the mySet1 set will contain all of the unique values from the mySet1 and mySet2 sets.

Now let's look at the subtract and subtracting methods. These methods will create a set with the values from the first set that are not in the second set:

```
var newSetSubtract = mySet1.subtracting(mySet2)
```

In this example, the newSetSubtract variable would contain the values "Two" and "Three" because those are the only two values that are not present in the second set.

We use the subtract method to perform the subtraction function in place without creating a new set.

```
mySet1.subtract(mySet2)
```

In this example, the mySet1 set will contain the values "Two" and "Three" because those are the only two values that are not in the mySet2 set.

Now let's look at the intersection methods. The intersection methods create a new set from the values that are common between the two sets:

```
var newSetIntersect = mySet1.intersection(mySet2)
```

In this example, the newSetIntersect variable will contain the values "One" and "abc" since they are the values that are common between the two sets.

We can use the `fromInterection()` method to perform the intersection function in place without creating a new set:

```
mySet1.fromIntersection(mySet2)
```

In this example, the `mySet1` set will contain the values `"One"` and `"abc"` since they are the values that are common between the two sets.

Finally, let's look at the `symmetricDifference` methods. These methods will create a new set with the values that are in either set but not in both:

```
var newSetExclusiveOr = mySet1.symmetricDifference(mySet2)
```

In this example, the `newSetExclusiveOr` variable will contain the values `"Two"`, `"Three"`, `"def"` and `"ghi"`.

To perform the `symmetricDifference` methods in place, we use the `fromSymmetricDifference()` method:

```
mySet1.fromSymmetricDifference(mySet2)
```

These four operations (the `union`, `subtraction`, `intersection`, and `symmetricDifference` methods) add additional functionality that is not present with arrays. Combined with faster lookup speeds as compared to an array, the set can be a very useful alternative when the order of the collection is not important and the instances in the collection must be unique.

Tuples

Tuples group multiple values into a single compound value. Unlike arrays and dictionaries, the values in a tuple do not have to be of the same type. While we are including the tuple in the chapter on collections, they really are not a collection; they are more like a type.

The following example shows how to define a tuple:

```
var team = ("Boston", "Red Sox", 97, 65, 59.9)
```

In the preceding example, we created an unnamed tuple that contains two strings, two integers, and one double. We can decompose the values from this tuple into a set of variables, as shown in the following example:

```
var team = ("Boston", "Red Sox", 97, 65, 59.9)
var (city, name, wins, loses, percent) = team
```

In the preceding code, the `city` variable will contain `Boston`, the `name` variable will contain `Red Sox`, the `wins` variable will contain `97`, the `loses` variable will contain `65`, and, finally, the `percent` variable will contain `0.599`.

We could also retrieve the values from a tuple by specifying the location of the value. The following example shows how we would retrieve the values by their location:

```
var team = ("Boston", "Red Sox", 97, 65, 59.9)
var city = team.0
var name = team.1
var wins = team.2
var loses = team.3
var percent = team.4
```

To avoid this decomposing step, we can create named tuples. A named tuple associates a name (key) with each element of the tuple. The following example shows how to create a named tuple:

```
var team = (city:"Boston", name:"Red Sox", wins:97, loses:65, percent:59.9)
```

To access the values from a named tuple, we use the dot syntax. In the preceding code, we will access the `city` element of the tuple like this: `team.city`. In the preceding code, the `team.city` element will contain `Boston`, the `team.name` element will contain `Red Sox`, the `team.wins` element will contain `97`, the `team.loses` element will contain `65`, and, finally, the `team.percent` element will contain `59.9`.

Tuples are incredibly useful and can be used for all sorts of purposes. I have found that they are very useful for replacing classes and structures that are designed to simply store data and do not contain any methods. We will learn more about classes and structures in Chapter 5, *Classes and Structures*.

Summary

In this chapter, we covered Swift collections and the tuple type. Having a good understanding of the native collection types of Swift is essential to architect and develop applications in Swift since all but the most basic of applications use collections to store data in memory.

4

Control Flow and Functions

While I was learning BASIC programming on my Vic-20, every month I would read several of the early computer magazines such as *Byte Magazine*. I remember one particular review that I read; it was for a game called *Zork*. While *Zork* was not a game that was available for my Vic-20, the concept of the game fascinated me because I was really into Sci-Fi and fantasy. I remember thinking how cool it would be to write a game like that, so I decided to figure out how to do it. One of the biggest concepts that I had to grasp at that time was controlling the flow of the application depending on the user's actions.

In this chapter, we will cover the following topics:

- What are conditional statements and how to use them
- What are loops and how to use them
- What are control transfer statements and how to use them
- How to create and use functions in Swift

What we have learned so far

Up to this point, we have been laying the foundation for writing applications with Swift. While it is possible to write a very basic application with what we have learned so far, it would be really difficult to write a useful application using only what we covered in the first three chapters.

Starting with this chapter, we will begin to move away from the foundations of the Swift language, and begin to learn the building blocks of application development with Swift. In this chapter, we will go over control flow and functions. To become a master of the Swift programming language, it is important that you fully understand and comprehend the concepts discussed in this chapter and in Chapter 5, *Classes and Structures*.

Before we cover control flow and functions, let's take a look at how curly brackets and parentheses are used in Swift.

Curly brackets

In Swift, unlike other C-like languages, curly brackets are required for conditional statements and loops. In other C-like languages, if there is only one statement to execute for a conditional statement or a loop, the curly brackets around that line are optional. This has lead to numerous errors and bugs, such as Apple's `goto fail` bug; therefore, when Apple was designing Swift, it was decided to require the use of curly brackets, even when there is only one line of code to execute. Let's look at some code that illustrates this requirement. This first example is not valid in Swift because it is missing the curly brackets; however, it will be valid in most other languages:

```
if (x > y)
   x = 0
```

In Swift, you are required to have the curly brackets, as illustrated in the following example:

```
if (x > y) {
   x = 0
}
```

Parentheses

Unlike other C-like languages, the parentheses around conditional expressions in Swift are optional. In the preceding example, we put parentheses around the conditional expression, but they are not required. The following example would be valid in Swift, but not valid in most C-like languages:

```
if x > y {
   x = 0
}
```

Control flow

Control flow, also known as flow of control, refers to the order in which statements, instructions, or functions are executed within an application. Swift supports all of the familiar control flow statements that are in C-like languages. These include loops (including `for` and `while`), conditional statements (including `if` and `switch`) and the transfer of the control statements (including `break` and `continue`). It is worthwhile to note that Swift 3 does not include the traditional C `for` loop; rather than the traditional `do...while` loop Swift has the `repeat...while` loop.

In addition to the standard C control flow statements, Swift has also added additional statements, such as the `for...in` loop, and enhanced some of the existing statements, such as the `switch` statement.

Let's begin by looking at conditional statements in Swift.

Conditional statements

A conditional statement will check a condition and execute a block of code only if the condition is true. Swift provides both the `if` and `if...else` conditional statements. Let's take a look at how to use these conditional statements to execute blocks of code if a specified condition is true.

The if statement

The `if` statement will check the conditional statement and if it is true it will execute the block of code. The `if` statement takes the following format:

```
if condition {
   block of code
}
```

Now, let's look at how to use the `if` statement:

```
let teamOneScore = 7
let teamTwoScore = 6
if teamOneScore > teamTwoScore {
    print("Team One Won")
}
```

In the preceding example, we begin by setting the `teamOneScore` and `teamTwoScore` constants. We then use the `if` statement to check whether the value of `teamOneScore` is greater than the value of `teamTwoScore`. If the value is greater, we print `Team One Won` to the console. If we run this code, we will indeed see that `Team One Won` is printed to the console, but if the value of `teamTwoScore` was greater than the value of `teamOneScore`, nothing is printed to the console. That would not be the best way to write an application because we would want the user to know which team actually won. The `if...else` statement can help us with this problem.

Conditional code execution with the if...else statement

The `if...else` statement will check a conditional statement and if it is true, it will execute a block of code. If the conditional statement is not true, it will execute a separate block of code. The `if...else` statement follows this format:

```
if condition {
    block of code if true
} else {
    block of code if not true
}
```

Let's modify the preceding example to use the `if...else` statement to tell the user which team won:

```
var teamOneScore = 7
var teamTwoScore = 6
if teamOneScore > teamTwoScore {
    print("Team One Won")
} else {
    print("Team Two Won")
}
```

This new version will print out `Team One Won`, if the value of `teamOneScore` is greater than the value of `teamTwoScore`; otherwise, it will print out the message, `Team Two Won`. What do you think the code will do if the value of `teamOneScore` is equal to the value of `teamTwoScore`? In the real world, we will have a tie, but in the preceding code, we will print out `Team Two Won`; this would not be fair to team one. In cases such as this, we can use multiple `else...if` statements and a plain `else` statement, as shown in the following example:

```
var teamOneScore = 7
var teamTwoScore = 6
if teamOneScore > teamTwoScore {
```

```
      print("Team One Won")
} else if teamTwoScore > teamOneScore {
      print("Team Two Won")
} else {
      print("We have a tie")
}
```

In the preceding code, if the value of `teamOneScore` is greater than the value of `teamTwoScore`, we print `Team One Won` to the console. We then have an `else if` statement and since the `if` statement is preceded by the `else` statement the conditional statement is checked only if the first `if` statement returns `false`. Finally, if both the `if` statements are false, then we assume that the values are equal and print `We have a tie` to the console.

A conditional statement checks the condition once, and if the condition is met it executes the block of code. What if we wanted to continuously execute the block of code until a condition is met? For this, we would use one of the looping statements that are in Swift. Let's take a look at looping statements in Swift.

The for loop

The `for` loop variants are probably the most widely used looping statements. While Swift does not offer the standard C-based `for` loop it does have the `for...in` loop. The standard C-based for loop was removed from the Swift language starting in Swift 3 because it was rarely used. You can read the full proposal to remove the `for` loop on the Swift evolution site (`https://github.com/apple/swift-evolution/blob/master/proposals/0007-remove-c-style-for-loops.md`). The `for...in` statement will execute a block of code for each item in a range, collection, or sequence.

Using the for...in loop

The `for...in` loop iterates over a collection of items or a range of numbers and executes a block of code for each item in the collection or range. The format for the `for...in` statement looks similar to this:

```
for variable in Collection/Range {
  block of code
}
```

As we can see in the preceding code, the `for...in` loop has two sections:

- `Variable`: This variable will change each time the `for...in` loop executes and hold the current item from the collection or range
- `Collection/Range`: This is the collection or range to iterate through

Let's take a look at how to use the `for...in` loop to iterate through a range of numbers:

```
for index in 1...5 {
    print(index)
}
```

In the preceding example, we iterate over a range of numbers from 1 to 5 and print each of the numbers to the console. This particular `for...in` statement uses the closed range operator (`...`) to give the `for...in` loop a range to go through. Swift also provides a second range operation called the half-open range operator (`..<`). The half-open range operator iterates through a range of numbers, but does not include the last number. Let's look at how to use the half-range operator:

```
for index in 1..<5 {
    print(index)
}
```

In the closed range operator example (`...`), we will see the numbers 1 through 5 printed to the console. In the half-range operator example, the last number (5) will be excluded; therefore, we will see the numbers 1 to 4 printed to the console.

Now, let's look at how to iterate over an array with the `for...in` loop:

```
var countries = ["USA","UK", "IN"]
for item in countries {
    print(item)
}
```

In the preceding example, we iterate through the `countries` array and print each element to the console. As we can see, iterating through an array with the `for...in` loop is safer, cleaner, and a lot easier than using the standard C-based `for` loop. Using the `for...in` loop prevents us from making common mistakes, such as using the <= (less than or equal to) operator rather than the less than (<) operator in our conditional statement.

Let's look at how to iterate over a dictionary with the `for...in` loop:

```
var dic = ["USA": "United States", "UK": "United Kingdom", "IN":"India"]

for (abbr, name) in dic {
  print("\(abbr) --  \(name)")
}
```

In the preceding example, we used the `for...in` loop to iterate through each key-value pair of a dictionary. In this example, each item in the dictionary is returned as a (key,value) tuple. We can decompose (key,value) tuple members as named constants within the body of the `for...in` loop. One thing to note is that, since a dictionary does not guarantee the order that items are stored in, the order that they are iterated over may not be the same as the order they were inserted in.

Now, let's look at another type of loop, the `while` loop.

The while loop

The `while` loop executes a block of code until a condition is met. Swift provides two forms of `while` loop; these are the `while` and `repeat...while` loops. In Swift 2.0, Apple replaced the `do...while` loop with the `repeat...while` loop. The `repeat...while` loop functions exactly as the `do...while` loop did. Apple now uses the `do` statement for error handling.

We use `while` loops when the number of iterations to perform is not known and is usually dependent on some business logic. A while loop is used when you want to run a loop zero or more times, while a `repeat...while` loop is used when you want to run the loop one or more times.

Using the while loop

The `while` loop starts by evaluating a conditional statement and then repeatedly executes a block of code if the conditional statement is true. The format for the `while` statement is as follows:

```
while condition {
  block of code
}
```

Let's look at how to use a `while` loop. In the following example, the `while` loop will continue to loop if a randomly-generated number is less than 4. In this example, we are using the `random()` function to generate a random number between 0 and 4:

```
var ran = 0
while ran < 4 {
ran = Int(random() % (5))
}
```

In the preceding example, we begin by initializing the `ran` variable to 0. The `while` loop then checks the `ran` variable, and if its value is less than 4, a new random number, between 0 and 4, is generated. The `while` loop will continue to loop while the randomly-generated number is less than 4. Once the randomly-generated number is equal to or greater than 4, the `while` loop will exit.

In the preceding example, the while loop checks the conditional statement prior to generating a new random number. What if we did not want to check the conditional statement prior to generating a random number? We could generate a random number when we first initialize the `ran` variable, but that would mean we would need to duplicate the code that generates the random numbers, and duplicating code is never an ideal solution. It would be preferable to use the `repeat...while` loop for such instances.

Using the repeat...while loop

The difference between the `while` and `repeat...while` loops is that `while` loops check the conditional statement prior to executing the block of code the first time; therefore, all the variables in the conditional statements need to be initialized prior to executing the `while` loop. The `repeat...while` loop will run through the loop block prior to checking the `conditional` statement for the first time; this means that we can initialize the variables in the conditional block of code. Use of the `repeat...while` loop is preferred when the conditional statement is dependent on the code in the loop block. The `repeat...while` loop takes the following format:

```
repeat {
   block of code
} while condition
```

Let's take a look at this specific example by creating a `repeat...while` loop where we initialize the variable we are checking, in the conditional `while` statement, within the loop block:

```
var ran: Int
repeat {
    ran = Int(random() % (5))
} while ran < 4
```

In the preceding example, we define the `ran` variable as an `Int`, but we do not initialize it until we enter the loop block and generate a random number. If we try to do this with the `while` loop (leaving the `ran` variable uninitialized), we will receive a `Variable used before being initialized` exception.

The switch statement

The `switch` statement takes a value, compares it to the several possible matches, and then executes the appropriate block of code based on the first successful match. The `switch` statement is an alternative to using the `if...else` statement when there could be several possible matches. The `switch` statement takes the following format:

```
switch value {
  case match1 :
    block of code
  case match2 :
    block of code
  ...... as many cases as needed
  default :
    block of code
}
```

Unlike the `switch` statements in most other languages, in Swift it does not fall through to the next `case` statement; therefore, we do not need to use a `break` statement to prevent the fall through. This is another safety feature that is built into Swift since one of the most common programming mistakes, with the `switch` statement, made by beginner programmers is to forget the `break` statement at the end of the `case` statement. Let's look at how to use the `switch` statement:

```
var speed = 300000000
switch speed {
case 300000000:
    print("Speed of light")
case 340:
    print("Speed of sound")
```

```
default:
    print("Unknown speed")
}
```

In the preceding example, the switch statement takes the value of the speed variable and compares it to the two case statements; if the value of speed matches either case, it will print out what the speed is. If the switch statement does not find a match, it will print out the Unknown speed message.

Every switch statement must have a match for all the possible values. This means that, unless we are matching against an enumeration, each switch statement must have a default case. Let's look at a case where we do not have a default case:

```
var num = 5
switch num {
case 1 :
    print("number is one")
case 2 :
    print("Number is two")
case 3 :
    print("Number is three")
}
```

If we put the preceding code into a Playground and attempt to compile the code, we will receive a switch must be exhaustive, consider adding a default clause error. This is a compile time error; therefore, we will not be notified until we attempt to compile the code.

It is possible to include multiple items in a single case. To do this we would need to separate the items with a comma. Let's look at how we would use the switch statement to tell us if a character is a vowel or a consonant:

```
var char : Character = "e"
switch char {
case "a", "e", "i", "o", "u":
    print("letter is a vowel")
case "b", "c", "d", "f", "g", "h", "j", "k", "l", "m",
"n", "p", "q", "r", "s", "t", "v", "w", "x", "y", "z":
    print("letter is a consonant")
default:
    print("unknown letter")
}
```

We can see in the preceding example that each case has multiple items. Commas separate these items and the switch statement will attempt to match the char variable to each item listed in the case statement.

It is also possible to check the value of a `switch` statement to see whether it is included in a range. To do this, we use a range operator in the `case` statement, as shown in the following example:

```
var grade = 93
switch grade {
case 90...100:
    print("Grade is an A")
case 80...89:
    print("Grade is a B")
case 70...79:
    print("Grade is an C")
case 60...69:
    print("Grade is a D")
case 0...59:
    print("Grade is a F")
default:
    print("Unknown Grade")
}
```

In the preceding example, the `switch` statement takes the `grade` variable; compares it with the `grade` ranges in each `case` statement, and prints out the appropriate grade.

In Swift, any `case` statement may contain an optional `guard` condition that can provide an additional condition to validate. The `guard` condition is defined with the `where` keyword. Let's say, in our preceding example, we had students who were receiving special assistance in the class and we wanted to define a grade of `D` for them in the range of 55 to 69. The following example shows how to do this:

```
var studentId = 4
var grade = 57
switch grade {
case 90...100:
    print("Grade is an A")
case 80...89:
    print("Grade is a B")
case 70...79:
    print("Grade is an C")
case 55...69 where studentId == 4:
    print("Grade is a D for student 4")
case 60...69:
    print("Grade is a D")
case 0...59:
    print("Grade is a F")
default:
    print("Unknown Grade")
}
```

One thing to keep in mind with the `guard` expression is that Swift will attempt to match the value starting with the first `case` statement and works its way down, checking each `case` statement in order. This means that, if we put the `case` statement with the `guard` expression after the Grade F `case` statement, then the `case` statement with the `guard` expression will never be reached. The following example illustrates this:

```
var studentId = 4
var grade = 57
switch grade {
case 90...100:
    print("Grade is an A")
case 80...89:
    print("Grade is a B")
case 70...79:
    print("Grade is an C")
case 60...69:
    print("Grade is a D")
case 0...59:
    print("Grade is a F")
//The following case statement would never be reached because the
//grades would always match one of the previous two
case 55...69 where studentId == 4:
    print("Grade is a D for student 4")
default:
    print("Unknown Grade")
}
```

 A good rule of thumb is that, if you are using a `guard` condition, always put the case statements with the `guard` condition before any similar case statements without `guard` expressions.

`Switch` statements are also extremely useful for evaluating enumerations. Since an enumeration has a finite number of values, if we provide a `case` statement for all the values in the enumeration, we do not need to provide a default case. The following example shows how we can use a `switch` statement to evaluate an enumeration:

```
enum Product {
    case Book(String, Double, Int)
    case Puzzle(String, Double)
}

var order = Product.Book("Mastering Swift 2", 49.99, 2015)

switch order {
case .Book(let name, let price, let year):
```

```
    print("You ordered the book \(name) for \(price)")
case .Puzzle(let name, let price):
    print("You ordered the Puzzle \(name) for \(price)")
}
```

In this example, we begin by defining an enumeration named `Product` with two values each with the associated values. We then create an `order` variable of the product type and use the `switch` statement to evaluate it. Notice that we did not put a default case at the end of the `switch` statement. If we added additional values to the `product` enumeration at a later time, we would need to either put a default case at the end of the `switch` statement or add additional `case` statements to handle the additional values.

Using case and where statements with conditional statements

As we saw in the last section, the `case` and `where` statements within a `switch` statement can be very powerful. We are able to use these statements with other conditional statements such as the `if`, `for`, and `while` statements. Using the `case` and `where` statements within our conditional statements can make our code much smaller and easier to read. Let's look at some examples, starting off with using the `where` statement to filter the results in a `for...in` loop.

Filtering with the where statement

In this section, we will see how we can use the `where` statement to filter the results of a `for...in` loop. For this example, we will take an array of integers and print out only the even numbers; however, before we look at how we would filter the results with the `where` statement, let's look at how we would do this without the `where` statement:

```
for number in 1...30 {
    if number % 2 == 0 {
        print(number)
    }
}
```

In this example, we use a `for...in` loop to cycle through the numbers 1 to 30. Within the `for...in` loop, we use an `if` conditional statement to filter out the odd numbers. In this simple example, the code is fairly easy to read, but let's see how we can use the `where` statement to use fewer lines of code and make them easier to read:

```
for number in 1...30 where number % 2 == 0 {
    print(number)
}
```

We still have the same `for...in` loop as the previous example; however, now we put the `where` statement at the end; in this particular example, we only loop through the even numbers. Using the `where` statement shortens our example by two lines and also makes it easier to read because the filter statement is on the same line as the `for...in` loop rather than being embedded in the loop itself.

Now let's look at how we could filter with the `for...case` statement.

Filtering with the for...case statement

In this next example, we will use the `for...case` statement to filter through an array of tuples and print out only the results that match our criteria. The `for...case` example is very similar to using the `where` statement that we saw earlier where it is designed to eliminate the need for an `if` statement within a loop to filter the results. In this example, we will use the `for...case` statement to filter through a list of World Series winners and print out the year(s) a particular team won the World Series:

```
var worldSeriesWinners = [
    ("Red Sox", 2004),
    ("White Sox", 2005),
    ("Cardinals", 2006),
    ("Red Sox", 2007),
    ("Phillies", 2008),
    ("Yankees", 2009),
    ("Giants", 2010),
    ("Cardinals", 2011),
    ("Giants", 2012),
    ("Red Sox", 2013),
    ("Giants", 2014),
    ("Royals", 2015)
]

for case let ("Red Sox", year) in worldSeriesWinners {
    print(year)
}
```

In this example, we create an array of tuples named `worldSeriesWinners`, where each tuple in the array contains the name of the team and the year that they won the World Series. We then use the `for...case` statement to filter through the array and only print out the years that the Red Sox won the World Series. The filtering is done within the `case` statement where `("Red Sox", year)` says that we want all the results that have the string, `"Red Sox"`, in the first item of the tuple and the value of the second item into the `year` constant. The `for` loop then loops through the results of the `case` statement, and we print out the value of the `year` constant.

The `for...case` statement also makes it very easy to filter out the nil values in an array of optionals. Let's take a look at an example of this:

```
let myNumbers: [Int?] = [1, 2, nil, 4, 5, nil, 6]

for case let .some(num) in myNumbers {
    print(num)
}
```

In this example, we create an array of optionals named `myNumbers` that may contain an integer value or may contain nil. As we will see in Chapter 10, *Using Optional Types*, an optional is defined as an enumeration internally, as shown in the following code:

```
enum Optional<Wrapped> {
    case none,
    case some(Wrapped)
}
```

If an optional is set to nil, it will have a value of `none`, but if it is not nil then it will have a value of `some` with an associated type of the actual value. In our example, when we filter for `.some(num)`, we are looking for any optional that has the value of `.some(non-nil value)`. As shorthand for `.some()`, we could use the question mark (?) symbol, as we will see in the following example.

We can also combine `for...case` with a `where` statement to do additional filtering, as shown in the following example:

```
let myNumbers: [Int?] = [1, 2, nil, 4, 5, nil, 6]

for case let num? in myNumbers where num > 3 {
    print(num)
}
```

This example is the same as the previous example except that we added the additional filtering with the `where` statement. In the previous example, we looped through all of the non-nil values, but in this example we loop through the non-nil values that are greater than 3. Let's see how we do this same filtering without the `case` or `where` statements:

```
for num in myNumbers {
    if let num = num {
        if num > 3 {
            print(num)
        }
    }
}
```

As we can see, using the `for...case` and `where` statements can greatly reduce the number of lines needed. It also makes our code much easier to read because all of the filtering statements are on the same line.

Let's look at one more filtering example. This time, we will look at the `if...case` statement.

Using the if...case statement

Using the `if...case` statement is very similar to using the `switch` statement. The `switch` statement is preferred when we have more than two cases we are trying to match, but there are instances where the `if...case` statement is needed. One of these times is when we are only looking for one or two possible matches, and we do not want to handle all of the possible matches. Let's look at an example of this:

```
enum Identifier {
    case Name(String)
    case Number(Int)
    case NoIdentifier
}

var playerIdentifier = Identifier.Number(42)

if case let .Number(num) = playerIdentifier {
    print("Player's number is \(num)")
}
```

In this example, we create an enumeration named `Identifier` that contains three possible values: `Name`, `Number`, and `NoIdentifier`. We create an instance of the `Identifier` enumeration named `playerIdentifier` with a value of `Number` and an associated value of `42`. We then use the `if-case` statement to see if the `playerIdentifier` has a value for `Number`, and if so, we print a message to the console.

Just like the `for...case` statement, we are able to do additional filtering with the `where` statement. The following example uses the same `Identifier` enumeration as we used in the previous example:

```
var playerIdentifier = Identifier.Number(2)

if case let .Number(num) = playerIdentifier, num == 2 {
    print("Player is either Xander Bogarts or Derek Jeter")
}
```

In this example, we still use the `if...case` statement to see if `playerIdentifier` has a value of `Number`, but we added the `where` statement to see if the associated value is equal to `2`; if so, we identify the player as either `Xander Bogarts or Derek Jeter`.

As we saw in our examples, using the `case` and `where` statements with our conditional statements can reduce the number of lines needed to do certain types of filtering. It can also make our code easier to read. Now let's take a look at control transfer statements.

Control transfer statements

Control transfer statements are used to transfer control to another part of the code. Swift offers six control transfer statements; these are `continue`, `break`, `fallthrough`, `guard`, `throws`, and `return`. We will look at the `return` statement in the *Functions* section later in this chapter and will discuss the `throws` statement in Chapter 8, *Writing Safer Code with Error Handling*. We will look at the remaining control transfer statements in this section.

The continue statement

The `continue` statement tells a loop to stop executing the code block and go to the next iteration of the loop. The following example shows how to use a `continue` statement to print out only odd numbers in a range:

```
for i in 1...10 {
    if i % 2 == 0 {
        continue
    }
```

```
        print("\(i) is odd")
    }
```

In the preceding example, we loop through a range of 1 through 10. For each iteration of the for...in loop, we use the remainder (%) operator to see whether the number is odd or even. If the number is even, the continue statement tells the loop to immediately go to the next iteration of the loop. If the number is odd, we print out the number is odd and then move ahead. The output of the preceding code is as follows:

```
1 is odd
3 is odd
5 is odd
7 is odd
9 is odd
```

Now, let's look at the break statement.

The break statement

The break statement immediately ends the execution of a code block within the control flow. The following example shows how to break out of a for loop when we encounter the first even number:

```
for i in 1...10 {
    if i % 2 == 0 {
        break
    }
    print("\(i) is odd")
}
```

In the preceding example, we loop through the range of 1 through 10. For each iteration of the for loop, we use the remainder (%) operator to see whether the number is odd or even. If the number is even, we use the break statement to immediately exit the loop. If the number is odd, we print out that the number is odd and then go to the next iteration of the loop. The preceding code has the following output:

```
1 is odd
```

The fallthrough statement

In Swift, `switch` statements do not fall through like other languages; however, we can use the `fallthrough` statement to force them to fall through. The `fallthrough` statement can be very dangerous because once a match is found, the next case defaults to true and that code block is executed. The following example illustrates this:

```
var name = "Jon"
var sport = "Baseball"
switch sport {
case "Baseball":
    print("\(name) plays Baseball")
    fallthrough
case "Basketball":
    print("\(name) plays Basketball")
    fallthrough
default:
    print("Unknown sport")
}
```

In the preceding example, since the first case, `Baseball`, matches the code and the remaining code blocks also execute, the output looks similar to this:

```
Jon plays Baseball
Jon plays Basketball
Unknown sport
```

The guard statement

In Swift and most modern languages, our conditional statements tend to focus on testing if a condition is true. As an example, the following code tests to see whether the variable x is greater than 10. If so, we perform some function; otherwise, we handle the error condition:

```
var x = 9
if x > 10 {
  // Functional code here
} else {
  // Do error condition
}
```

This type of code leads to having our functional code embedded within our checks and with the error conditions tucked away at the end of our functions, but what if that is not what we really want? Sometimes, it may be nice to take care of our error conditions at the beginning of the function. I know, in our simple example, we could easily check if x is less than or equal to 10 and if so perform the error condition, but not all the conditional statements are that easy to rewrite, especially the items such as optional binding.

In Swift, we have the guard statement. The guard statement focuses on performing a function if a condition is false; this allows us to trap errors and perform the error conditions early in our functions. We could rewrite our previous example using the guard statement like this:

```
var x = 9
guard x > 10 else {
  // Do error condition
    return
}
// Functional code here
```

In this new example, we check to see whether the variable x is greater than 10, and if not, we perform our error condition. If the variable x is greater than 10, our code continues. You will notice that we have a return statement embedded within the guard condition code. The code within the guard statement must contain a transfer of control statement; this is what prevents the rest of the code from executing. If we forget the transfer of control statement, Swift will show a compile time error.

Let's look at some more examples of the guard statement. The following example shows how we would use the guard statement to verify that an optional contains a valid value:

```
func guardFunction(str: String?) {
    guard let goodStr = str else {
        print("Input was nil")
        return
    }
    print("Input was \(goodStr)")
}
```

In this example, we create a function named guardFunction() that accepts an optional containing a string or nil value. We then use the guard statement with optional binding to verify that the string optional does not contain a nil. If it does contain nil, then the code within the guard statement is executed and the return statement is used to exit the function. The really nice thing about using the guard statement with optional binding is that the new variable is in scope for the rest of the function rather than just within the scope of the optional binding statement.

Now that we have seen how the control flow statements work in Swift, let's introduce functions and classes in Swift.

Functions

In Swift, a function is a self-contained block of code that performs a specific task. Functions are generally used to logically break our code into reusable named blocks. The function's name is used to call the function.

When we define a function, we can also optionally define one or more parameters (also known as arguments). Parameters are named values that are passed into the function by the code that calls it. These parameters are generally used within the function to perform the task of the function. We can also define default values for the parameters to simplify how the function is called.

Every Swift function has a type associated with it. This type is referred to as the return type and it defines the type of data returned from the function to the code that called it. If a value is not returned from a function, the return type is `Void`.

Let's look at how to define functions in Swift.

Using a single-parameter function

The syntax used to define a function in Swift is very flexible. This flexibility makes it easy for us to define simple C style functions, or more complex functions, with local and external parameter names. Let's look at some examples of how to define functions. The following example accepts one parameter and does not return any value back to the code that called it (return type-`Void`):

```
func sayHello(name: String) -> Void {
let retString = "Hello " + name
   print( retString)
}
```

In the preceding example, we defined a function named `sayHello` that accepts one variable that is named `name`. Inside the function, we print out a `Hello` greeting to the name of the person. Once the code within the function gets executed, the function exits and control is returned back to the code that called it. Rather than printing out the greeting, if we want to return the greeting back to the code that called it, we can add a return type, as follows:

```
func sayHello2(name: String) ->String {
    let retString = "Hello " + name
    return retString
}
```

The `->` string defines that the return type associated with the function is a string. This means that the function must return a string variable back to the code that calls it. Inside the function, we build a string constant with the greeting message and then use the `return` keyword to return the string constant.

Calling a Swift function is very similar to how we call functions or methods in other languages such as C or Java. The following example shows how to call the `sayHello(name:)` function, which prints the greeting message to the screen from within the function:

```
sayHello(name:"Jon")
```

Now, let's look at how to call the `sayHello2(name:)` function, which returns a value back to the code that called it:

```
var message = sayHello2(name:"Jon")
print(message)
```

In the preceding example, we call the `sayHello2(name:)` function and put the value returned in the `message` variable. If a function defines a return type, such as the `sayHello2(name:)` function does, it must return a value of that type to the code that called it. Therefore, every possible conditional path within the function must end by returning a value of the specified type. This does not mean that the code that called the function has to retrieve the returned value. As an example, both lines in the following examples are valid:

```
sayHello2(name:"Jon")
var message = sayHello2(name: "Jon")
```

If you do not specify a variable for the return value to go into, the value is dropped. When you compile your code you will receive a warning if a function returns a value and you do not put it into a variable or a constant. You can avoid the warning by using the underscore as shown in this next example:

```
_ = sayHello2(name:"Jon")
```

The underscore tells the compiler that you are aware of the return value but you do not want to use it. Let's look at how we would define multiple parameters for our functions.

Using a multi-parameter function

We are not limited to just one parameter with our functions, we can also define multiple parameters. To create a multi-parameter function, we list the parameters in the parentheses and separate the parameter definitions with commas. Let's look at how to define multiple parameters in a function:

```
func sayHello(name: String, greeting: String) {
    print("\(greeting) \(name)")
}
```

In the preceding example, the function accepts two arguments: `name` and `greeting`. We then print a `greeting` to the console using both the parameters.

Calling a multi-parameter function is a little different from calling a single-parameter function. When calling a multi-parameter function, we separate the parameters with commas. We also need to include the parameter name for all the parameters. The following example shows how to call a multi-parameter function:

```
sayHello(name:"Jon", greeting:"Bonjour")
```

We do not need to supply an argument for each parameter of the function if we define default values. Let's look at how to configure default values for our parameters.

Defining a parameter's default values

We can define default values for parameters by using the equal to operator (=) within the function definition when we declare the variables. The following example shows how to declare a function with parameter default values:

```
func sayHello(name: String, greeting: String = "Bonjour") {
    print("\(greeting) \(name)")
}
```

In the function declaration, we define one parameter without a default value (`name: String`) and one parameter with a default value (`greeting: String = "Bonjour"`). When a parameter has a default value declared, we are able to call the function with or without setting a value for that parameter. The following example shows how to call the `sayHello()` function without setting the `greeting` parameter, and also how to call it with setting the `greeting` parameter:

```
sayHello(name:"Jon")
sayHello(name:"Jon", greeting: "Hello")
```

In the `sayHello(name:"Jon")` line, the `sayHello()` function will print out the message `Bonjour Jon` since it uses the default value for the `greeting` parameter. In the `sayHello(name:"Jon", greeting: "Hello")` line, the `sayHello()` function will print out the message `Hello Jon` since we override the default value for the `greeting` parameter.

We can declare multiple parameters with default values and override only the ones we want by using the parameter names. The following example shows how we would do this by overriding one of the default values when we call it:

```
func sayHello4(name: String, name2: String = "Kim", greeting: String =
"Bonjour") {
    print"\(greeting) \(name) and \(name2)")
}

sayHello4(name:"Jon", greeting: "Hello")
```

In the preceding example, we declare one parameter without a default value (`name: String`) and two parameters with default values (`name2: String = "Kim"`, `greeting: String = "Bonjour"`). We then call the function leaving the `name2` parameter with its default value, but override the default value of the `greeting` parameter.

The preceding example would print out the message, `Hello Jon and Kim`.

Returning multiple values from a function

There are a couple of ways to return multiple values from a Swift function. One of the most common ways is to put the values into a collection type (array or dictionary) and return the collection. The following example shows how to return a collection type from a Swift function:

```
func getNames() -> [String] {
    let retArray = ["Jon", "Kim", "Kailey", "Kara"]
    return retArray
}

var names = getNames()
```

In the preceding example, we declare the `getNames()` function with no parameters and a return type of `[String]`. The return type of `[String]` specifies the return type as an array of `String` types.

One of the drawbacks to returning a collection type is that the values of the collection must be of the same type, or we must declare our collection type to be of the `Any` type. In the preceding example, our array could only return `String` types. If we needed to return numbers with our strings, we could return an array of `Any` types and then use typecasting to specify the object type. However, this would not be a very good design for our application since it would be very prone to errors. A better way to return values of different types would be to use a tuple type.

When we return a tuple from a function, it is recommended that we use a named tuple to allow us to use the dot syntax to access the returned values. The following example shows how to return a named tuple from a function and access the values from the named tuple that is returned:

```
func getTeam() -> (team:String, wins:Int, percent:Double) {
    let retTuple = ("Red Sox", 99, 0.611)
 return retTuple
}

var t = getTeam()
print("\(t.team) had \(t.wins) wins")
```

In the preceding example, we define the `getTeam()` function, which returns a named tuple that contains three values-`String`, `Int`, and `Double`. Within the function, we create the tuple that we are going to return. Notice that we do not need to define the tuple that we are going to return as a named tuple as long as the value types within the tuple match the value types in the function definition. We can then call the function, as we would any other function, and use the dot syntax to access the values of the tuple that is returned. In the preceding example, the code would print out the following line:

```
Red Sox had 99 wins
```

Returning optional values

In the previous sections, we returned non-nil values from our function; however, that is not always what we need our code to do. What happens if we need to return a nil value from a function? The following code would throw an `expression does not conform to type 'NilLiteralConvertible'` exception:

```
func getName() ->String {
    return nil
}
```

This code throws an exception because we define the return type as a string value; however, we are attempting to return `nil`. If there is a reason to return `nil`, we need to define the return type as an optional type to let the code calling it know that the value may be `nil`. To define the return type as an optional type, we use the question mark (?) in the same way we did when we defined a variable as an optional type. The following example shows how to define an optional return type:

```
func getName() ->String? {
    return nil
}
```

The preceding code would not throw an exception.

We can also set a tuple as an optional type or any value within a tuple as an optional type. The following example shows how we would return a tuple as an optional type:

```
func getTeam2(id: Int) -> (team:String, wins:Int, percent:Double)? {
    if id == 1 {
        return ("Red Sox", 99, 0.611)
    }
    return nil
}
```

[100]

In the following example, we could return a tuple as defined within our function definition or a `nil`; either option is valid. If we needed an individual value within our tuple to be `nil`, we would need to add an optional type within our tuple. The following example shows how to return a `nil` within our tuple:

```
func getTeam() -> (team:String, wins:Int, percent:Double?) {
    let retTuple: (String, Int, Double?) = ("Red Sox", 99, nil)
    return retTuple
}
```

In the preceding example, we can set the `percent` value to either a `Double` value or `nil`.

Adding external parameter names

In the preceding examples in this section, the parameters were defined similarly to how we would define the parameters in C code, where we define the parameter names and value types. When we call the function, we also call the function similarly to how we would call functions in C code, where we use the function name and specify the values we are passing to the function within parenthesis. In Swift, we are not limited to this syntax; we can also use external parameter names.

External parameter names are used when we call a function to indicate the purpose of each parameter. If we want to use external parameter names with our functions, we need to define an external parameter name for each parameter in addition to its local parameter name. The external parameter name is added before the local parameter name in the function definition. The external and local parameter names are separated by a space.

Let's look at how to use external parameter names. But before we do so, let's review how we have previously defined functions. In the next two examples, we will define a function without external parameter names and then we will redefine that function with external parameter names:

```
func winPercentage(team: String, wins: Int, loses: Int) -> Double {
    return Double(wins) / Double(wins + loses)
}
```

In the preceding example, we define the `winPercentage()` function that accepts three parameters. These parameters are `team`, `wins`, and `loses`. The `team` parameter is a `String` type and the `wins` and `loses` parameters are `Int` types. The following line of code shows how to call the `winPercentage()` function:

```
var per = winPercentage(team: "Red Sox", wins: 99, loses: 63)
```

Now, let's define the same function with external parameter names:

```
func winPercentage(BaseballTeam team: String, withWins wins: Int, andLoses
losses: Int) -> Double {
   return Double(wins) / Double(wins + losses)
}
```

In the preceding example, we redefine the `winPercentage` function with external parameter names. In this redefinition, we have the same three parameters: `team`, `wins`, and `losses`. The difference lies in how we define the parameters. When using external parameters, we define each parameter with both an external parameter name and a local parameter name separated by a space. In the preceding example, the first parameter has an external parameter name of `BaseballTeam`, an internal parameter name of `team`, and a type of `String`.

When we call a function with external parameter names, we need to include the external parameter names in the function call. The following code shows how to call the function in the preceding example:

```
var per = winPercentage(BaseballTeam:"Red Sox", withWins:99, andLoses:63)
```

While using external parameter names requires more typing, it does make your code easier to read. In the preceding example, it is easy to see that the function is looking for the name of a baseball team, the second parameter is the number of wins, and the last parameter is the number of losses.

Using variadic parameters

A **variadic** parameter is one that accepts zero or more values of a specified type. Within the function's definition, we define a variadic parameter by appending three periods(...) to the parameter's type name. The values of a variadic parameter are made available to the function as an array of the specified type. The following example shows how we would use a variadic parameter with a function:

```
func sayHello(greeting: String, names: String...) {
   for name in names {
      print("\(greeting) \(name)")
   }
}
```

In the preceding example, the sayHello() function takes two parameters. The first parameter is a String type, which is the greeting to use. The second parameter is a variadic parameter of the String type; the names to send the greeting to. Within the function, a variadic parameter is an array that contains the type specified; therefore, in our example, the names parameter is an array of string values. In this example, we use a for...in loop to access the values within the names parameter.

The following line of code shows how to call the sayHello() function with a variadic parameter:

```
sayHello(greeting:"Hello", names: "Jon", "Kim")
```

The preceding line of code will print two greetings: Hello Jon and Hello Kim.

Inout parameters

If we want to change the value of a parameter and we want those changes to persist once the function ends, we need to define the parameter as an inout parameter. Any changes made to an inout parameter are passed back to the variable that was used in the function call.

Two caveats to keep in mind when we use inout parameters are that these parameters cannot have default values and they cannot be a variadic parameter.

Let's look at how to use the inout parameters to swap the values of two variables:

```
func reverse( first: inout String, second: inout String) {
    let tmp = first
    first = second
    second = tmp
}
```

This function will accept two parameters and swap the values of the variables that are used in the function call. When we make the function call, we put an ampersand (&) in front of the variable name indicating that the function can modify its value. The following example shows how to call the reverse function:

```
var one = "One"
var two = "Two"
reverse(first: &one, second: &two)
print("one: \(one)  two: \(two)")
```

In the preceding example, we set variableone to the value One and variable two to the value Two. We then call the reverse function with the one and two variables. Once the swap function returns, the variable named one will contain the value Two, while the variable named two will contain the value One.

Nesting functions

All the functions that we have shown so far are examples of global functions. Global functions are defined at a global scope within the class or file that they are in. Swift also allows us to nest one function within another. Nested functions can only be called within the enclosed function; however, the enclosed function can return a nested function that allows it to be used outside the scope of the enclosed function. We will cover returning a function in Chapter 12, *Working with Closures*.

Let's look at how to nest functions by creating a simple sort function that will take an array of integers and sort it:

```
func sort( numbers: inout [Int]) {
    func reverse( first: inout Int, second: inout Int) {
        let tmp = first
        first = second
        second = tmp
    }
    var count = numbers.count
    while count > 0 {
        for var i in 1..<count {
            if numbers[i] < numbers[i-1] {
                reverse(first: &numbers[i], second: &numbers[i-1])
            }
        }
        count -= 1
    }
}
```

In the preceding code, we begin by creating a global function named sort that accepts an inout parameter, that is, an array of Int. Within the sort function, the first thing we do is define the nested function that is named reverse. A function needs to be defined in the code prior to calling it, so it is good practice to put all the nested functions at the start of the global function so that we know they are defined prior to calling them. The reverse function simply swaps the two values that are passed in.

Within the body of the `sort` function, we implement the logic for the simple sort. Within that logic, we compare two numbers in the array, and if the numbers need to be reversed, we call the nested `reverse` function to swap the two numbers. This example shows how we can effectively use a nested function to organize our code to make it easy to maintain and read. Let's look at how to call the global sort function:

```
var nums: [Int] = [6,2,5,3,1]

sort(numbers: &nums)

for value in nums {
    print("--\(value)")
}
```

The preceding code creates an array of five integers and then passes the array to the `sort` function. When the `sort` function returns the `nums` array, it contains a sorted array.

 Nested functions, when used properly, can be very useful. However, it is really easy to overuse them. Before creating a nested function, you might want to ask yourself why you want to use a nested function and what problem you are solving by using it.

Putting it all together

To reinforce what we learned in this chapter, let's look at one more example. For this example, we will create a function that will test to see if a string value contains a valid IPv4 address or not. An IPv4 address is the address assigned to a computer that uses the **Internet Protocol** (**IP**) to communicate. An IP address consists of four numeric values, ranging from 0-255, separated by a dot (period). An example of a valid IP address is 10.0.1.250:

```
func isValidIP(ipAddr: String?) -> Bool {

    guard let ipAddr = ipAddr else {
        return false
    }
    let octets = ipAddr.characters.split { $0 == "."}.map{String($0)}
    guard octets.count == 4 else {
        return false
    }
    func validOctet(octet: String) -> Bool {
        guard let num = Int(String(octet)),
            num >= 0 && num < 256 else {
                return false
        }
```

```
        return true
    }
    for octet in octets {
        guard validOctet(octet: octet) else {
            return false
        }
    }
    return true

}
```

Since the parameter for the `isValidIp()` function is an optional type, the first thing we do is verify that the `ipAddr` parameter is not nil. To do this, we used a `guard` statement with optional binding; if the optional binding fails, we return a Boolean `false` value because nil is not a valid IP address.

If the `ipAddr` parameter contains a non-nil value, we then split the string into an array of strings, at the dots. Since an IP address is supposed to contain four numbers separated by a dot, we use the `guard` statement again to check whether the array contains four elements. If it does not, we return `false` because we know that the `ipAddr` parameter did not contain a valid IP address.

Next, we create a nested function named `validOctet()` that has one String parameter named `octet`. This nested function will verify that the `octet` parameter contains a numeric value between 0 and 255. If so, it will return a Boolean `true` value; otherwise, it will return a `false` Boolean value.

Finally, we loop through values in the array that we created by splitting the original `ipAddr` parameter at the dots and pass the values to the `validOctet()` nested function. If all four values get verified by the `validOctet()` function, we have a valid IP address and we return a Boolean `true` value; however, if any of the values fail the `validOctet()` function, we return a Boolean `false` value.

Summary

In this chapter, we covered control flow and functions in Swift. It is essential to understand the concepts in this chapter before going on. Every application that we write, beyond the simple Hello World applications, will rely very heavily on control flow statements and functions.

Control flow statements are used to make decisions within our application, and functions will be used to group our code into the sections that are reusable and organized.

5
Classes and Structures

The first programming language that I learned was BASIC. It was a good language to begin programming with, but once I traded in my Commodore Vic-20 for a PCjr (yes, I had a PCjr and I really enjoyed it), I realized that there were other, more advanced languages out there, and I spent a lot of time learning Pascal and C. It wasn't until I started college that I heard the term *object-oriented language*. At that time, object-oriented languages were so new that there were no real courses on them, but I was able to experiment a little with C++. After I graduated, I left object-oriented programming behind, and it really wasn't until several years later, when I started to experiment with C++ again, that I really discovered the power and flexibility of object-oriented programming.

In this chapter, we will cover the following topics:

- Creating and using classes and structures
- Adding properties and property observers to classes and structures
- Adding methods to classes and structures
- Adding initializers to classes and structures
- Using access controls
- Creating a class hierarchy
- Extending a class
- Understanding memory management and ARC

What are classes and structures?

In Swift, classes and structures are very similar. If we really want to master Swift, it is very important to understand what makes classes and structures so similar and also what sets them apart because they are the building blocks of our applications. Apple describes classes and structures as:

Classes and structures are general-purpose, flexible constructs that become the building blocks of your program's code. You define properties and methods to add functionality to your classes and structures by using the already familiar syntax of constants, variables, and functions.

Let's begin by taking a quick look at some of the similarities between classes and structures.

Similarities between classes and structures

In Swift, classes and structures are more similar than they are in other languages, such as Objective-C. The following is a list of some of the features that classes and structures share:

- **Properties**: These are used to store information in our classes and structures
- **Methods**: These provide functionality for our classes and structures
- **Initializers**: These are used when initializing instances of our classes and structures
- **Subscripts**: These provide access to values using the subscript syntax
- **Extensions**: These help in extending both classes and structures

Now, let's take a quick look at some of the differences between classes and structures.

Differences between classes and structures

While classes and structures are very similar, there are also several very important differences. The following is a list of some of the differences between classes and structures in Swift:

- **Type**: A structure is a value type while a class is a reference type
- **Inheritance**: A structure cannot inherit from other types while a class can
- **Deinitializers**: Structures cannot have custom deinitializers while a class can

Throughout this chapter, we will be emphasizing the differences between classes and structures to help us understand when to use each. Before we really delve into classes and structures, let's take a look at the difference between value types (structures) and reference types (classes). In order to understand when to use classes and structures and how to properly use them, it is important to understand the difference between value and reference types.

Value versus reference types

Structures are value types. This means that, when we pass instances of a structure within our application, we pass a copy of the structure and not the original structure. Classes are reference types, which means that, when we pass an instance of a class within our application, we pass a reference to the original instance. It is very important to understand this difference between value and reference types. We will give a very high-level view here, and will provide additional details in the *Memory management* section at the end of this chapter.

When we pass structures within our application, we are passing copies of the structures and not the original structures. Since a function gets its own copy of the structure, it can change it as needed, without affecting the original instance of the structure.

When we pass an instance of a class within our application, we are passing a reference to the original instance of the class. Since we are passing the instance of the class to a function, the function gets a reference to the original instance; therefore, any changes made within the function will remain once the function exits.

To illustrate the difference between value and reference types, let's look at a real-world object–a book. If we had a friend who wanted to read *Mastering Swift 3 for Linux*, we could either buy them their own copy or share ours.

If we bought our friend their own copy of the book, then any notes they made within the book would remain in their copy of the book and would not be reflected in our copy. This is how *pass by value* works with structures and variables. Any changes that are made to the structure or variable within the function are not reflected in the original instance of the structure or variable.

If we share our copy of the book, then any notes they make within the book will stay in the book when they return it to us. This is how *pass by reference* works. Any changes that are made to the instance of the class remains when the function exits.

To read more about value versus reference types, see the *Memory management* section at the end of this chapter.

Creating a class or structure

We use the same syntax to define classes and structures. The only difference is we define a class using the `class` keyword, and a structure by using the `struct` keyword. Let's look at the syntax used to create both classes and structures:

```
class MyClass {
  // MyClass definition
}

struct MyStruct {
  // MyStruct definition
}
```

In the preceding code, we define a new class named `MyClass` and a new structure named `MyStruct`. This effectively creates two new Swift types named `MyClass` and `MyStruct`. When we name a new type, we want to use the standard naming convention set by Swift where the name is in camel case, with the first letter being uppercase. Any method or property defined within the class or structure should also be named using camel case with the first letter being lowercase.

Empty classes and structures are not that useful, so let's look at how we can add properties to our classes and structures.

Properties

Properties associate values with a class or a structure. There are two types of properties, which are as follows:

- **Stored properties**: They store variable or constant values as part of an instance of a class or structure. Stored properties can also have property observers, which can monitor the property for changes and respond with custom actions when the value of the property changes.
- **Computed properties**: They do not store a value by themselves, but retrieve and possibly set other properties. The value returned by a computed property can also be calculated when it is requested.

Stored properties

A stored property is a variable or constant that is stored as part of an instance of a class or structure. These are defined with the var and let keywords. Let's look at how we will use stored properties in classes and structures. In the following code, we will create a structure named MyStruct and a class named MyClass. The structure and the class both contain two stored properties, c and v. The stored property c is a constant because it is defined with the let keyword, and v is a variable because it is defined with the var keyword. Let's take a look at the following code:

```
struct MyStruct {
  let c = 5
  var v = ""
}

class MyClass {
  let c = 5
  var v = ""
}
```

As we can see from the example, the syntax to define a stored property is the same for both classes and properties. Let's look at how we would create an instance of both the structure and class. The following code creates an instance of the MyStruct structure named myStruct and an instance of the MyClass class named myClass:

```
var myStruct = MyStruct()
var myClass = MyClass()
```

One of the differences between a structure and a class is that, by default, a structure creates an initializer that lets us populate the stored properties when we create an instance of the structure. Therefore, we could also create an instance of MyStruct like this:

```
var myStruct = MyStruct(v: "Hello")
```

In the preceding example, the initializer is used to set the variable v, and the c constant will contain the number 5 that is set in the struct itself. If, for example, we did not give the constant an initial value, as shown in the following example, the default initializer would be used to set the constant as well:

```
struct MyStruct {
  let c: Int
  var v = ""
}
```

The following example shows how the initializer for this new `struct` would work:

```
var myStruct = MyStruct(c: 10, v: "Hello")
```

This allows us to define a constant, where we set the value when we initialize the class or structure at runtime rather than hard-coding the value of the constant in our code.

The order in which the parameters appear in the initializer is the order that we defined them in. In the previous example, we defined the c constant first; therefore, it is the first parameter in the initializer. We defined the v parameter second; therefore it is the second parameter in the initializer.

To set or read a stored property, we use the standard dot syntax. Let's look at how we would set and read stored properties in Swift:

```
var x = myClass.c
myClass.v = "Howdy"
```

Before we move on to computed properties, let's create both a structure and class that will represent an employee. We will be using and expanding these throughout this chapter to show how classes and structures are similar and how they differ:

```
struct EmployeeStruct {
  var firstName = ""
  var lastName = ""
  var salaryYear = 0.0
}

public class EmployeeClass {
  var firstName = ""
  var lastName = ""
  var salaryYear = 0.0
}
```

The employee structure is named `EmployeeStruct` and the employee class is named `EmployeeClass`. Both the class and structure have three stored properties: `firstName`, `lastName`, and `salaryYear`.

Within our structure and class, we can now access these properties by using the name of the property and the `self` keyword. Every instance of a structure or class has a property named `self`. This property refers to the instance itself; therefore, we can use it to access the properties within the instance. The following examples show how we can access the properties using the `self` keyword:

```
self.firstName = "Jon"
self.lastName = "Hoffman"
```

Computed properties

Computed properties are properties that do not have backend variables that are used to store the values associated with the property. The values of a computed property are usually computed when code requests it. You can think of a computed property as a function disguised as a property. Let's take a look at how we would define a read-only computed property:

```
var salaryWeek: Double {
get{
  return self.salaryYear/52
  }
}
```

To create a read-only computed property, we begin by defining it as if it were a normal variable with the `var` keyword, followed by the variable name, colon, and the variable type. What comes next is different; we add a curly bracket at the end of the declaration and then define a `getter` method that is called when the value of our computed property is requested. In this example, the `getter` method divides the current value of the `salaryYear` property by `52` to get the employee's weekly salary.

We can simplify the definition of the read-only computed property by removing the `get` keyword. We would rewrite the `salaryWeek` function like this:

```
var salaryWeek: Double {
  return self.salaryYear/52
}
```

Computed properties are not limited to being read-only, we can also write to them. To enable the salaryWeek property to be writeable, we would need to add a setter method. The following example shows how we would add a setter method that will set the salaryYear property, based on the value being passed into the salaryWeek property:

```
var salaryWeek: Double {
  get {
    return self.salaryYear/52
  }
  set (newSalaryWeek){
    self.salaryYear = newSalaryWeek*52
  }
}
```

We can simplify the setter definition by not defining a name for the new value. In this case, the value would be assigned to a default variable name, newValue. The salaryWeek computed property could be rewritten like this:

```
var salaryWeek: Double {
  get{
    return self.salaryYear/52
  }
  set{
    self.salaryYear = newValue*52
  }
}
```

The salaryWeek computed property, as written in the preceding example, could be added to either the EmployeeClass class or the EmployeeStruct structure without any modifications. Let's see how we would do this by adding the salaryWeek property to our EmployeeClass class:

```
public class EmployeeClass {
  var firstName = ""
  var lastName = ""
  var salaryYear = 0.0
  var salaryWeek: Double {
    get{
      return self.salaryYear/52
    }
    set (newSalaryWeek){
      self.salaryYear = newSalaryWeek*52
    }
  }
}
```

Now, let's look at how we would add the `salaryWeek` computed property to the `EmployeeStruct` structure:

```
struct EmployeeStruct {
    var firstName = ""
    var lastName = ""
    var salaryYear = 0.0
    var salaryWeek: Double {
        get{
            return self.salaryYear/52
        }
        set (newSalaryWeek){
            self.salaryYear = newSalaryWeek*52
        }
    }
}
```

As we can see, the class and structure definitions are the same so far, except for the initial `class` or `struct` keywords that are used to define them.

We read and write to a computed property exactly as we would a stored property. Code that is external to the class or structure should not be aware that the property is a computed property. Let's see this in action by creating an instance of the `EmployeeStruct` structure:

```
var f = EmployeeStruct(firstName: "Jon", lastName: "Hoffman", salaryYear:
39000)

print(f.salaryWeek) //prints 750.00 to the console
f.salaryWeek = 1000
print(f.salaryWeek) //prints 1000.00 to the console
print(f.salaryYear) //prints 52000.00 to the console
```

The preceding example starts off by creating an instance of the `EmployStruct` structure with the `salaryYear` value being set to `39,000`. Next, we print the value of the `salaryWeek` property to the console. This value is currently `750.00`. We then set the `salaryWeek` property to `1000.00` and print out both the `salaryWeek` and `salaryYear` properties to the console. The values of the `salaryWeek` and `salaryYear` properties are now `1000.00` and `52000` respectively. As we can see, in this example, setting either the `salaryWeek` or `salaryYear` property changes the values returned by both.

Computed properties can be very useful for offering different views of the same data. For example, if we had a value that represented the length of something, we could store the length in centimeters and then use computed properties that calculate the values for meters, millimeters, and kilometers.

Now, let's take a look at property observers.

Property observers

Property observers are called every time the value of the property is set. We can add property observers to any non-lazy stored property. We can also add property observers to any inherited stored or computed property by overriding the property in the subclass. We will cover this in the *Overriding properties* section a little later in this chapter.

There are two property observers that we can set in Swift–willSet and didSet. The willSet observer is called right before the property is set, and the didSet observer is called right after the property is set.

One thing to note about property observers is that they are not called when the value is set during initialization. Let's look at how we would add a property observer to the salary property of our EmployeeClass class and EmployeeStruct structure:

```
var salaryYear: Double = 0.0 {
  willSet(newSalary) {
    print("About to set salaryYear to \(newSalary)")
  }
  didSet {
    if salaryWeek > oldValue {
      print("\(firstName) got a raise")
    }
    else {
      print("\(firstName) did not get a raise")
    }
  }
}
```

When we add a property observer to a stored property, we need to include the type of the value being stored within the definition of the property. In the preceding example, we did not need to define our salaryYear property as a Double type; however, when we add property observers the definition is required.

After the property definition, we define a `willSet` observer that simply prints out the new value that the `salaryYear` property will be set to. We also define a `didSet` observer that will check whether the new value is greater than the old value. If so, it will print out that the employee got a raise; otherwise, it will print out that the employee did not get a raise.

As with the getter in computed properties, we do not need to define the name for the new value for the `willSet` observer. If we do not define a name, the new value is put in a constant named `newValue`. The following example shows how we would rewrite the previous `willSet` observer without defining a name for the new value:

```
willSet {
    print("About to set salaryYear to \(newValue)")
}
```

As we have seen, properties are mainly used to store information associated with a class or structure, and methods are mainly used to add the business logic to a class or structure. Let's look at how we would add methods to a class or structure.

Methods

Methods are functions that are associated with a class or structure. A method, like a function, will encapsulate the code for a specific task or functionality that is associated with the class or structure. Let's look at how we would define a method in classes and structures. The following code will return the full name of the employee by using the `firstName` and `lastName` properties:

```
func getFullName() -> String {
    return firstName + " " + lastName
}
```

We define this method exactly as we would define any function. A method is simply a function that is associated with a specific class or structure, and everything that we learned about functions in the previous chapters applies to methods. The `getFullName()` function can be added directly to the `EmployeeClass` class or `EmployeeStruct` structure without any modification.

To access a method, we use the same dot syntax we used to access properties. The following code shows how we would access the `getFullName()` method of a class and a structure:

```
var e = EmployeeClass()
var f = EmployeeStruct(firstName: "Jon", lastName: "Hoffman", salaryYear:
50000)
```

```
e.firstName = "Jon"
e.lastName = "Hoffman"
e.salaryYear = 50000.00

print(e.getFullName()) //Jon Hoffman is printed to the console
print(f.getFullName()) //Jon Hoffman is printed to the console
```

In the preceding example, we initialize an instance of both the `EmployeeClass` class and `EmployeeStruct` structure. We populate the structure and class with the same information and then use the `getFullName()` method to print the full name of the employee to the console. In both cases, `Jon Hoffman` is printed to the console.

There is a difference in how we define methods for classes and structures, which need to update property values. Let's look at how we would define a method that gives an employee a raise within the `EmployeeClass` class:

```
func giveRaise(amount: Double) {
  self.salaryYear += amount
}
```

If we add the preceding code to our `EmployeeClass`, it works as expected; when we call the method with an amount, the employee gets a raise. However, if we try to add this method as it is written to the `EmployeeStruct` structure, we receive the `Left side of mutating operator isn't mutable: 'self is immutable'` error. By default, we are not allowed to update property values within a method of a structure. If we want to modify a property, we can opt into mutating behavior for that method by adding the `mutating` keyword before the `func` keyword of the method declaration. Therefore, the following code would be the correct way to define the `giveRaise()` method for the `EmployeeStruct` structure:

```
mutating func giveRase(amount: Double) {
    self.salaryYear += amount
}
```

In the preceding examples, we used the `self` property. Every instance of a type has a property called `self`, which is the instance itself. We use the `self` property to refer to the current instance of the type within the instance itself, so when we write `self.salaryYear`, we ask for the value of the `salaryYear` property of the current instance.

The `self` property can be used to distinguish between a local variable and an instance variable that have the same name. Let's look at an example that illustrates this:

```
func compareFirstName(firstName: String) -> Bool {
  return self.firstName == firstName
}
```

In the preceding example, the method accepts an argument with the name, `firstName`. There is also a property that has this name. We use the `self` property to specify that we want the instance property with the name, `firstName`, and not the local variable with this name.

Other than the `mutating` keyword being required for methods that change the value of the structure's properties, methods can be defined and used exactly as functions are defined and used. Therefore, everything we learned about functions in the previous chapter can be applied to methods.

There are times when we want to initialize properties or perform some business logic when a class or structure is first initialized. For this, we will use an initializer.

Custom initializers

Initializers are called when we initialize a new instance of a particular type (a class or structure). Initialization is the process of preparing an instance for use. The initialization process can include setting initial values for stored properties, verifying external resources are available, or setting up the UI properly. Initializers are generally used to ensure that the instance of the class or structure is properly initialized prior to first use.

Initializers are special methods that are used to create a new instance of a type. We define an initializer exactly as we would define other methods, but we must use the `init` keyword as the name of the initializer to tell the compiler that this method is an initializer. In its simplest form, the initializer does not accept any arguments. Let's look at the syntax used to write a simple initializer:

```
init() {
  //Perform initialization here
}
```

This format works for both classes and structures. By default, all classes and structures have an empty default initializer that we can override if we choose to. We saw these default initializers when we used the `EmployeeClass` class and `EmployeeStruct` structure in the previous section. Structures also have an additional default initializer, which we saw with the `EmployeeStruct` structure, that accepts a value for each stored property and initializes them with those values. Let's look at how we would add custom initializers to our `EmployeeClass` class and `EmployeeStruct` structure. In the following code, we create three custom initializers that will work for both the `EmployeeClass` class and the `EmployeeStruct` structure:

```
init() {
  self.firstName = ""
  self.lastName = ""
  self.salaryYear = 0.0
}
init(firstName: String, lastName: String) {
  self.firstName = firstName
  self.lastName = lastName
  self.salaryYear = 0.0
}
init(firstName: String, lastName: String, salaryYear: Double) {
  self.firstName = firstName
  self.lastName = lastName
  self.salaryYear = salaryYear
}
```

The first initializer, `init()`, when used, will set all of the stored properties to their default values. The second initializer, `init(firstName: String, lastName: String)`, when used, will populate the `firstName` and `lastName` properties with the values of the arguments. The third initializer, `init(firstName: String, lastName: String, salaryYear: Double)`, will populate all the properties with the values of the arguments.

In the previous example, we can see that in Swift an initializer does not have a return value. This means that we do not have to define the return type for the initializer or have a return statement within the initializer. Let's look at how we would use these initializers:

```
var g = EmployeeClass()
var h = EmployeeStruct(firstName: "Me", lastName: "Moe")
var i = EmployeeClass(firstName: "Me", lastName: "Moe", salaryYear: 45000)
```

The variable `g` uses the `init()` initializer to create an instance of the `EmployeeClass` class; therefore, all the properties of this `EmployeeClass` instance contain their default values.

The h variable uses the `init(firstName: String, lastName: String)` initializer to create an instance of the `EmployeeStruct` structure; therefore, the `firstName` property of the structure is set to Me and the `lastName` property is set to Moe, which are the two arguments passed into the initializer. The `salaryYear` property is still set to the default value of 0.0.

The i variable uses the `init(firstName: String, lastName: String, salaryYear: Double)` initializer to create an instance of the `EmployeeClass` class; therefore, the `firstName` property is set to Me, the `lastName` property is set to Moe, and the `salaryYear` is set to 45000.

Since all the initializers are identified with the `init` keyword, the parameters and parameter types are used to identify which initializer to use. Therefore, Swift provides automatic external names for all of these parameters. In the previous example, we can see that, when we use an initializer that has parameters, we include the parameter names. Let's take a look at internal and external parameter names with initializers.

Internal and external parameter names

Just like functions, the parameters associated with an initializer can have separate internal and external names. Unlike functions, if we do not supply external parameter names for our parameters, Swift will automatically generate them for us. In the previous examples, we did not include external parameter names in the definition of the initializers, so Swift created them for us using the internal parameter name as the external parameter name.

If we wanted to supply our own parameter names, we would do so by putting the external function name before the internal function name, exactly as we do with any normal function. Let's look at how we would define our own external parameter names by redefining one of the initializers within our `EmployeeClass` class:

```
init(employeeWithFirstName firstName: String, lastName:   String, andSalary
salaryYear: Double) {
  self.firstName = firstName
  self.lastName = lastName
  self.salaryYear = salaryYear
}
```

In the preceding example, we created the `init(employeeWithFirstName firstName:` `String, lastName lastName: String, andSalary salaryYear: Double)` initializer. This initializer will create an instance of the `EmployeeClass` class and populate the instance properties with the value of the arguments. In this example, each of the parameters has both external and internal property names. Let's look at how we would use this initializer, with the external property names, to create an instance of the `EmployeeClass` class:

```
var i = EmployeeClass(employeeWithFirstName: "Me", lastName:  "Moe",
andSalary: 45000)
```

Notice that we are now using the external parameter names as we defined in our initializer. Using external parameter names can help make our code more readable and differentiate between different initializers.

So, what will happen if our initializer fails? For example, what if our class relies on a specific resource, such as a web service that is not currently available? This is where failable initializers come in.

Failable initializers

A failable initializer is an initializer that may fail to initialize the resources needed for a class or a structure, thereby rendering the instance unusable. When using a failable initializer, the result of the initializer is an optional type, containing either a valid instance of the type or nil.

An initializer can be made failable by adding a question mark (?) after the `init` keyword. Let's look at how we would create a failable initializer that will not allow a new employee to be initialized with a salary below $20,000 a year:

```
init?(firstName: String, lastName: String, salaryYear: Double) {
  self.firstName = firstName
  self.lastName = lastName
  self.salaryYear = salaryYear
  if self.salaryYear < 20000 {
    return nil
  }
}
```

In the previous example, we did not include a `return` statement within the initializer because Swift does not need to return the initialized instance; however, in a failable initializer, if the initialization fails, we will return `nil`. If the initializer successfully initializes the instance, we do not need to return anything. Therefore, in our example, if the yearly salary that is passed in is below $20,000 a year, we return `nil`, indicating that the initialization failed; otherwise, nothing will be returned. Let's look at how we would use a failable initializer to create an instance of a class or structure:

```
if let f = EmployeeClass(firstName: "Jon", lastName: "Hoffman",
  salaryYear: 29000) {
  print(f.getFullName())
} else {
  print("Failed to initialize")
}
```

In the previous example, we initialize the instance of the `EmployeeClass` class with a yearly salary greater than $20,000; therefore, the instance gets initialized correctly and the full name of `Jon Hoffman` is printed to the console. Now let's try to initialize an instance of the `EmployeeClass` class with a yearly salary less than $20,000 to see how it fails:

```
if let f = EmployeeClass(firstName: "Jon", lastName: "Hoffman", salaryYear:
19000) {
  print(f.getFullName())
  print(f.compareFirstName(firstName: "Jon"))
} else {
  print("Failed to initialize")
}
```

In the example, the yearly salary that we are attempting to initialize for our employee is less than $20,000; therefore, the initialization fails and a `Failed to initialize` message is printed to the console.

There are times when we want to restrict access to certain parts of our code. This enables us to hide implementation details and only expose the interfaces we want to expose. This feature is handled with named access controls.

Access controls allow us to restrict the access to, and visibility of, parts of our code. This allows us to hide implementation details and only expose the interfaces we want the external code to access. We can assign specific access levels to both classes and structures. We can also assign specific access levels to properties, methods, and initializers that belong to our classes and structures.

In Swift, there are four access levels:

- **Public**: This is the most visible access control level. It allows us to use the property, method, class, and so on anywhere we want to import the module. Basically, anything can use an item that has an access control level set to public. This level is primarily used by frameworks to expose the framework's public API.
- **Internal**: This is the default access level. This access level allows us to use the property, method, class, and so on in the defining source as well as the module that the source is in (the application or framework). If this level is used in a framework, it lets other parts of the framework use the item but code outside the framework will be unable to access it.
- **Private**: This is the least visible access control level. It only allows us to use the property, method, class, and so on in the source file that defines it.

- **Fileprivate**: This access control allows access to the properties and methods from any code within the same source file that the item is defined in.

If we are writing code that will be self-contained within a single application and there is no need for it to be made available outside the application, then we can largely ignore access controls. The default access level of internal already matches this requirement. We may, however, want to hide parts of the implementation, which can be done by setting the access level to private, but that should be an exception and not the rule.

When we are developing frameworks, access controls really become useful. We need to mark public-facing interfaces as public, so other modules such as applications that import the framework can use them. We would then use the internal and private access control levels to mark the interfaces that we want to use internally to the framework and the source file, respectively.

To define access levels, we place the name of the level before the definition of the entity. The following code shows examples of how we would add access levels to several entities:

```
private struct EmployeeStruct {}
public class EmployeeClass {}
internal class EmployeeClass2 {}
public var firstName = "Jon"
internal var lastName = "Hoffman"
private var salaryYear = 0.0
public func getFullName() -> String {}
private func giveRaise(amount: Double) {}
```

There are some limitations with access controls, but these limitations are there to ensure that access levels in Swift follow a simple guiding principle–*no entity can be defined in terms of another entity that has a lower (more restrictive) access level*. What this means is that we cannot assign a higher (less restrictive) access level to an entity when it relies on another entity that has a lower (more restrictive) access level.

As shown in the following examples:

- We cannot mark a method as being public when one of the arguments or the return type has an access level of private because external code would not have access to the private type
- We cannot set the access level of a method or property to public when the class or structure has an access level of private because external code would not be able to access the constructor when the class is private

Inheritance

The concept of inheritance is a basic object-oriented development concept. Inheritance allows a class to be defined as having a certain set of characteristics and then other classes can be derived from that class. The derived class inherits all of the features of the class it is inheriting from (unless the derived class overrides those characteristics) and then usually adds additional characteristics of its own.

With inheritance, we can create what is known as a class hierarchy. In a class hierarchy, the class at the top of the hierarchy is known as the **base class** and the derived classes are known as **subclasses**. We are not limited to only creating subclasses from a base class; we can also create subclasses from other subclasses. The class that a subclass is derived from is known as the parent or superclass. In Swift, a class can have only one parent class. This is known as single inheritance.

 Inheritance is one of the fundamental differences that separate classes from structures. Classes can be derived from a parent or superclass, but a structure cannot.

Subclasses can call and access the properties, methods, and subscripts of their superclass. They can also override the properties, methods, and subscripts of their superclass. Subclasses can add property observers to properties that they inherit from a superclass, so they can be notified when the values of the properties change. Let's look at an example that illustrates how inheritance works in Swift.

We will start off by defining a base class named `Plant`. The `Plant` class will have two properties, `height` and `age`. It will also have one method, `growHeight()`. The `height` property will represent the height of the plant, the `age` property will represent the age of the plant, and the `growHeight()` method will be used to increase the height of the plant. Here is how we would define the `Plant` class:

```
class Plant {
    var height = 0.0
    var age = 0
    func growHeight(inches: Double) {
        self.height +=  inches;
    }
}
```

Now that we have our `Plant` base class, let's see how we can define a subclass of it. We will name this subclass `Tree`. The `Tree` class will inherit the `age` and `height` properties of the `Plant` class and add one additional property named `limbs`. It will also inherit the `growHeight()` method of the `Plant` class and add two additional methods: `limbGrow()`, where a new limb is grown, and `limbFall()`, where one of the limbs falls off the tree. Let's have a look at the following code:

```
class Tree: Plant {
  private var limbs = 0
  func limbGrow() {
    self.limbs += 1
  }
  func limbFall() {
    self.limbs -= 1
  }
}
```

We indicate that a class has a superclass by adding a colon and the name of the superclass to the end of the class definition. In the `Tree` example, we indicated that the `Tree` class has a superclass named `Plant`.

Now, let's look at how we could use the `Tree` class that inherited the `age` and `height` properties from the `Plant` class:

```
var tree = Tree()
tree.age = 5
tree.height = 4
tree.limbGrow()
tree.limbGrow()
```

The preceding example begins by creating an instance of the `Tree` class. We then set the `age` and `height` properties to 5 and 4, respectively, and add two limbs to the tree by calling the `limbGrow()` method twice.

We now have a base class named `Plant` that has a subclass named `Tree`. This means that the super (or parent) class of `Tree` is the `Plant` class. This also means that one of the subclasses (or child classes) of `Plant` is named `Tree`. There are, however, lots of different kinds of trees in the world. Let's create two subclasses from the `Tree` class. These subclasses will be the `PineTree` class and the `OakTree` class:

```
class PineTree: Tree {
    var needles = 0
}

class OakTree: Tree {
    var leaves = 0
}
```

The following diagram shows the class hierarchy that we just created:

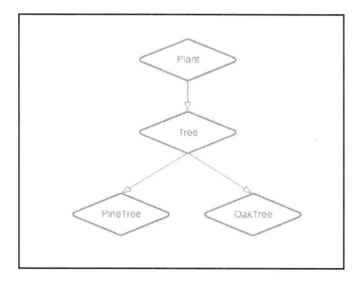

It is important to keep in mind that, in Swift, a class can have multiple subclasses; however, a class can have only one superclass. There are times when a subclass needs to provide its own implementation of a method or property that it inherited from its superclass. This is known as **overriding**.

Overriding methods and properties

To override a method, property, or subscript, we need to prefix the definition with the `override` keyword. This tells the compiler that we intend to override something in the superclass and that we did not make a duplicate definition by mistake. The `override` keyword does prompt the Swift compiler to verify that the superclass (or one of its parents) has a matching declaration that can be overridden. If it cannot find a matching declaration in one of the superclasses, an error will be thrown.

Overriding methods

Let's look at how we would override a method. We will start by adding a `getDetails()` method to the `Plant` class that we will then override in the child classes. The following code shows how the new `Plant` class looks with the `getDetails()` method added:

```
class Plant {
  var height = 0.0
  var age = 0
  func growHeight(inches: Double) {
    self.height +=  inches;
  }
  func getDetails() -> String {
    return "Plant Details"
  }
}
```

Now let's see how we would override the `getDetails()` method in the `Tree` class:

```
class Tree: Plant {
  private var limbs = 0
  func limbGrow() {
    self.limbs += 1
  }
  func limbFall() {
    self.limbs -= 1
  }
  override func getDetails() -> String {
    return "Tree Details"
  }
}
```

The thing to note here is that we do not use the `override` keyword in the `Plant` class because it is the first class to implement this method; however, we do include it in the `Tree` class since we are overriding the `getDetails()` method from the `Plant` class. Now, let's see what happens if we call the `getDetails()` method from an instance of the `Plant` and `Tree` classes:

```
var plant = Plant()
var tree = Tree()
print("Plant: \(plant.getDetails())")
print("Tree: \(tree.getDetails())")
```

The previous example would print the following two lines to the console:

```
Plant: Plant Details
Tree: Tree Details
```

As we can see, the `getDetails()` method in the `Tree` subclass overrides the `getDetails()` method of its parent `Plant` class.

Inside the `Tree` class, we can still call the `getDetails()` method (or any overridden method, property, or subscript) of its superclass by using the `super` prefix. Let's see how we would call the `getDetails()` method of the `Plant` class from an instance of the `Tree` class. We will begin by replacing the `getDetails()` method in the `Plant` class with the following method, which will generate a string containing the values of the `height` and `age` properties. Let's take a look at the following code:

```
func getDetails() -> String {
    return "Height: \(height)  age: \(age)"
}
```

In the preceding code, we are changing the `getDetails()` method to return a string that contains the `height` and `age` of the plant. Now, let's replace the `getDetails()` method for the `Tree` class with the following method:

```
override func getDetails() -> String {
  let details = super.getDetails()
  return "\(details)  limbs: \(limbs)"
}
```

In the preceding example, we begin by calling the `getDetails()` method of the superclass (the `Plant` class in this case) to get a string containing the tree's `height` and `age`. We then build a new string object that contains the results of the `getDetails()` method from the superclass, adds the number of limbs to it, and then returns it. Let's look at what happens if we call the `getDetails()` method of the `Tree` class:

```
var tree = Tree()
tree.age = 5
tree.height = 4
tree.limbGrow()
tree.limbGrow()
print(tree.getDetails())
```

If we run the preceding code, the following line would be printed to the console:

```
Height:  4.0  age:  5  limbs:  2
```

As we can see, the string that is returned contains the `height` and `age` information from the `Plant` class and the limbs information from the `Tree` class.

We can also chain the overridden methods. Let's see what happens if we add the following method to the `OakTree` class:

```
override func getDetails() -> String {
  let details = super.getDetails()
  return "\(details)  Leaves:  \(leaves)"
}
```

When we call the `getDetails()` method of an instance of the `OakTree` class, it calls the `getDetails()` method of its superclass (the `Tree` class). The `getDetails()` method of the `Tree` class also calls the `getDetails()` method of its superclass (the `Plant` class). The `getDetails()` method of the `Tree` class will finally create a string instance that contains the `height` and `age` from the `Plant` class, the `limbs` from the `Tree` class, and the `leaves` from the `OakTree` class. Let's look at an example of this:

```
var tree = OakTree()
tree.age = 5
tree.height = 4
tree.leaves = 50
tree.limbGrow()
tree.limbGrow()
print(tree.getDetails())
```

If we run the preceding code, we see the following line printed to the console:

```
Height:  4.0  age:  5  limbs:  2  Leaves:  50
```

Overriding properties

We can provide custom `getter` and `setter` to override any inherited property. When we override a property, we must provide the name and the type of property we are overriding, so the compiler can verify that one of the classes in the class hierarchy has a matching property to override. While overriding, properties are not as common as overriding methods; it is good for us to know how to do this when we need.

Let's see how we would override a property by adding the following method to our `Plant` class:

```
var description: String {
  get {
    return "Base class is Plant."
  }
}
```

The `description` property is a basic read-only property. This property returns the string, `Base class is Plant`. Now let's override this property by adding the following property to the `Tree` class:

```
override var description: String {
  return "\(super.description)  I am a Tree class."
}
```

When we override a property, we use the same `override` keyword that we use when we override a method. The `override` keyword tells the compiler that we want to override a property, so the compiler can verify that another class in the class hierarchy contains a matching property to override. We then implement the property as we would any other property. Calling the `description` property of the tree would result in the `Base class is Plant. I am a Tree class.` string being returned.

There are times when we want to prevent a subclass from overriding the properties and methods. There are also times when we want to prevent an entire class from being subclassed. Let's see how we do this.

Preventing overrides

To prevent overrides or subclassing, we use the `final` keyword. To use the `final` keyword, we add it before the item's definition. Examples are `final func`, `final var`, and `final class`.

Any attempt to override an item marked final will throw a compile-time error.

Protocols

There are times when we would like to describe the implementation (methods, properties, and other requirements) of a class without actually providing the implementation. For this, we use protocols.

Protocols define a blueprint of methods, properties, and other requirements for a class or a structure. A class or a structure can then provide an implementation that conforms to those requirements. The class or structure that provides the implementation is said to conform to the protocol.

Protocol syntax

The syntax to define a protocol is very similar to how we define a class or a structure. The following example shows the syntax used to define a protocol:

```
protocol MyProtocol {
  //protocol definition here
}
```

We state that a class or structure conforms to a particular protocol by placing the name of the protocol after the class or structure's name, separated by a colon. Here is an example of how we would state that a class conforms to the MyProtocol protocol:

```
class myClass: MyProtocol {
  //class implementation here
}
```

A class or a structure can conform to multiple protocols. We list the protocols that the class or structure conforms to by separating them with commas. The following example shows how we would state that our class conforms to multiple protocols:

```
class MyClass: MyProtocol, AnotherProtocol, ThirdProtocol {
  // class implementation here
}
```

When we need a class to inherit from a superclass and implement a protocol, we list the superclass first, followed by the protocols. The following example illustrates this:

```
Class MyClass: MySuperClass, MyProtocol, MyProtocol2 {
  // Class implementation here
}
```

Property requirements

A protocol can require that the conforming class or structure provide certain properties with a specified name and type. The protocol does not say if the property should be a stored or computed property because the implementation details are left up to the conforming class or structure.

When defining a property within a protocol, we must specify whether the property is a read-only or a read/write property by using the get and set keywords. Let's look at how we would define properties within a protocol by creating a FullName protocol:

```
protocol FullName {
  var firstName: String {get set}
  var lastName: String {get set}
}
```

The FullName protocol defines two properties, which any class or structure that conforms to the protocol must implement. These are the firstName and lastName properties. Both these properties in the FullName protocol are read/write properties. If we wanted to specify that the property is read-only, we would define it with only the get keyword, like this:

```
var readOnly: String {get}
```

Let's see how we would create a Scientist class that conforms to this protocol:

```
class Scientist: FullName {
  var firstName = ""
  var lastName = ""
}
```

If we had forgotten to include either the firstName or lastName property, we would have received a Scientist does not conform to protocol 'FullName' error message. We also need to make sure that the type of the property is the same. For example, if we changed the lastName definition in the Scientist class to var lastName = 42, we would also receive a Scientist does not conform to protocol 'FullName' error message because the protocol specifies that we must have a lastName property of the string type.

Method requirements

A protocol can require that the conforming class or structure provide certain methods. We define a method within a protocol exactly as we do within a normal class or structure, except without the curly braces or method body. Let's add a `getFullName()` method to our `FullName` protocol and `Scientist` class.

The following example shows how the `FullName` protocol would look with the `getFullName()` method added:

```
protocol FullName {
  var firstName: String {get set}
  var lastName: String {get set}

  func getFullName() -> String
}
```

Now, we will need to add a `getFullName()` method to our Scientist class so that it will properly conform to the `FullName` protocol:

```
class Scientist: FullName {
  var firstName = ""
  var lastName = ""
  var field = ""

  func getFullName() -> String {
    return "\(firstName) \(lastName) studies \(field)"
  }
}
```

Structures can conform to Swift protocols exactly as classes do. The following example shows how we can create a `FootballPlayer` structure that conforms to the `FullName` protocol:

```
struct FootballPlayer: FullName {
    var firstName = ""
    var lastName = ""
    var number = 0
    func getFullName() -> String {
        return "\(firstName) \(lastName) has the number \(number)"
    }
}
```

When a class or structure conforms to a Swift protocol, we can be sure that it has implemented the required properties and methods. This can be very useful when we want to ensure that certain properties or methods are implemented over various classes, as our preceding examples show.

Protocols are also very useful when we want to decouple our code from requiring specific classes or structures. The following code shows how we would decouple our code using the `FullName` protocol, the `Scientist` class, and the `FootballPlayer` structure that we have already built:

```
var scientist = Scientist()
scientist.firstName = "Kara"
scientist.lastName = "Hoffman"
scientist.field = "Physics"

var player = FootballPlayer();
player.firstName = "Dan"
player.lastName = "Marino"
player.number = 13

var person: FullName
person = scientist
print(person.getFullName())
person = player
print(player.getFullName())
```

In the preceding code, we begin by creating an instance of the `Scientist` class and the `FootballPlayer` structure. We then create a `person` variable that is of the `FullName` (protocol) type and set it to the `scientist` instance that we just created. We then call the `getFullName()` method to retrieve our description. This will print out the `Kara Hoffman studies Physics` message to the console.

We then set the `person` variable equal to the `player` instance and call the `getFullName()` method again. This will print out the `Dan Marino has the number 13` message to the console.

As we can see, the `person` variable does not care what the actual implementation class or structure is. Since we defined the `person` variable to be of the `FullName` type, we can set the `person` variable to an instance of any class or structure that conforms to the `FullName` protocol.

We will read more about protocols in Chapter 6, *Using Protocols and Protocol Extensions* and also in Chapter 7, *Protocol Oriented Design*.

Extensions

With extensions, we can add new properties, methods, initializers, and subscripts, or make an existing class or structure conform to a protocol. One thing to note is that extensions cannot override the existing functionality.

To define an extension, we use the `extension` keyword, followed by the type that we are extending. The following example shows how we would create an extension that extends the string class:

```
extension String {
  //add new functionality here
}
```

Let's see how extensions work by adding a `reverse()` method and a `firstLetter` property to Swift's standard string class:

```
extension String {
    var firstLetter: Character? {
        get {
            return self.characters.first
        }
    }

    func reverse() -> String {
        var reverse = ""
        for letter in self.characters {
            reverse = "\(letter)" + reverse
        }
        return reverse
    }
}
```

When we extend an existing class or structure, we define properties, methods, initializers, and subscripts in exactly the same way as we would normally define them in a standard class or structure. In the string extension example, we see that we define the `reverse()` method and the `firstLetter` property exactly as we would define them in a normal class.

We would then use these properties, methods, initializers and subscripts, added by the extensions, exactly as we would use them normally. Here is an example of how we would use the `reverse()` method that we just added to the `String` type:

```
var test = "abc"
print(test.reverse())
```

Extensions are very useful for adding additional functionality to classes and structures from external frameworks, even for Apple's frameworks, as demonstrated in the examples. It is preferred to use extensions to add additional functionality to classes from external frameworks rather than subclassing because it allows us to use the classes provided by the frameworks throughout our code.

Memory management

As I mentioned at the start of this chapter, structures are value types and classes are reference types. What this means is that, when we pass an instance of a structure within our application, such as a parameter of a method, we create a new instance of the structure in the memory. This new instance of the structure is only valid while the application is in the scope where the structure was created. Once the structure goes out of scope, the new instance of the structure is destroyed and the memory is released. This makes memory management of structures pretty easy and somewhat painless.

Classes, on the other hand, are of the reference type. This means that we allocate the memory for the instance of the class only once when it is initially created. When we want to pass an instance of the class within our application, as either a function argument or by assigning it to a variable, we really pass a reference to where the instance is stored in the memory. Since the instance of a class may be referenced in multiple scopes (unlike a structure), it cannot be automatically destroyed, and memory is not released when it goes out of scope if it is referenced in another scope. Therefore, Swift needs some form of memory management to track and release the memory used by instances of classes when the class is no longer needed. Swift uses **Automatic Reference Counting (ARC)** to track and manage memory usage.

With ARC, for the most part, memory management in Swift simply works. ARC will automatically track the references to instances of classes, and when an instance is no longer needed (no references pointing to it), ARC will automatically destroy the instance and release the memory. There are a few instances where ARC requires additional information about relationships to properly manage the memory. Before we look at the instances where ARC needs help, let's look at how ARC works.

How ARC works

Whenever we create a new instance of a class, ARC allocates the memory needed to store that class. This ensures that there is enough memory to store the information associated with that instance of the class, and also locks the memory so that nothing overwrites it. When the instance of the class is no longer needed, ARC will release the memory allocated for the class so that it can be used for other purposes. This ensures that we are not tying up memory that is no longer needed.

If ARC were to release the memory for an instance of a class that we still needed, it would not be possible to retrieve the class information from memory. If we did try to access the instance of the class after the memory was released, our application might crash. To ensure memory is not released for an instance of a class that is still needed, ARC counts how many times the instance is referenced (how many active properties, variables, or constants are pointing to the instance of the class). Once the reference count for an instance of a class equals zero (nothing is referencing the instance), the memory is marked for release.

All of the previous examples run properly, but the following examples will not. When we run sample code, ARC does not release objects that we create; this is by design so that we can see how the application runs and also the state of the objects at each step. Let's look at an example of how ARC works.

We begin by creating a `MyClass` class with the following code:

```
class MyClass {
  var name = ""
  init(name: String) {
    self.name = name
    print("Initializing class with name \(self.name)")
  }
  deinit {
   print("Releasing class with name \(self.name)")
  }
}
```

This class is very similar to our previous `MyClass` class, except that we add a deinitializer that is called just before an instance of the class is destroyed and removed from memory. This deinitializer prints out a message to the console that lets us know that the instance of the class is about to be removed.

Now, let's look at the code that shows how ARC creates and destroys instances of a class:

```
var class1ref1: MyClass? = MyClass(name: "One")
var class2ref1: MyClass? = MyClass(name: "Two")
var class2ref2: MyClass? = class2ref1
print("Setting class1ref1 to nil")
class1ref1 = nil
print("Setting class2ref1 to nil")
class2ref1 = nil
print("Setting class2ref2 to nil")
class2ref2 = nil
```

In the example, we begin by creating two instances of the MyClass class named class1ref1 (which stands for class 1 reference 1) and class2ref1 (which stands for class 2 reference 1). We then create a second reference to class2ref1 named class2ref2. Now, in order to see how ARC works, we need to begin setting the references to nil. We start out by setting class1ref1 to nil. Since there is only one reference to class1ref1, the deinitializer will be called. Once the deinitializer completes its task, in our case, it prints a message to the console letting us know that the instance of the class has been destroyed and the memory has been released.

We then set the class2ref1 to nil, but a second reference to this class (class2ref2) prevents ARC from destroying the instance so that the deinitializer is not called. Finally, we set class2ref2 to nil, which allows ARC to destroy this instance of the MyClass class.

If we run this code, we will see the following output, which illustrates how ARC works:

```
Initializing class with name One
Initializing class with name Two
Setting class1ref1 to nil
Releasing class with name One
Setting class2ref1 to nil
Setting class2ref2 to nil
Releasing class with name Two
```

From the example, it seems that ARC handles memory management very well. However, it is possible to write code that will prevent ARC from working properly.

Strong reference cycles

A strong reference cycle is where the instances of two classes hold a strong reference to each other, preventing ARC from releasing either instance. Strong reference cycles are a lot easier to understand with an example, so let's create one. In this project, we start off by creating two classes named `MyClass1` and `MyClass2` with the following code:

```
class MyClass1 {
    var name = ""
    var class2: MyClass2?

  init(name: String) {
      self.name = name
      print("Initializing class with name \(self.name)")
  }
  deinit {
      print("Releaseing class with name \(self.name)")
  }
}

class MyClass2 {
    var name = ""
    var class1: MyClass1?

  init(name: String) {
      self.name = name
      print("Initializing class2 with name \(self.name)")
  }
  deinit {
      print("Releaseing class2 with name \(self.name)")
  }

}
```

As we can see from the code, `MyClass1` contains an instance of `MyClass2`; therefore, the instance of `MyClass2` cannot be released until `MyClass1` is destroyed. We can also see from the code that `MyClass2` contains an instance of `MyClass1`; therefore, the instance of `MyClass1` cannot be released until `MyClass2` is destroyed. This creates a cycle of dependency in which neither instance can be destroyed until the other one is destroyed. Let's see how this works by running the following code:

```
var class1: MyClass1? = MyClass1(name: "Class1")
var class2: MyClass2? = MyClass2(name: "Class2")
//class1 and class2 each have a reference count of 1
class1?.class2 = class2
//Class2 now has a reference count of 2
```

```
class2?.class1 = class1
//class1 now has a reference count of 2
print("Setting classes to nil")
class2 = nil
//class2 now has a reference count of 1, not destroyed
class1 = nil
//class1 now has a reference count of 1, not destroyed
```

As we can see from the comments in the example, the reference counter for each instance never reaches zero; therefore, ARC cannot destroy the instances, thereby creating a memory leak. A memory leak is where an application continues to use memory but does not properly release it. This can eventually cause an application to crash.

To resolve a strong reference cycle, we need to prevent one of the classes from keeping a strong hold on the instance of the other class, thereby allowing ARC to destroy them both. Swift provides two ways of doing this, by letting us define the properties as either a weak reference or an unowned reference.

The difference between a weak reference and an unowned reference is that the instance which a weak reference refers to can be nil, whereas the instance that an unowned reference is referring to cannot be nil. This means that when we use a weak reference, the property must be an optional property since it can be nil. Let's see how we would use unowned and weak references to resolve a strong reference cycle. Let's start by looking at the unowned reference technique.

We begin by creating two more classes, `MyClass3` and `MyClass4`:

```
class MyClass3 {
    var name = ""
    unowned let class4: MyClass4

    init(name: String, class4: MyClass4) {
        self.name = name
        self.class4 = class4
        print("Initializing class3 with name \(self.name)")
    }
    deinit {
        print("Releasing class3 with name \(self.name)")
    }
}

class MyClass4{
    var name = ""
    var class3: MyClass3?

    init(name: String) {
```

```
        self.name = name
        print("Initializing class4 with name \(self.name)")
    }
    deinit {
        print("Releasing class4 with name \(self.name)")
    }
}
```

The `MyClass4` class looks pretty similar to the `MyClass1` and `MyClass2` classes in the preceding example. What is different here is the `MyClass3` class. In the `MyClass3` class, we set the `class4` property to `unowned`, which means it cannot be nil and it does not keep a strong reference to the `MyClass4` instance that it is referring to. Since the `class4` property cannot be `nil`, we also need to set it when the class is initialized.

Now, let's see how we can initialize and deinitialize the instances of these classes with the following code:

```
var class4 = MyClass4(name: "Class4")
var class3: MyClass3? = MyClass3(name: "class3", class4: class4)
class4.class3 = class3
print("Classes going out of scope")
```

In the preceding code, we create an instance of the `MyClass4` class and then use that instance to create an instance of the `MyClass3` class. We then set the `class3` property of the `MyClass4` instance to the `MyClass3` instance we just created. This creates a reference cycle of dependency between the two classes again, but this time, the `MyClass3` instance does not keep a strong hold on the `MyClass4` instance, allowing ARC to release both instances when they are no longer needed.

If we run this code, we see the following output, showing that both the `MyClass3` and `MyClass4` instances are released and the memory is freed:

```
Initializing class4 with name Class4
Initializing class3 with name class3
Classes going out of scope.
Releasing class4 with name Class4
Releasing class3 with name class3
```

Now let's look at how we would use a weak reference to prevent a strong reference cycle. We begin by creating two new classes:

```
class MyClass5 {
  var name = ""
  var class6: MyClass6?
  init(name: String) {
    self.name = name
```

```
      print("Initializing class5 with name \(self.name)")
    }
    deinit {
      print("Releasing class5 with name \(self.name)")
    }
}

class MyClass6 {
  var name = ""
  weak var class5: MyClass5?
  init(name: String) {
    self.name = name
    print("Initializing class6 with name \(self.name)")
  }
  deinit {
    print("Releasing class6 with name \(self.name)")
  }
}
```

The MyClass5 and MyClass6 classes look very similar to the MyClass1 and MyClass2 classes we created earlier to show how a strong reference cycle works. The big difference is that we define the class5 property in the MyClass6 class as a weak reference.

Now, let's see how we can initialize and deinitialize instances of these classes with the following code:

```
var class5: MyClass5? = MyClass5(name: "Class5")
var class6: MyClass6? = MyClass6(name: "Class6")
class5?.class6 = class6
class6?.class5 = class5
print("Classes going out of scope ")
```

In the preceding code, we create instances of the MyClass5 and MyClass6 classes and then set the properties of those classes to point to the instance of the other class. Once again, this creates a cycle of dependency, but since we set the class5 property of the MyClass6 class to weak, it does not create a strong reference, allowing both instances to be released.

If we run the code, we will see the following output, showing that both the MyClass5 and MyClass6 instances are released and the memory is freed:

```
Initializing class5 with name Class5
Initializing class6 with name Class6
Classes going out of scope.
Releasing class5 with name Class5
Releasing class6 with name Class6
```

It is recommended that we avoid creating circular dependencies, as shown in this section, but there are times when we need them. For those times, remember that ARC does need some help to release them.

Summary

As this chapter ends, we end the introduction to the Swift programming language. At this point, we have enough knowledge of the Swift language to begin writing our own applications; however, there is still much to learn.

In the following chapters, we will look in greater depth at some of the concepts that we already discussed, such as optionals and subscripts. We will also show how we perform common tasks with Swift, such as parsing common file formats and handling concurrency. Finally, some chapters will help us write better code such as a sample Swift style guide, and a chapter on design patterns.

6
Using Protocols and Protocol Extensions

While watching the presentations from WWDC 2015 about protocol extensions and **Protocol-Oriented Programming** (**POP**), I will admit that I was very sceptical. I have worked with **Object-Oriented Programming** (**OOP**) for so long that I was unsure if this new programming paradigm would solve all of the problems that Apple was claiming it would. Since I am not one to let my skepticism get in the way of trying something new, I set up a new project that mirrored the one I was currently working on, but wrote the code using Apple's recommendations for protocol-oriented programming. I also used protocol extensions extensively in the code. I can honestly say that I was amazed by how much cleaner the new project was compared to the original one. I believe that protocol extensions are going to be one of those defining features that set one programming language apart from the rest. I also believe that many major languages will soon have similar features.

In this chapter, you will learn:

- How protocols are used as a type
- How to implement polymorphism in Swift using protocols
- How to use protocol extensions
- Why we would want to use protocol extensions

While protocol extensions are basically syntactic sugar they are, in my opinion, one of the most important additions to the Swift programming language. With protocol extensions, we are able to provide method and property implementations to any type that conforms to a protocol. To really understand how useful protocols and protocol extensions are, let's get a better understanding of protocols.

While classes, structures, and enumerations can all conform to protocols in Swift, in this chapter we will be focusing on classes and structures. Enumerations are used when we need to represent a finite number of cases and, while there are valid use cases for having an enumerations conform to a protocol, they are very rare in my experience. Just remember that, anywhere that we refer to a class or structures, we can also use an enumeration.

Let's begin exploring protocols by seeing how they are full-fledged types in Swift.

Protocols as types

Even though no functionality is implemented in a protocol, they are still considered a full-fledged type in the Swift programming language and can be used like any other type. What this means is we can use protocols as a parameter type or as a return type in a function. We can also use them as the type for variables, constants, and collections. Let's take a look at some examples. For these few examples, we will use the `PersonProtocol` protocol:

```
protocol PersonProtocol {
    var firstName: String {get set}
    var lastName: String {get set}
    var birthDate: NSDate {get set}
    var profession: String {get}
    init (firstName: String, lastName: String, birthDate: NSDate)
}
```

In this first example, we will see how we would use protocols as a parameter type or return type in functions, methods, or initializers:

```
func updatePerson(person: PersonProtocol) -> PersonProtocol {
    // Code to update person goes here
    return person
}
```

In this example, the `updatePerson()` function accepts one parameter of the `PersonProtocol` protocol type and then returns a value of the `PersonProtocol` protocol type. Now let's see how we can use protocols as a type for constants, variables, or properties:

```
var myPerson: PersonProtocol
```

In this example, we create a variable of the `PersonProtocol` protocol type that is named `myPerson`. We can also use protocols as the item type to store in collections such as arrays, dictionaries, or sets:

```
var people: [PersonProtocol] = []
```

In this final example, we create an array of `PersonProtocol` protocol types. As we can see from these three examples, even though the `PersonProtocol` protocol does not implement any functionality, we can still use protocols when we need to specify a type. We cannot, however, create an instance of a protocol. This is because no functionality is implemented in a protocol. As an example, if we tried to create an instance of the `PersonProtocol` protocol, we would receive the `error: protocol type 'PersonProtocol' cannot be instantiated` error, as shown in the following example:

```
var test = PersonProtocol(firstName: "Jon", lastName: "Hoffman", birthDate:
bDateProgrammer)
```

We can use the instance of any class or structure that conforms to our protocol anywhere that the protocol type is required. As an example, if we defined a variable to be of the `PersonProtocol` protocol type, we could then populate that variable with any class or structure that conforms to the `PersonProtocol` protocol. For this example, let's assume that we have two types named `SwiftProgrammer` and `FootballPlayer`, which conform to the `PersonProtocol` protocol:

```
var myPerson: PersonProtocol

myPerson = SwiftProgrammer(firstName: "Jon", lastName: "Hoffman",
birthDate: bDateProgrammer)
print("\(myPerson.firstName) \(myPerson.lastName)")

myPerson = FootballPlayer(firstName: "Dan", lastName: "Marino", birthDate:
bDatePlayer)
print("\(myPerson.firstName) \(myPerson.lastName)")
```

In this example, we start off by creating the `myPerson` variable of the `PersonProtocol` protocol type. We then set the variable with an instance of the `SwiftProgrammer` type and print out the first and last names. Next, we set the `myPerson` variable to an instance of the `FootballPlayer` type and print out the first and last names again. One thing to note is that Swift does not care if the instance is a class or structure. It only matters that the type conforms to the `PersonProtocol` protocol type. Therefore, this code would be perfectly valid if the `SwiftProgrammer` type were a structure and the `FootballPlayer` type were a class.

As we saw earlier, we can use our `PersonProtocol` protocol as the type for an array. This means that we can populate the array with instances of any type that conforms to the `PersonProtocol` protocol. Once again, it does not matter if the type is a class or a structure as long as it conforms to the `PersonProtocol` protocol. Here is an example of this:

```
var programmer = SwiftProgrammer(firstName: "Jon", lastName: "Hoffman",
birthDate: bDateProgrammer)

var player = FootballPlayer(firstName: "Dan", lastName: "Marino",
birthDate: bDatePlayer)

var people: [PersonProtocol] = []
people.append(programmer)
people.append(player)
```

In this example, we create an instance of the `SwiftProgrammer` type and an instance of the `FootballPlayer` type. We then add both instances to the `people` array.

Polymorphism with protocols

What we were seeing in the previous examples is a form of polymorphism. The word polymorphism comes from the Greek roots *Poly*, meaning many, and *morphe*, meaning form. In programming languages, polymorphism is a single interface to multiple types (many forms). In the previous example, the single interface was the `PersonProtocol` protocol and the multiple types were any type that conforms to that protocol.

Polymorphism gives us the ability to interact with multiple types in a uniform manner. To illustrate this, we can extend our previous example where we created an array of the `PersonProtocol` types and loop through the array. We can then access each item in the array using the properties and methods define in the `PersonProtocol` protocol, regardless of the actual type. Let's see an example of this:

```
for person in people {
    print("\(person.firstName) \(person.lastName):
        \(person.profession)")
}
```

If we ran this example, the output would look similar to this:

```
Jon Hoffman: Swift Programmer
Dan Marino: Football Player
```

We have mentioned a few times in this chapter that, when we define the type of a variable, constant, collection type, and so on to be a protocol type, we can then use the instance of any type that conforms to that protocol. This is a very important concept to understand and is one of the many things that make protocols and protocol extensions so powerful.

When we use a protocol to access instances, as shown in the previous example, we are limited to using only properties and methods that are defined in the protocol. If we want to use properties or methods that are specific to the individual types, we would need to cast the instance to that type.

Type casting with protocols

Type casting is a way to check the type of an instance and/or to treat the instance as a specified type. In Swift, we use the `is` keyword to check if an instance is a specific type and the `as` keyword to treat the instance as a specific type.

To start with, let's see how we would check the instance type using the `is` keyword. The following example shows how this is done:

```
for person in people {
  if person is SwiftProgrammer {
    print("\(person.firstName) is a Swift Programmer")
  }
}
```

In this example, we use the `if` conditional statement to check whether each element in the people array is an instance of the `SwiftProgrammer` type; if so, we print that the person is a Swift programmer to the console. While this is a good method to check whether we have an instance of a specific class or structure, it is not very efficient if we wanted to check for multiple types. It is a lot more efficient to use the `switch` statement, as shown in the next example:

```
for person in people {
    switch (person) {
    case is SwiftProgrammer:
        print("\(person.firstName) is a Swift Programmer")
    case is FootballPlayer:
        print("\(person.firstName) is a Football Player")
    default:
        print("\(person.firstName) is an unknown type")
    }
}
```

In the previous example, we showed how to use the `switch` statement to check the instance type for each element of the array. To do this check, we use the `is` keyword in each of the `case` statements in an attempt to match the instance type.

In `Chapter 4`, *Control Flow and Functions*, we saw how to filter conditional statements with the `where` statement. We can also use the `where` statement with the `is` keyword to filter the array, as shown in the following example:

```
for person in people where person is SwiftProgrammer {
    print("\(person.firstName) is a Swift Programmer")

}
```

Now let's look at how we can cast an instance of a class or structure to a specific type. To do this, we can use the `as` keyword. Since the cast can fail if the instance is not of the specified type, the `as` keyword comes in two forms: `as?` and `as!`. With the `as?` form, if the casting fails, it returns a `nil`; with the `as!` form, if the casting fails, we get a runtime error. Therefore, it is recommended we use the `as?` form unless we are absolutely sure of the instance type or we perform a check of the instance type prior to doing the cast.

Let's look at how we would use the `as?` keyword to cast an instance of a class or structure to a specified type:

```
for person in people {
    if let p = person as? SwiftProgrammer {
        print("\(person.firstName) is a Swift Programmer")
    }
}
```

Since the `as?` keyword returns an optional, we can use optional binding to perform the cast, as shown in this example. If we are sure of the instance type, we can use the `as!` keyword. The following example shows how to use the `as!` keyword when we filter the results of the array to only return instances of the `SwiftProgrammer` type:

```
for person in people where person is SwiftProgrammer {
  let p = person as! SwiftProgrammer
}
```

Now that we have covered the basics of protocols let's delve into one of the most exciting features of Swift: protocol extensions.

Protocol extensions

Protocol extensions allow us to extend a protocol to provide method and property implementations to conforming types. They also allow us to provide common implementations to all confirming types, eliminating the need to provide an implementation in each individual type or the need to create a class hierarchy. While protocol extensions may not seem too exciting, once you see how powerful they really are, they will transform the way you think about and write code.

Let's begin by looking at how we would use protocol extensions with a very simplistic example. We will start off by defining a protocol called `DogProtocol` as follows:

```
protocol DogProtocol {
    var name: String {get set}
    var color: String {get set}
}
```

With this protocol, we are saying that any type that conforms to the `DogProtocol` protocol, must have the two properties of the `String` type, with names of: `name` and `color`. Now let's define the three types that conform to this protocol. We will name these types `JackRussel`, `WhiteLab`, and `Mutt` as follows:

```
struct JackRussel: DogProtocol {
    var name: String
    var color: String
}

class WhiteLab: DogProtocol {
    var name: String
    var color: String
    init(name: String, color: String) {
        self.name = name
        self.color = color
    }
}

struct Mutt: DogProtocol {
    var name: String
    var color: String
}
```

We purposely created the `JackRussel` and `Mutt` types as structures and the `WhiteLab` type as a class to show the differences between how the two types are set up. We also wanted to illustrate how they are treated the same way when it comes to protocols and protocol extensions. The biggest difference that we can see in this example is that structure types provide a default initiator, but in the class, we must provide the initiator to populate the properties.

Now let's say that we want to provide a method named `speak` to each type that conforms to the `DogProtocol` protocol. Prior to protocol extensions, we would start off by adding the method definition to the protocol, as shown in the following code:

```
protocol DogProtocol {
    var name: String {get set}
    var color: String {get set}
    func speak() -> String
}
```

Once the method is defined in the protocol, we would then need to provide an implementation of the method in every type that conforms to the protocol. Depending on the number of types that conformed to this protocol, this could take a bit of time to implement. The following code sample shows how we might implement this method:

```
struct JackRussel: DogProtocol {
    var name: String
    var color: String
     func speak() -> String {
        return "Woof Woof"
    }
}

class WhiteLab: DogProtocol {
    var name: String
    var color: String
    init(name: String, color: String) {
        self.name = name
        self.color = color
    }
    func speak() -> String {
        return "Woof Woof"
    }

}

struct Mutt: DogProtocol {
    var name: String
    var color: String
```

```
    func speak() -> String {
        return "Woof Woof"
    }

}
```

While this method works, it is not very efficient because whenever we update the protocol, we would need to update all the types that conform to it and we may be duplicating a lot of code, as shown in this example. Another concern is that if we need to change the default behavior of the speak() method, we would have to go in each implementation and change the speak() method. This is where protocol extensions come in.

With protocol extensions, we could take the speak() method definition out of the protocol itself. We can then define it, with the default behavior, in protocol extension. The following code shows how we would define the protocol and the protocol extension:

```
protocol DogProtocol {
    var name: String {get set}
    var color: String {get set}
}

extension DogProtocol {
    func speak() -> String {
        return "Woof Woof"
    }
}
```

We begin by defining DogProtocol with the original two properties. We then create a protocol extension that extends DogProtocol and contains the default implementation of the speak() method. With this code, there is no need to provide an implementation of the speak() method in each of the types that conform to DogProtocol because they automatically receive the implementation as part of the protocol. Let's see how this works by setting our three types that conform to DogProtocol back to their original implementations; they should receive the speak() method from the protocol extension:

```
struct JackRussel: DogProtocol {
    var name: String
    var color: String
}
class WhiteLab: DogProtocol {
    var name: String
    var color: String
    init(name: String, color: String) {
        self.name = name
        self.color = color
    }
}
```

```
    }

    struct Mutt: DogProtocol {
        var name: String
        var color: String
    }
```

We can now use each of the types as shown in the following code:

```
    let dash = JackRussel(name: "Dash", color: "Brown and White")
    let lily = WhiteLab(name: "Lily", color: "White")
    let buddy = Mutt(name: "Buddy", color: "Brown")
    let dSpeak = dash.speak()  // returns "woof woof"
    let lSpeak = lily.speak()  // returns "woof woof"
    let bSpeak = buddy.speak() // returns "woof woof"
```

As we can see in this example, by adding the `speak()` method to the `DogProtocol` protocol extension, we are automatically adding that method to all the types that conform to `DogProtocol`. The `speak()` method in the `DogProtocol` protocol extension can be considered a default implementation of the `speak()` method because we are able to override it in the type implementations. As an example, we could override the `speak()` method in the `Mutt` structure, as shown in the following code:

```
    struct Mutt: DogProtocol {
        var name: String
        var color: String
        func speak() -> String {
            return "I am hungry"
        }
    }
```

When we call the `speak()` method for an instance of the `Mutt` type, it will return the string, `I am hungry`.

Now that we have seen how to use protocols and protocol extensions, let's look at a more real-world example. In numerous apps across multiple platforms (iOS, Android, and Windows), I have had the requirement to validate user input as it is entered. This validation can be done very easily with regular expressions; however, we do not want various regular expressions littered throughout our code. It is very easy to solve this problem by creating different classes or structures that contains the validation code; however, we would have to organize these classes to make them easy to use and maintain. Prior to protocol extensions in Swift, I would use protocols to define the validation requirements and then create a structure that would conform to the protocol for each validation that I needed. Let's take a look at this pre-protocol extension method.

A regular expression is a sequence of characters that define a particular pattern. This pattern can then be used to search a string to see whether the string matches the pattern or contains a match for the pattern. Most major programming languages contain a regular expression parser, and if you are not familiar with regular expressions, it may be worthwhile to learn more about them.

The following code shows the `TextValidating` protocol, which defines the requirements for any type that we want to use for text validation:

```
protocol TextValidating {
    var regExMatchingString: String {get}
    var regExFindMatchString: String {get}
    var validationMessage: String {get}
    func validateString(str: String) -> Bool
    func getMatchingString(str: String) -> String?
}
```

The Swift API Design Guidelines (https://swift.org/documentation/api-design-guidelines/) state that protocols that describe what something is should be named like a noun while protocols that describe a capability should be named with one of these suffixes: able, ible or ing. With this in mind we will name our text validation protocol `TextValidating`.

In this protocol, we define three properties and two methods that any type that conforms to `TextValidating` must implement. The three properties are:

- `regExMatchingString`: This is a regular expression string used to verify that the input string contains only valid characters.
- `regExFindMatchString`: This is a regular expression string used to retrieve a new string from the input string containing only valid characters. This regular expression is generally used when we need to validate the input in real time, as the user enters information, because it will find the longest matching prefix of the input string.
- `validationMessage`: This is the error message to display if the input string contains non-valid characters.

The two methods for this protocol are as follows:

- `validateString`: This method will return `true` if the input string contains only valid characters. The `regExMatchingString` property will be used in this method to perform the match.

- getMatchingString: This method will return a new string that contains only valid characters. This method is generally used when we need to validate the input in real time as the user enters information because it will find the longest matching prefix of the input string. We will use the regExFindMatchString property in this method to retrieve the new string.

Now let's see how we would create a structure that conforms to this protocol. The following structure would be used to verify that the input string contains only alpha characters:

```swift
class AlphaValidation1: TextValidating {
    static let sharedInstance = AlphaValidation1()
    private init(){}
    let regExFindMatchString = "^[a-zA-Z]{0,10}"
    let validationMessage = "Can only contain Alpha characters"
    var regExMatchingString: String { get {
        return regExFindMatchString + "$"
        }
    }
    func validateString(str: String) -> Bool {
        if let _ = str.range(of:regExMatchingString, options:
            .regularExpression) {
            return true
        } else {
            return false
        }
    }
    func getMatchingString(str: String) -> String? {
        if let newMatch = str.range(of:regExFindMatchString, options:
            .regularExpression) {
            return str.substring(with:newMatch)
        } else {
            return nil
        }
    }
}
```

In this implementation, the regExFindMatchString and validationMessage properties are stored properties, and the regExMatchingString property is a computed property. We also implement the validateString() and getMatchingString() methods within the structure.

Normally, we would have several different types that conform to
TextValidating protocol where each one would validate a different type of input. As we
can see from the AlphaValidation1 structure, there is a bit of code involved with each
validation type. A lot of the code would also be duplicated in each type. The code for both
methods (validateString() and getMatchingString()) and the
regExMatchingString property would be duplicated in every validation class. This is not
ideal, but if we wanted to avoid creating a class hierarchy with a super class that contains
the duplicate code (I personally prefer using value types over classes), we would have no
other choice. Now let's see how we would implement this using protocol extensions.

With protocol extensions, we need to think about the code a little differently. The big
difference is, we neither need, nor want, to define everything in the protocol. With standard
protocols or when we use a class hierarchy, all the methods and properties that you want to
access using the generic superclass or protocol interface would have to be defined within
the superclass or protocol. With protocol extensions, it is preferable for us not to define a
property or method in the protocol if we are going to be defining it within the protocol
extension. Therefore, when we rewrite our text validation types with protocol extensions,
TextValidating would be greatly simplified and would look similar to this:

```
protocol TextValidating {
    var regExFindMatchString: String {get}
    var validationMessage: String {get}
}
```

In the original TextValidating protocol, we defined three properties and two methods.
As we can see in this new protocol, we are only defining two properties. Now that we have
our TextValidating protocol defined, let's create the protocol extension for it:

```
extension TextValidating {
    var regExMatchingString: String { get {
        return regExFindMatchString + "$"
        }
    }
    func validateString(str: String) -> Bool {
        if let _ = str.range(of:regExMatchingString, options:
            .regularExpression) {
            return true
        } else {
            return false
        }
    }
    func getMatchingString(str: String) -> String? {
        if let newMatch = str.range(of:regExFindMatchString, options:
            .regularExpression) {
            return str.substring(with: newMatch)
```

```
        } else {
            return nil
        }
    }
}
```

In the `TextValidating` protocol extension, we define the two methods and the third property that were defined in the original `TextValidating`, but were not defined in the new one. Now that we have created our protocol and protocol extension, we are able to define our text validation types. In the following code, we define three structures that we will use to validate text when a user types it in:

```
struct AlphaValidation: TextValidating {
    static let sharedInstance = AlphaValidation()
    private init(){}
    let regExFindMatchString = "^[a-zA-Z]{0,10}"
    let validationMessage = "Can only contain Alpha characters"
}

struct AlphaNumericValidation: TextValidating {
    static let sharedInstance = AlphaNumericValidation()
    private init(){}
    let regExFindMatchString = "^[a-zA-Z0-9]{0,15}"
    let validationMessage = "Can only contain Alpha Numeric characters"
}


struct DisplayNameValidation: TextValidating {
    static let sharedInstance = DisplayNameValidation()
    private init(){}
    let regExFindMatchString = "^[\\s?[a-zA-Z0-9\\-_\\s]]{0,15}"
    let validationMessage = "Display Name can contain only contain
        Alphanumeric Characters"
}
```

In each text validation structure, we create a static constant and a private initiator so that we can use the structure as a singleton. For more information on the singleton pattern, please see *The Singleton design pattern* section of Chapter 17, *Adopting Design Patterns in Swift*.

After we define the singleton pattern, all we do in each type is set the values for the `regExFindMatchString` and `validationMessage` properties. Now, we have virtually no duplicate code. The only code that is duplicated is the code for the singleton pattern and that is not something we would want to put in the protocol extension because we would not want to force that pattern on all the conforming types.

To use the text validation structures, we would use the `validateString()` method to see if a string instance matched the regular expression and the `getMatchingString()` method to return a new string with the invalid characters removed from the original string instance. The following example shows how we would use these methods:

```
var myString1 = "abcxyz"
var myString2 = "abc123"

let validation = AlphaValidation.sharedInstance

let valid1 = validation.validateString(str: myString1)
let newString1 = validation.getMatchingString(str: myString1)

let valid2 = validation.validateString(str: myString2)
let newString2 = validation.getMatchingString(str: myString2)
```

In this example the `valid2` constant would be true because the value of `myString1` matches the regular expression defined in the `AlphaValidation` type while the `valid2` constant would be false because the value of `myString2` does not match. The `newString1` constant would contain the same value as the `myString1` constant because the original string matched the regular expression while `newString2` would contain `abc` because the remainder of the characters do not match the regular expression.

Summary

In this chapter, we saw that protocols are treated as full-fledged types by Swift. We also saw how polymorphism can be implemented in Swift with protocols. We concluded this chapter with an in-depth look at protocol extensions and how we would use them in Swift.

Protocols and protocol extensions are the backbone of Apple's new protocol-oriented programming paradigm. This new model for programming has the potential to change the way we write and think about code. While we did not specifically cover protocol-oriented programming in this chapter, understanding the topics in this chapter gives us the solid understanding of protocols and protocol extensions needed to learn about this new programming model.

7
Protocol-Oriented Design

When Apple announced Swift 2 at the **World Wide Developers Conference** (**WWDC**) in 2016, they also declared that Swift was the world's first **Protocol-Oriented Programming** (**POP**) language. By its name we might assume that POP is all about the protocol; however that would be a wrong assumption. POP is about so much more than just the protocol; it is actually a new way of not only writing applications but also thinking about programming.

In this chapter we will learn:

- The difference between OOP and POP design
- What is protocol-oriented design?
- What is protocol composition?
- What is protocol inheritance?

Within days after *Dave Abrahams* did his presentation on POP at the WWDC 2016, there were numerous tutorials on the Internet about POP that took a very object-oriented approach to it. By this statement I mean the approach taken by these tutorials focused on replacing the superclass with protocols and protocol extensions. While protocols and protocol extensions are arguably two of the more important concepts of POP, these tutorials seem to be missing some very important concepts.

In this chapter, we will be comparing a protocol-oriented design with an object-oriented design to highlight some of the conceptual differences between the two. We will see how we can use protocols and protocol extensions to replace superclasses but we will also see how we can use POP to create a cleaner and easier-to-maintain code base. To do this we will look at how we would define animal types for a video game in both an object-oriented and also a protocol-oriented way, to appreciate the advantages of both. Let's start off by defining the requirements for our animals.

Requirements

When we develop applications we usually have a set of requirements that we need to develop towards. With that in mind, let's define the requirements for the animal types that we will be creating in this chapter:

- We will have three categories of animal: sea, land, and air.
- Animals may be members of multiple categories. For example an alligator can be a member of both the land and sea categories.
- Animals may be able to attack and/or move when they are on a tile that matches the categories they are in.
- Animals will start off with a certain number of hit points and if those hit points reach 0 or less then they will die.
- For our example here we will define two animals (`Lion` and `Alligator`) but we know that the number of animal types will grow as we develop the game.

We will start off by looking at how we would design our animal types with an object-oriented approach.

Object-oriented design

Before we start writing code, let's create a very basic class diagram that shows how we would design the `Animal` class hierarchy. I usually start off by doing a very basic diagram that simply shows the classes themselves without much detail. This helps me picture the class hierarchy in my mind. The following diagram shows the class hierarchy for our object-oriented design:

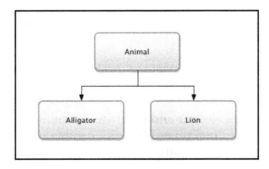

This diagram shows that we have one superclass named `Animal` and two subclasses named `Alligator` and `Lion`. We may think that, with the three categories (land, air, and sea), we would want to create a larger class hierarchy where the middle layer would contain the classes for the land, air, and sea animals. This would allow us to separate the code for each category; however it is not possible with our requirements. The reason this is not possible is that any of the animal types can be members of multiple categories and with a class hierarchy each class can have one and only one superclass. This means that our `Animal` superclass will need to contain the code required for each of the three categories. Lets take a look at the code for the `Animal` superclass.

We will start the `Animal` superclass off by defining ten properties. These properties will define what type of animal it is and what type of attacks/movement it can do. We also define a property that will keep track of the hit points for the animal. The animal dies when its hit points reach zero.

We defined these as private variables because we need to set them in the subclass; however we do not want external entities to change them. The preference is for these to be constants; however a subclass can not set/change the value of a constant defined in a superclass. In order for this to work the subclass needs to be defined in the same physical file as the superclass. You can refer to Apple's page on access controls for more details at `https://developer.apple.com/library/ios/documentation/Swift/Conceptual/Swift_Programming_Language/AccessControl.html`.

 When we are writing applications for the iOS or Mac OS platforms using Xcode, managing access controls is pretty easy because the Xcode IDE can tell us what properties/methods we have access to. This becomes significantly harder to do when we are developing on the Linux platform using a text editor.

```
class Animal
{
    private var landAnimal = false
    private var landAttack = false
    private var landMovement = false

    private var seaAnimal = false
    private var seaAttack = false
    private var seaMovement = false

    private var airAnimal = false
    private var airAttack = false
    private var airMovement = false
```

```
    private var hitPoints = 0
}
```

Next, we will define an initializer that will set the properties. We will set all of the properties to `false` by default and the hit points to 0. It will be up to the subclasses to set the appropriate properties that apply for that particular type:

```
init()
{
    landAnimal = false
    landAttack = false
    landMovement = false
    airAnimal = false
    airAttack = false
    airMovement = false
    seaAnimal = false
    seaAttack = false
    seaMovement = false
    hitPoints = 0
}
```

Since our properties are private we need to create some `getter` methods so we can retrieve the values of the properties. We will also create a couple of additional methods that will verify whether the animal is alive and also a method that will deduct hit points when the animal takes a hit:

```
func isLandAnimal() -> Bool { return landAnimal }
func canLandAttack() -> Bool { return landAttack }
func canLandMove() -> Bool { return landMovement }
func isSeaAnimal() -> Bool { return seaAnimal }
func canSeaAttack() -> Bool { return seaAttack }
func canSeaMove() -> Bool { return seaMovement }
func isAirAnimal() -> Bool { return airAnimal }
func canAirAttack() -> Bool { return airAttack }
func canAirMove() -> Bool { return airMovement }

func doLandAttack() {}
func doLandMovement() {}
func doSeaAttack() {}
func doSeaMovement() {}
func doAirAttack() {}
func doAirMovement() {}

func takeHit(amount: Int) { hitPoints -= amount }
func hitPointsRemaining() -> Int { return hitPoints }
func isAlive() -> Bool { return hitPoints > 0 ? true : false }
}
```

One big disadvantage to this design, as we noted earlier, is that all of the subclasses need to be in the same physical file as the `Animal` superclass. Given how large the classes can be, we may do not want all of these types in the same file. To avoid this we could set the properties to internal or public but that would not prevent the values from being changed by other instances of other types. This is a major drawback in an object-oriented design.

We can now create the `Alligator` and `Lion` classes as subclasses of the `Animal` class:

```
class Lion: Animal {

  override init() {
    super.init()
    landAnimal = true
    landAttack = true
    landMovement = true
    hitPoints = 20
  }

  override func doLandAttack() { print("Lion Attack") }
  override func doLandMovement() { print("Lion Move") }
}

class Alligator: Animal {

  override init() {
    super.init()
    landAnimal = true
    landAttack = true
    landMovement = true

    seaAnimal = true
    seaAttack = true
    seaMovement = true
    hitPoints = 35
  }

  override func doLandAttack() { print("Alligator Land Attack") }
  override func doLandMovement() { print("Alligator Land Move") }
  override func doSeaAttack() { print("Alligator Sea Attack") }
  override func doSeaMovement() { print("Alligator Sea Move") }

}
```

As we can see, these classes override the functionality needed for each animal. The `Lion` class contains the functionality for a land animal and the `Alligator` class contains the functionality for both a land and sea animal. Since both classes have the same `Animal` superclass we can use polymorphism to access them through the interface provided by the `Animal` superclass:

```
var animals = [Animal]()

var an1 = Alligator()
var an2 = Alligator()
var an3 = Lion()

animals.append(an1)
animals.append(an2)
animals.append(an3)

for (index, animal) in animals.enumerated() {
  if animal.isAirAnimal() {
  print("Animal at \(index) is Air")
}
if animal.isLandAnimal() {
  print("Animal at \(index) is Land")
}
if animal.isSeaAnimal() {
  print("Animal at \(index) is Sea")
}
}
```

The way we designed the animal types here would definitely work but there are several drawbacks to this design. The first drawback is the large monolithic `Animal` superclass. Those familiar with designing characters for video games will probably realize how much functionality is actually missing from the `Animal` superclass and its subclasses. This is on purpose so we can focus on the design and not all of the functionality. For those who are not familiar with designing characters for video games, trust me when I say that this class will get a lot bigger when we add all of the functionality needed.

Another drawback is not being able to define constants in the superclass that the subclasses can set. We could define various initiators for the superclass that would correctly set the constants for the different animal categories; however these initiators could become pretty complex and hard to maintain as we add additional animals. The builder pattern could help us with the initiation but, as we are about to see, a protocol-oriented design would be even better.

One final drawback that I am going to point out is the use of flags (`landAnimal`, `seaAnimal` and `airAnimal` properties) to define the type of animal. If we accidentally set these flags wrong then the animal will not behave correctly. As an example, if we set the `seaAnimal` flag rather than the `landAnimal` flag in the `Lion` class then the lion would not be able to move or attack on land. Trust me, it is very easy, even for the most experienced developers, to set flags wrongly.

Now let's look at how we would define this same functionality in a protocol-oriented way.

Protocol-oriented design

Just like with the object-oriented design, we will start off with a type diagram that shows the types needed and the relationships between them. The following diagram shows our protocol-oriented design:

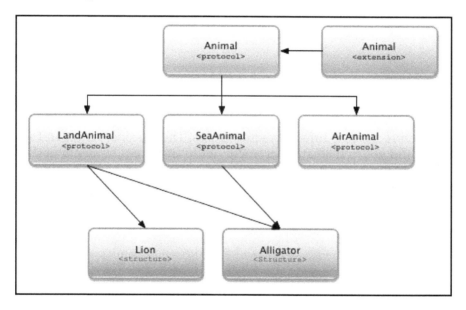

As we can see, our POP design is quite a bit different from our OOP design. In this design we use three techniques that make POP significantly different from OOP. These techniques are protocol inheritance, protocol composition, and protocol extensions. It is important to understand these concepts so, before we go into our design, let's look at what protocol inheritance and protocol composition are. We looked at *protocol extensions* in the last chapter.

Protocol inheritance

Protocol inheritance is where one protocol can inherit the requirements from one or more other protocols. This is similar to class inheritance in OOP but instead of inheriting functionality we are inheriting requirements. We can also inherit requirements from multiple protocols whereas a class, in Swift, can have one (and only one) superclass. Let's look at a quick example of protocol inheritance. Let's start off by defining protocols named `Name`, `Age`, `Fur`, and `Hair`:

```
protocol Name {
    var firstName: String {get set}
    var lastName: String {get set}
}

protocol Age {
    var age: Double {get set}
}

protocol Fur {
    var furColor: String {get set}
}

protocol Hair {
    var hairColoe: String {get set}
}
```

Each of the four protocols has different requirements. There is one thing that I would like to point out. If you find yourself creating protocols with single requirements as shown in this example you probably want to reconsider your overall design. Protocols should not be this granular because we end up with too many protocols and they become hard to manage.

Now let's see how we can use these protocols and protocol inheritance to create other protocols. We will define two more protocols named `Person` and `Dog`:

```
protocol Person: Name, Age, Hair {
    var height: Double {get set}
}

protocol Dog: Name, Age, Fur {
    var breed: String {get set}
}
```

Any type that conforms to the `Person` protocol will need to fulfill the requirements of the `Name`, `Age`, and `Hair` protocols as well as the requirements defined in the `Person` protocol itself. Any type that conforms to the `Dog` protocol will need to fulfill the requirements of the `Name`, `Age`, and `Fur` protocols as well as the requirements defined in the `Dog` protocol itself.

Protocol inheritance is extremely powerful because we are able to define several smaller protocols and mix/match them to create larger protocols. Definitely be careful not to create protocols that are too granular.

Protocol composition

Protocol composition allows types to conform to more than one protocol. This is one of the many advantages that POP has over OOP. With OOP a class can have only one superclass. This can lead to very large monolithic superclasses as we saw in the *Object-oriented design* section of this chapter. With POP we are encouraged to create multiple smaller protocols with very specific requirements. Let's look at how protocol composition works.

To our example from the *Protocol inheritance* section, let's add another protocol named `Occupation`:

```
protocol Occupation {
    var occupationName: String {get set}
    var yearlySalary: Double {get set}
    var experienceYears: Double {get set}
}
```

Now let's create a new type name `Programmer` that will conform to both the `Person` and `Occupation` protocols:

```
struct Programmer: Person, Occupation {
    var firstName: String
    var lastName: String
    var age: Double
    var hairColoe: String
    var height: Double
    var occupationName: String
    var yearlySalary: Double
    var experienceYears: Double
}
```

In this example the `Programmer` structure conforms to all of the requirements from the `Person` and `Occupation` protocols. Keep in mind that the `Person` protocol is a composite of the requirements from the `Name`, `Age`, `Hair`, and `Person` protocols, therefore the `Programmer` type actually conforms to all of those protocols plus the `Occupation` protocol.

Once again, I want to warn you not to make your protocols too granular. Protocol inheritance and composition are really powerful features but can also cause problems if used wrongly.

Animal – protocol-oriented design

Now let's begin rewriting the animal types in a protocol-oriented way. We will start off by defining our `Animal` protocol:

```
protocol Animal {
    var hitPoints: Int {get set}
}
```

In the `Animal` protocol, the only item that we are defining is the `hitPoints` property. This protocol would also contain any additional items that are common to all animals. To be consistent with our OOP design, we only need to add the `hitPoints` property to this protocol.

Next, we need to add an `Animal` protocol extension that will contain the functionality that is common for all types that conform to the protocol. Our `Animal` protocol extension would contain the following code:

```
extension Animal {
    mutating func takeHit(amount: Int) { hitPoints -= amount }
    func hitPointsRemaining() -> Int { return hitPoints }
    func isAlive() -> Bool { return hitPoints > 0 ? true : false }
}
```

The `Animal` protocol extension contains the same `takeHit()`, `hitPointsRemaining()`, and `isAlive()` methods that we saw in the `Animals` superclass from the OOP example. Any type that conforms to the `Animal` protocol will automatically receive these three methods.

Now let's define our `LandAnimal`, `SeaAnimal`, and `AirAnimal` protocols. These protocols will define the requirements for land, sea, and air animals respectively:

```
protocol LandAnimal: Animal {
    var landAttack: Bool {get}
```

```
    var landMovement: Bool {get}
    func doLandAttack()
    func doLandMovement()
}

protocol SeaAnimal: Animal {
    var seaAttack: Bool {get}
    var seaMovement: Bool {get}
    func doSeaAttack()
    func doSeaMovement()
}

protocol AirAnimal: Animal {
    var airAttack: Bool {get}
    var airMovement: Bool {get}
    func doAirAttack()
    func doAirMovement()
}
```

Unlike the `Animal` superclass in the OOP example, these three protocols only contain the functionality needed for their particular type of animal. Each of these protocols only contains four lines of code while the `Animal` superclass, from the OOP example, contains significantly more. This makes our protocol design much easier to read and manage. The protocol design is also much safer because the functionality for the various animal types is isolated in its own protocol rather than being embedded in a giant superclass. We also avoid the use of flags to define the animal category and instead define the category of the animal by what protocols they are conforming too.

Now let's look at how we would create our `Lion` and `Alligator` types using the protocol-oriented design:

```
struct Lion: LandAnimal {
    var hitPoints = 20
    let landAttack = true
    let landMovement = true

    func doLandAttack() { print("Lion Attack") }
    func doLandMovement() { print("Lion Move") }
}

struct Alligator: LandAnimal, SeaAnimal {
    var hitPoints = 35
    let landAttack = true
    let landMovement = true
    let seaAttack = true
    let seaMovement = true
    func doLandAttack() { print("Alligator Land Attack") }
```

```
    func doLandMovement() { print("Alligator Land Move") }
    func doSeaAttack() { print("Alligator Sea Attack") }
    func doSeaMovement() { print("Alligator Sea Move") }
}
```

Notice that we specify that the `Lion` type conforms to the `LandAnimal` protocol while the `Alligator` type conforms to both the `LandAnimal` and `SeaAnimal` protocols. As we saw earlier, having a single type that conforms to multiple protocols is called **protocol composition** and is what allows us to use smaller protocols rather than one giant monolithic superclass as we did in the OOP example.

Both the `Lion` and `Alligator` types originate from the `Animal` protocol; therefore we can still use polymorphism as we did in the OOP example where we use the `Animal` type to store instances of the `Lion` and `Alligator` types. Let's see how this works:

```
var animals = [Animal]()

var an1 = Alligator()
var an2 = Alligator()
var an3 = Lion()

animals.append(an1)
animals.append(an2)
animals.append(an3)


for (index, animal) in animals.enumerated() {
    if let animal = animal as? AirAnimal {
        print("Animal at \(index) is Air")
    }
    if let animal = animal as? LandAnimal {
        print("Animal at \(index) is Land")
    }
    if let animal = animal as? SeaAnimal {
        print("Animal at \(index) is Sea")
    }
}
```

In this example, we create an array that will contain animal types named `animals`. We then create two instances of the `Alligator` type and one instance of the `Lion` type and add all three instances to the `animals` array. Finally, we use a `for...in` loop to loop through the array and print out the animal type based on the protocol that the instance conform too.

Using the where statement with protocols

When we use a protocol-oriented design, as we just saw, we are able to use the `where` statement to filter instances of our types. For example, if we only want to get the instances that conform to the `SeaAnimal` protocol we can create a `for` loop such as this:

```
for (index, animal) in animals.enumerated() where animal is SeaAnimal {
    print("Only Sea Animal: \(index)")
}
```

This will retrieve only those animals that conform to the `SeaAnimal` protocol. This is a lot safer than just checking the flags because, as we pointed out earlier, it is really easy to set the wrong flag in our code, which would introduce all sorts of weird behavior.

Summary

When we read through this chapter and see some of the advantages that POP has over OOP, we might concluded that POP is clearly superior to OOP. However, this assumption would not be entirely correct.

OOP has been around since the 1970s and is a tried and tested programming paradigm. POP is the new kid on the block and was designed to correct some of the issues with OOP. I have personally used the POP paradigm in a couple of projects and I am very excited about its possibilities.

OOP and POP have similar philosophies, such as creating custom types that model real-world objects and polymorphism to use a single interface to interact with multiple types. The difference lies in how these philosophies are implemented.

To me, the code base in a project that uses POP is much safer, easier to read, and easier to maintain as compared to a project that uses OOP. This does not mean that I am going to stop using OOP all together. I can still see plenty of need for class hierarchies and inheritance.

Remember, when we are designing our application we should always use the right tool for the job. We would not want to use a chain saw to cut a piece of 2 x 4 lumber, but we also would not want to use a skilsaw to cut down a tree. Therefore, the winner is the programmer who can choose from different programming paradigms rather than being limited to one.

If you would like to read more about POP, you can read my book *Swift 3 Protocol-Oriented Programming – Second Edition*.

8
Writing Safer Code with Error Handling

When I first started writing applications with Objective-C, one of the most noticeable deficiencies was the lack of exception handling. Most modern programming languages, such as Java and C#, use `try...catch` blocks or something similar to handle exceptions. While Objective-C did have the `try...catch` block, it wasn't used within the Cocoa frameworks themselves, and it never felt like a true part of the language. I have significant experience with C, so I was able to understand how Apple frameworks received and responded to errors, and, to be honest, in some cases, I actually preferred this method, even though I had grown accustomed to exception handling with Java and C#. When Swift was first introduced, I was hoping that Apple would put true error handling into the language so we would have the option of using it; however, it was not in the initial release of Swift. When Swift 2 was released, Apple added additional error handling to Swift. While this error handling may look similar to exception handling in Java and C#, there are some very significant differences.

We will cover the following topics in this chapter:

- How we handled errors before Swift 2
- How to use the `do...catch` block in Swift
- How to represent errors

Error handling prior to Swift 2.0

Error handling is the process of responding to, and recovering from, error conditions within our applications. Prior to Swift 2.0, error reporting followed the same pattern as Objective-C; however, with Swift, we have the added benefit of using optional return values, where returning a nil would indicate an error within the function.

In the simplest form of error handling, the return value from the function indicates whether it was successful or not. This return value could be something as simple as a Boolean true/false value or something more complex, such as an enumeration, whose values would indicate what actually went wrong if the function was unsuccessful. If we needed to report additional information about the error that occurred, we could add an NSError out parameter of the NSErrorPointer type, but this wasn't the easiest of approaches, and these errors tended to be ignored by developers. The following example illustrates how errors were generally handled prior to Swift 2.0. (Note: this code does not work in Swift 3.0):

```
var str = "Hello World"
var error: NSError

var results = str.writeToFile(path, atomically: true, encoding:
NSUTF8StringEncoding, error: &error)

if results {
  // successful code here
} else {
    println("Error writing filer: \(error)")
}
```

While handling errors in this manner works well, and can be modified to suit most needs, it definitely is not the perfect solution. There are a couple of issues with this solution, the biggest being that it is easy for developers to ignore both the error value that is returned and the error itself. While most experienced developers will be very careful to check for errors, sometimes it is hard for novice developers to understand what and when to check, especially if the function does not contain an NSError parameter.

In addition to using NSError, we could also raise and catch exceptions using the NSException class; however, very few developers actually use this method. Even within the Cocoa and Cocoa Touch frameworks, this method of exception handling was rarely used.

While using the NSError class and returning values to handle errors does work well, there were many people, including myself, who were disappointed that Apple did not include additional error handling when Swift was originally released. Native error handling was finally introduced in Swift starting with Swift 2.0.

Native error handling

Languages such as Java and C# generally refer to the error handling process as **exception handling**; within the Swift documentation, Apple refers to this process as **error handling**. While, externally, Java and C# exception handling may look very similar to Swift's error handling, there are some significant differences that those familiar with exception handling in the other languages will notice throughout this chapter.

Representing errors

Before we can really understand how error handling works in Swift, we must first see how we would represent an error. In Swift, errors are represented by values of types that conform to the Error protocol. Swift's enumerations are very well suited to modeling error conditions because, generally, we have a finite number of error conditions to represent.

Let's look at how we would use an enumeration to represent an error. For this, we will define a fictitious error named MyError with three error conditions: Minor, Bad, and Terrible:

```
enum MyError: Error {
    case Minor
    case Bad
    case Terrible
}
```

In this example, we define that the MyError enumeration conforms to the Error protocol. We then define the three error conditions: Minor, Bad, and Terrible.We can also use associated values with our error conditions to allow us to add additional details about the error condition. Let's say that we wanted to add a description to the Terrible error condition. We would do it like this:

```
enum MyError: Error {
    case Minor
    case Bad
    case Terrible (description: String)
}
```

Those who are familiar with exception handling in Java and C# can see that representing errors in Swift is a lot cleaner and easier because we do not need to create a lot of boilerplate code or a full class. With Swift, we simply define an enumeration with our error conditions. Another advantage that we have is that it is very easy to define multiple error conditions and group them together so all the related error conditions are of one type.

Now let's see how we would model errors in Swift. For this example, let's look at how we would assign numbers to players in a baseball team. In a baseball team, every new player who is called up is assigned a unique number for that team. This number must also be within a certain range. In this case, we would have three error conditions: number is too large, number is too small, or number is not unique. The following example shows how we might represent these error conditions:

```
enum PlayerNumberError: Error {
    case NumberTooHigh(description: String)
    case NumberTooLow(description: String)
    case NumberAlreadyAssigned
}
```

With the `PlayerNumberError` type, we define three very specific error conditions that tell us exactly what is wrong. These error conditions are also grouped together in one type, since they are all related to assigning players numbers.

This method of defining errors allows us to define very specific errors that let our code know exactly what went wrong if an error condition occurs, and, as we see in our example, it also lets us group our errors so that all of the related errors can be defined in the same type.

Now that we know how to represent errors, let's look at how we would throw errors.

Throwing errors

When an error occurs in a function, the code that called the function must be made aware of it, this is called **throwing the error**. When a function throws an error, it assumes that the code that called the function, or some code further up the chain, will catch, and recover appropriately from, the error.

To throw an error from a function, we use the throws keyword. This keyword lets the code that called it know that an error may be thrown from the function. Unlike exception handling in other languages, we do not list the specific error types that may be thrown.

Since we do not list the specific error types that may be thrown from a function within the function's definition, it would be good practice to list them in the documentation and comments for the function so that other developers who use our function know what error types to catch.

Soon, we will look at how we would throw errors but first, let's add a fourth error to the `PlayerNumberError` type that we defined earlier. This error condition is thrown if we are trying to retrieve a player by his or her number, but no player has assigned that number.

The new `PlayerNumberError` type will now look similar to this:

```
enum PlayerNumberError: Error {
    case NumberTooHigh(description: String)
    case NumberTooLow(description: String)
    case NumberAlreadyAssigned
    case NumberDoesNotExist
}
```

To demonstrate how to throw errors, we will begin by creating a `BaseballTeam` structure that will contain a list of players for a given team. These players will be stored in a dictionary object named `players`. We will use the player's numbers as the key, since we know that each player must have a unique number. The `BaseballPlayer` type, which will be used to represent a single player, will be a `typealias` for a tuple type, and is defined like this:

```
typealias BaseballPlayer = (firstName: String, lastName: String, number:
Int)
```

In this `BaseballTeam` structure, we will have two methods. The first one will be named `addPlayer()`. This method will have one parameter of the `BaseballPlayer` type and will attempt to add the player to the team. This method can also throw one of three error conditions: `NumberTooHigh`, `NumberTooLow`, or `NumberAlreadyExists`. Here is how we would write this method:

```
mutating func addPlayer(player: BaseballPlayer) throws {

    guard player.number < maxNumber else {
        throw PlayerNumberError.NumberTooHigh(description: "Max
            number is \(maxNumber)")
    }

    guard player.number > minNumber else {
        throw PlayerNumberError.NumberTooLow(description: "Min
            number is \(minNumber)")
    }

    guard players[player.number] == nil else {
        throw PlayerNumberError.NumberAlreadyAssigned
    }
    players[player.number] = player
}
```

In the method's definition, we see that the `throws` keyword is added. The `throws` keyword lets any code that calls this method know that it may throw an error, and that the errors must be handled. We then use the three `guard` statements. These `guard` statements are used to verify that the number is not too large, not too small, and is unique in the `players` dictionary. If any of the conditions are not met, we throw the appropriate error using the `throw` keyword. If we make it through all three checks, the player is added to the `players` dictionary.

The second method that we will be adding to the `BaseballTeam` struct is the `getPlayerByNumber()` method. This method will attempt to retrieve the baseball player that is assigned a given number. If no player is assigned that number, this method will throw a `PlayerNumberError.NumberDoesNotExist` error. The `getPlayerByNumber()` method will look similar to this:

```
func getPlayerByNumber(number: Int) throws -> BaseballPlayer {
    if let player = players[number] {
        return player
    }
else {
        throw PlayerNumberError.NumberDoesNotExist
    }
}
```

In this method definition, we see that it can throw an error because we use the `throws` keyword within the definition. When we use the `throws` keyword, it must be placed before the `return` type in the method definition.

Within the method, we attempt to retrieve the baseball player with the number that is passed into the method. If we are able to retrieve the player, we return it; otherwise, we throw the `PlayerNumberError.NumberDoesNotExist` error. Notice that if we throw an error from a method that has a return type, we do not need to return a value.

Now let's see how we would catch an error with Swift.

Catching errors

When an error is thrown from a function, we can catch it in the code that called the function; this is done using the `do...catch` block. The `do...catch` block takes the following syntax:

```
do {
    try [Some function that throws]
    [Any additional code]
```

```
} catch [pattern] {
   [Code if function threw error]
}
```

If an error is thrown, it is propagated out until it is handled by a `catch` clause. The `catch` clause consists of the `catch` keyword, followed by a pattern to match the error against. If the error matches the pattern, the code within the `catch` block is executed. If, for some reason, the error is never caught, we will receive a runtime error and our application will probably crash.

Let's look at how we would use the `do...catch` block by calling both the `getPlayerByNumber()` and `addPlayer()` methods of the `BaseballTeam` structure. Let's look at the `getPlayerByNumber()` method first, since it only throws one error condition:

```
do {
    let player = try myTeam.getPlayerByNumber(number: 34)
    print("Player is \(player.firstName) \(player.lastName)")
} catch PlayerNumberError.NumberDoesNotExist {
    print("No player has that number")
}
```

Within this example, the `do...catch` block calls the `getPlayerByNumber()` method of the `BaseballTeam` structure. This method will throw the `PlayerNumberError.NumberDoesNotExist` error condition if no player on the team has been assigned this number; therefore, we attempt to match that error in our `catch` statement.

Any time an error is thrown within a `do...catch` block, the remainder of the code within the block is skipped and the code within the `catch` block, which matches the error, is executed. Therefore, in our example, if the `PlayerNumberError.NumberDoesNotExist` error is thrown by the `getPlayerByNumber()` method, then the `print()` function is never reached.

We do not have to include a pattern after the `catch` statement. If a pattern is not included after the `catch` statement, or if we put in an underscore, the `catch` statement will match all error conditions. For example, either one of the following two `catch` statements will catch all errors:

```
do {
    // our statements
} catch {
    // our error conditions
}
```

```
do {
    // our statements
} catch _ {
    // our error conditions
}
```

If we want to capture the error, we can use the `let` keyword, as shown in the following example:

```
do {
    // our statements
} catch let error {
    print("Error:  \(error)")
}
```

Now let's look at how we could use the `catch` statement, similar to a `switch` statement, to catch different error conditions. For this, we will call the `addPlayer()` method of our `BaseballTeam` struct:

```
do {
    try myTeam.addPlayer(player:("David", "Ortiz", 34))
} catch PlayerNumberError.NumberTooHigh(let description) {
    print("Error: \(description)")
} catch PlayerNumberError.NumberTooLow(let description) {
    print("Error: \(description)")
} catch PlayerNumberError.NumberAlreadyAssigned {
    print("Error: Number already assigned")
}
```

In this example, we have three `catch` statements. Each `catch` statement has a different pattern to match; therefore, they will each match a different error condition. If we recall, the `PlayerNumberError.NumberTooHigh` and `PlayerNumberError.NumberTooLow` error conditions have associated values. To retrieve the associated value, we use the `let` statement within the parentheses, as shown in the example.

It is always good practice to make your last `catch` statement an empty `catch` so that it will catch any error that did not match any of the patterns in the previous `catch` statements. Therefore, the previous example should be rewritten to look like this:

```
do {
    try myTeam.addPlayer(player:("David", "Ortiz", 34))
} catch PlayerNumberError.NumberTooHigh(let description) {
    print("Error: \(description)")
} catch PlayerNumberError.NumberTooLow(let description) {
    print("Error: \(description)")
} catch PlayerNumberError.NumberAlreadyAssigned {
```

```
        print("Error: Number already assigned")
    } catch {
        print("Error: Unknown Error")
    }
```

We can also let the errors propagate out rather than immediately catching them. To do this, we just need to add the `throws` keyword to the function definition. For instance, in the following example, rather than catching the error, we could let it propagate out to the code that called the function like this:

```
func myFunc() throws {
    try myTeam.addPlayer(player:("David", "Ortiz", 34))
}
```

If we are certain that an error will not be thrown, we can call the function using a forced-try expression, which is written as `try!`. The forced-try expression disables error propagation and wraps the function call in a runtime assertion that no error will be thrown from this call. If an error is thrown, we will get a runtime error, so be very careful when using this expression.

When I am working with exceptions in languages such as Java and C#, I see a lot of empty `catch` blocks. This is where we need to catch the exception because one might be thrown; however, we do not want to do anything with it. In Swift, the code would look something like this:

```
do {
    let player = try myTeam.getPlayerByNumber(number: 34)
    print("Player is \(player.firstName) \(player.lastName)")
} catch {}
```

Seeing code like this is one of the things that I dislike about exception handling. Well, the Swift developers have an answer for this: The `try?` keyword. The `try?` keyword attempts to perform an operation that may throw an error. If the operation succeeds, the results are returned in the form of an optional; however, if the operation fails with an error being thrown, the operation returns a nil and the error is discarded.

Since the results of the `try?` keyword are returned in the form of an optional, we would normally want to use this keyword with optional binding. We could rewrite the previous example like this:

```
if let player = try? myTeam.getPlayerByNumber(number: 34) {
    print("Player is \(player.firstName) \(player.lastName)")
}
```

As we can see, the `try?` keyword makes our code much cleaner and easier to read.

If we need to perform some cleanup action, regardless of whether we had any errors or not, we can use the `defer` statement. We use the `defer` statement to execute a block of code just before code execution leaves the current scope. The following example shows how we would use the `defer` statement:

```
func deferFunction()  {
    print("Function started")
    var str: String?
    defer {
    print("In defer block")
        if let s = str {
            print("str is \(s)")
        }
    }
    str = "Jon"
    print("Function finished")
}
```

If we called this function, the first line that is printed to the console would be `Function started`. The execution of the code would skip over the `defer` block and `Function finished` would be printed to the console next. Finally, the `defer` block of code would be executed just before we leave the function's scope, and we would see the message, `In defer block`. The following is the output from this function:

```
Function started
Function finished
In defer block
str is Jon
```

The `defer` block will always be called before execution leaves the current scope, even if an error is thrown. The `defer` block is very useful when we need to perform some cleanup functions prior to leaving a function.

The `defer` statement is very useful when we want to make sure we perform all the necessary cleanup, even if an error is thrown. For example, if we successfully opened a file to write to, we will always want to make sure we close that file, even if we have an error during the write operation. We could then put the file-closed functionality in a `defer` block to make sure that the file is always closed prior to leaving the current scope.

Summary

In this chapter, we looked at Swift's error handling features. This feature is really important for writing safe code. While we are not required to use this feature in our custom types, it does give us a uniform manner to handle and respond to errors. Apple has also started to use this error handling in their frameworks. It is recommended that we use error handling in our code.

9
Custom Subscripting

Custom subscripts were added to Objective-C in 2012. At the time, *Chris Lattner* was already two years into developing Swift, and, like other good features, subscripts were added to the Swift language. I have not used custom subscripts in many other languages; however, I do find myself using subscripts extensively when I am developing in Swift. The syntax for using subscripts in Swift seems like a more natural part of the language, possibly because they were part of the language when it was released and not added in later. Once you start using subscripts in Swift, you may find them indispensible.

In this chapter, you will learn the following topics:

- What custom subscripts are
- How to add custom subscripts to classes, structures, or enumerations
- How to create read/write and read-only subscripts
- How to use external names without custom subscripts
- How to use multidimensional subscripts

Introducing subscripts

Subscripts, in the Swift language, are used as shortcuts for accessing elements of a collection, list, or sequence. We can use them in our custom types to set or retrieve the values by index rather than using `getter` and `setter` methods. Subscripts, if used correctly, can significantly enhance the usability and readability of our custom types.

We can define multiple subscripts for a single type. When a type has multiple subscripts, the appropriate subscript will be chosen, based on the type of index passed into the subscript. We can also set external parameter names for our subscripts, which can help distinguish between subscripts that have the same type.

We use custom subscripts just like we use subscripts for arrays and dictionaries. For example, to access an element in an array, we will use the `anArray[index]` syntax, and to access an element of a dictionary, we will use the same syntax `aDictionary[key]`. When we define a custom subscript for our custom types, we also access them with the same syntax, `ourType[key]`.

When creating custom subscripts, we should try to make them feel as if they are a natural part of the class, structure, or enumeration. As mentioned earlier, subscripts can significantly enhance the usability and readability of our code, but if we try to overuse them, they will not feel natural and will be hard to use.

In this chapter, we will look at several examples of how we can create and use custom subscripts. We will also show an example of how not to use a subscript. Before we show how to use custom subscripts, let's review how subscripts are used with Swift arrays to see how subscripts are used within the Swift language itself. We should use subscripts in a similar manner to how Apple uses them within the language to make our custom subscripts easy to understand and use.

Subscripts with Swift arrays

The following example shows how to use subscripts to access and change the values of an array:

```
var arrayOne = [1,2,3,4,5,6]
print(arrayOne[3])  //Displays '4'
arrayOne[3] = 10
print(arrayOne[3])  //Displays '10'
```

In the preceding example, we create an array of integers and then use the subscript syntax to display and change the item of element number 3 in the array. Subscripts are mainly used to get or retrieve information from a collection. We generally do not use subscripts when specific logic needs to be applied to determine which item to select. For example, we will not use subscripts to append an item to the end of the array or to retrieve the number of items in the array. To append an item to the end of an array, or to get the number of items in an array, we will use functions or properties like this:

```
arrayOne.append(7)  //append 7 to the end of the array
arrayOne.count  //returns the number of items in an array
```

Subscripts in our custom types should follow the same standard set by the Swift language itself, so other developers that use our types are not confused by the implementation. The key to knowing when to use subscripts, and when not to, is to understand how the subscript will be used.

Read and write custom subscripts

Let's see how to define a subscript that is used to read and write to a backend array. Reading and writing to a backend storage class is one of the most common uses for custom subscripts but, as we will see in this chapter, we do not need to have a backend storage class. The following code shows how to use a subscript to read and write to an array:

```
class MyNames {
    private var names:[String] = ["Jon", "Kim", "Kailey", "Kara"]
    subscript(index: Int) -> String {
        get {
            return names[index]
        }
        set {
            names[index] = newValue
        }
    }
}
```

As we can see, the syntax is similar to how we can define properties within a class using the `get` and `set` keywords. The difference is that we declare the subscript using the `subscript` keyword. We then specify one or more inputs and the return type.

We can now use the custom subscript, just like we used subscripts with arrays and dictionaries. The following code shows how to use the subscript in the preceding example:

```
var nam = MyNames()
print(nam[0])  //Displays 'Jon'
nam[0] = "Buddy"
print(nam[0])  //Displays 'Buddy'
```

In the preceding code, we create an instance of the `MyNames` class. We then display the original name at index 0, change the name at index 0, and redisplay it. In this example, we use the subscript that we defined in the `MyNames` class to retrieve and set elements of the `names` array within the `MyNames` class.

While we could just make the `names` array property available for external code to read and write directly to, this would lock our code into using an array to store the data. If we ever want to change the backend storage mechanism to a dictionary object, or even an SQLite database, we will be unable to do so because all of the external code would also have to be changed. Subscripts are very good at hiding how we store information within our custom types; therefore, external code that uses these custom types does not rely on the specific storage implementations.

We would also be unable to verify that the external code was inserting valid information into the array if we gave direct access to it. With subscripts, we can add validation to our setters to verify that the data being passed in is correct before adding it to the array. This can be very useful, whether we are creating a framework or a library.

Read-only custom subscripts

We can also make the subscript read-only by either not declaring a `setter` method within the subscript or by not implicitly declaring a `getter` or `setter` method. The following code shows how to declare a read-only property by not declaring a `setter` method:

```
//No getter/setters implicitly declared
subscript(index: Int) ->String {
  return names[index]
}
```

The following example shows how to declare a read-only property by only declaring a `getter` method:

```
//Declaring only a getter
subscript(index: Int) ->String {
  get {
    return names[index]
  }
}
```

In the first example, we do not define either a `getter` or `setter` method; therefore, Swift sets the subscript as read-only and the code acts as if it was in a getter definition. In the second example, we specifically set the code in a getter definition. Both examples are valid read-only subscripts.

Calculated subscripts

While the preceding example is very similar to using the stored properties in a class or structure, we can also use subscripts in a similar manner to computed properties. Let's see how to do this:

```
struct MathTable {
    var num: Int
    subscript(index: Int) -> Int {
        return num * index
    }
}
```

In the previous example, we used an array as the backend storage mechanism for the subscript. In this example, we use the value of the subscript to calculate the return value. We will use this subscript as follows:

```
var table = MathTable(num: 5)
print(table[4])
```

This example will display the calculated value of 5 (the number defined in the initialization) times 4 (the subscript value), which is equal to 20.

Subscript values

In the preceding subscript examples, all of the subscripts accepted integers as the value for the subscript. However, we are not limited to integers. In the following example, we could use a String type as the value for the subscript. The subscript will also return a String type:

```
struct Hello {
    subscript (name: String) ->String {
        return "Hello \(name)"
    }
}
```

In this example, the subscript takes a string as the value within the subscript and returns a message, saying Hello. Let's see how to use this subscript:

```
var hello = Hello()
print(hello["Jon"])
```

This example will display the message, Hello Jon, to the console.

External names for subscripts

As we mentioned earlier in this chapter, we can have multiple subscript signatures for our custom types. The appropriate subscript will be chosen, based on the type of index passed into it. There are times when we may wish to define multiple subscripts that have the same type. For this, we could use external names, similar to how we define external names for the parameters of a function.

Let's rewrite the original `MathTable` structure to include two subscripts that each accept an integer as the subscript type; however, one will perform a multiplication operation, and the other will perform an addition operation:

```
struct MathTable {
  var num: Int
  subscript(multiply index: Int) -> Int {
    return num * index
  }
  subscript(addition index: Int) -> Int {
    return num + index
  }
}
```

As we can see, in this example we define two subscripts and each subscript is an integer type. The difference between the two subscripts is the external name within the definition. In the first subscript, we define an external name of `multiply` because we multiply the value of the subscript by the `num` property within this subscript. In the second subscript, we define an external name of `addition` because we add the value of the subscript to the `num` property within the subscript.

Let's see how to use these two subscripts:

```
var table = MathTable(num: 5)
print(table[multiply: 4])  //Displays 20 because 5*4=20
print(table[addition: 4])  //Displays 9 because 5+4=9
```

If we run this example, we will see that the correct subscript is used, based on the external name within the subscript.

Using external names within our subscript is very useful if we need multiple subscripts of the same type; however, I would not recommend using external names unless they are needed to distinguish between multiple subscripts.

Multidimensional subscripts

While the most common subscripts are the ones that take a single parameter, subscripts are not limited to single parameters. They can take any number of input parameters, and these parameters can be of any type.

Let's see how we could use a multidimensional subscript to implement a Tic-Tac-Toe board. A Tic-Tac-Toe board looks similar to this:

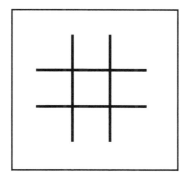

The board can be represented by a two-dimensional array where each dimension has three elements. Each player will then take a turn placing their pieces (typically, x or o) on the board until one player has three pieces in a row or the board is full.

Let's see how we could implement a Tic-Tac-Toe board using a multidimensional array and multidimensional subscripts:

```
struct TicTacToe {
  var board = [["","",""],["","",""],["","",""]]
  subscript(x: Int, y: Int) -> String {
    get {
      return board[x][y]
    }
    set {
      board[x][y] = newValue
    }
  }
}
```

We start the Tic-Tac-Toe structure by defining a 3×3 array that will represent the game board. We then define a subscript that can be used to set and retrieve player pieces on the board. The subscript will accept two integer values. Multiple parameters are defined by putting the parameters between parentheses. In our example, we are defining the subscript with the parameters, (x: Int, y: Int). We can then use the x and y variable names within our subscripts to access the values that are passed in.

Let's see how to use this subscript to set the user's pieces on the board:

```
var board = TicTacToe()
board[1,1] = "x"
board[0,0] = "o"
```

If we run this code, we will see that we added the player x piece to the center square and the player o piece to the upper left square, so our game board will look similar to this:

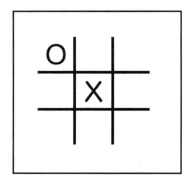

We are not limited to using only one type in our multidimensional subscripts, so we can use multiple types. For example, we could have a subscript of the (x: Int, y:Double, z: String) type.

We can also add external names for our multidimensional subscript types to help identify what values are used and to distinguish between the subscripts that have the same types. Let's take a look at how to use multiple types and external names with subscripts by creating a subscript that will return an array of string instances, based on the values of the subscript:

```
struct SayHello {
   subscript(messageText message:String, messageName name:String,    number
number:Int) -> [String]{
   var retArray: [String] = []
     for _ in 0..<number {
       retArray.append("\(message) \(name)")
     }
```

```
        return retArray
    }
}
```

In the `SayHello` structure, we define our subscript like this:

```
subscript(messageText message:String,messageName name:String, number
number:Int) -> [String]
```

This defines a subscript with three elements. Each element has an external name (`message`, `name`, and `number`) and an internal name (`message`, `name`, and `number`). The first two elements are of the `String` type and the last one is an `Int` type. We use the first two elements to create a message for the user that will repeat the number of times defined by the last (`number`) element. We will use this subscript as follows:

```
var message = SayHello()
var ret = message[messageText:"Bonjour",messageName:"Jon",number:5]
```

If we run this code, we will see that the `ret` variable contains an array of five strings, where each string equals `Bonjour Jon`.

When not to use a custom subscript

As we have seen in this chapter, creating custom subscripts can really enhance our code; however, we should avoid overusing them or using them in a way that is not consistent with the standard subscript usage. The way to avoid overusing subscripts is to examine how subscripts are used in Swift's standard libraries.

Let's take a look at the following example:

```
class MyNames {
  private var names:[String] = ["Jon", "Kim", "Kailey", "Kara"]
  var number: Int {
    get {
      return names.count
    }
  }
  subscript(add name: String) -> String {
    names.append(name)
    return name
  }
  subscript(index: Int) -> String {
    get {
      return names[index]
    }
```

```
    set {
      names[index] = newValue
    }
  }
}
```

In the preceding example, within the `MyNames` class, we define an array of names that is used within our application. As an example, let's say that, within our application, we display this list of names and allow users to add names to it. Within the `MyNames` class, we then define the following subscript, which allows us to append a new name to the array:

```
subscript(add name: String) -> String {
  names.append(name)
  return name
}
```

This would be a poor use of subscripts because its usage is not consistent with how subscripts are used within the Swift language. This might cause confusion when the class is used in the future. It would be more appropriate to rewrite this subscript as a function such as this:

```
func append(name: String) {
  names.append(name)
}
```

Remember, when you are using custom subscripts make sure that you are using them appropriately. As a general rule we should use subscripts in our custom types similarly to how they are used in the Swift language itself.

Summary

As we saw in this chapter, adding support for subscripts to our custom types can greatly enhance their readability and usability. We saw that subscripts can be used to add an abstraction layer between our backend storage class and external code. Subscripts can also be used, in a similar manner to computed properties, where the subscript is used to calculate a value. As we noted, the key with subscripts is to use them appropriately and in a manner that is consistent with subscripts in the Swift language.

10
Using Optional Types

When I first started using Swift, the concept that I had the most trouble learning was optional types. Coming from an Objective-C, C, Java, and Python background, I was able to relate most of Swift's features to how things worked in one of the other languages that I knew, but optionals were different. There really was nothing like optionals in the other languages that I used, so it took a lot of reading to fully understand them. While we covered optionals in `Chapter 2`, *Learning About Variables, Constants, Strings, and Operators*, which gave a brief overview of what optionals are, we really need to cover them in more detail to fully understand what optionals are, how to properly use them, and why they are so important in the Swift language.

In this chapter, we will cover the following topics:

- An introduction to optional types
- The need for optional types in Swift
- Unwrapping an optional
- Optional binding
- Optional chaining

Introducing optionals

When we declare variables in Swift, they are, by default, non-optional, which means that they must contain a valid, non-nil value. If we try to set a non-optional variable to nil, it will result in a `Nil cannot be assigned to type '{type}'` error, where `{type}` is the type of the variable.

For example, the following code will throw an error when we attempt to set the `message` variable to `nil` because `message` is a non-optional type:

```
var message: String = "My String"
message = nil
```

It is very important to understand that nil in Swift is very different from nil in Objective-C or other C-based languages. In these languages, nil is a pointer to a non-existent object; however, in Swift, nil is the absence of a value. This concept is very important in fully understanding optionals in Swift.

A variable defined as an optional can contain a valid value or it can indicate the absence of a value. We indicate an absence of a value by assigning it a special nil value. Optionals of any type can be set to nil, whereas in Objective-C only objects can be set to nil.

To really understand the concept behind optionals, let's look at a line of code that defines an optional:

```
var myString: String?
```

The question mark (?) at the end indicates that the `myString` variable is an optional. When we look at this code, it would be wrong to read it as if the `myString` variable is a `String` type that is optional. We should actually read this line of code as the `myString` variable is an optional type, which may contain a `String` type or no value. The subtle difference between the two lines actually makes a big difference in understanding how optionals work.

Optionals are a special type in Swift. When we defined the `myString` variable, we actually defined it as an optional type. To understand this, let's look at some more code:

```
var myString1: String?
var myString2: Optional<String>
```

These two declarations are equivalent. Both lines declare an optional type that may contain a `String` type or have no value. In Swift, we can think of the absence of a value as being set to nil, but always remember that this is different than setting something to nil in Objective-C. In this book, when we refer to nil, we are referring to how Swift uses nil and not to how Objective-C uses nil.

The optional type is an enumeration with two possible values, None and Some(T), where T is the associated value of the appropriate type. If we set the optional to nil, then it will have a value of None, and if we set a value, then the optional will have a value of Some with an associated value of the appropriate type. In Chapter 2, *Learning About Variables, Constants, Strings, and Operators*, we explained that an enumeration in Swift may have associated values. Associated values allow us to store additional information along with the enumeration's member values.

Internally, an optional is defined as follows:

```
enum Optional<T> {
  case None
  case Some(T)
}
```

Here, T is the type to associate with the optional. The T symbol is used to define a generic. We can read more about generics in Chapter 11, *Working with Generics*. For now, just remember that the T symbol represents any type.

The need for optional types in Swift

Now, the burning question is why does Swift need optionals? To understand this question, we should examine what problems optionals are designed to solve.

In most languages, it is possible to create a variable without giving it an initialized value. For example, in Objective-C, both of these lines of code are valid:

```
int i;
MyObject *m;
```

Now, let's say that the MyObject class has the following method:

```
-(int)myMethodWithValue:(int)i {
    return i*2;
}
```

This method takes the value passed in from the i parameter, multiplies it by 2, and returns the results. Let's try to call this method using the following code:

```
MyObject *m;
NSLog(@"Value: %d",[m myMethodWithValue:5]);
```

Our first thought might be that this code would display `Value:  10`, since we are passing the value of 5 to a method that doubles the value passed in; however, this would be incorrect. In reality, this code would display `Value:  0` because we did not initialize the m object prior to using it.

When we forget to initialize an object or set a value for a variable, we can get unexpected results at runtime, as we just demonstrated. The unexpected results can be, at times, very difficult to track down.

With optionals, Swift is able to detect problems such as this at compile time and alert us before it becomes a runtime issue. If we expect a variable or object to always contain a value prior to using it, we will declare the variable as a non-optional (this is the default declaration). Then we would receive an error if we try to use it prior to initializing it. Let's look at an example of this. The following code would display an error because we are attempting to use a non-optional variable prior to initializing it:

```
var myString: String
print(myString)
```

If a variable is declared as an optional, it is good programming practice to verify that it contains a valid value before attempting to use it. We should only declare a variable as an optional if there is a valid reason for the variable to contain no value. This is the reason Swift declares variables as non-optional by default.

Now that we (hopefully) have a better understanding of what optionals are and what types of problems they are designed to solve, let's look at how to use them.

Defining an optional

Typically, to define an optional type, we put a question mark after the type in the variable declaration. Keep in mind that the type we define in the variable's declaration is actually the associated value in the optional enumeration. The following code shows us how we would typically declare an optional:

```
var myOptional: String?
```

This code declares an optional variable that might contain a string or no value (nil). When a variable is declared like this, by default, it is set to no value.

Using optionals

There are a number of ways that we can use optionals within our code. The key to using optionals is to always verify that they contain a valid value prior to accessing them. We use the term **unwrapping** to refer to the process of retrieving a value from an optional.

Forced unwrapping optionals

To unwrap or retrieve the value of an optional, we place an exclamation mark (!) after the variable name. Forced unwrapping, in this manner, can be very dangerous and should be used only if we are certain that the value is not nil.

When we use the exclamation mark to unwrap an optional, we are telling the compiler that we know the optional contains a value, and to go ahead and give it to us. Let's look at how to do this:

```
var myString1: String?
myString1 = "test"
var test: String = myString1!
```

This code will work as we expect it to, where the `test` variable will contain the `test` string; however, if the line that set the `myString1` optional to `test` was removed, we would receive a runtime error when we run the application. Note that the compiler will not alert us of an issue because we are using the exclamation point to unwrap the optional; therefore, the compiler assumes that we know what we are doing and will happily compile the code for us. We should verify that the `myString1` optional contains a valid value prior to unwrapping it. The following example is one way to do this:

```
var myString1: String?
myString1 = "test"
if myString1 != nil {
    var test:String = myString1!
}
```

Now, if the line that sets the `myString1` optional to `test` was removed, we would not receive a runtime error because we are only unwrapping the `myString` optional, if it contains a valid (non-nil) value.

Unwrapping optionals, as we just described, is not the most optimal way, and it is not recommended that we unwrap optionals in this manner. We can combine the verification and unwrapping into one step called **optional binding**.

Optional binding

Optional binding is the recommended way to unwrap an optional. With optional binding, we perform a check to see whether the optional contains a valid value and, if so, unwrap it into a temporary variable or constant. This is all performed in one step.

Optional binding is performed with the `if` or `while` conditional statements. It takes the following format, if we want to put the value of the optional in a constant:

```
if let constantName = optional {
    statements
}
```

If we need to put the value in a variable, instead of a constant, we can use the `var` keyword instead of the `let` keyword, as shown in the following example:

```
if var variableName = optional {
    statements
}
```

The following example shows how to perform optional binding:

```
var myString3: String?
myString3 = "Space"
if let tempVar = myString3 {
    print(tempVar)
} else {
    print("No value")
}
```

In the example, we define the `myString3` variable as an optional type. If the `myString3` optional contains a valid value, then we set the new variable named `tempvar` to the value of the `myString3` optional and print the value to the console. If the `myString3` optional does not contain a value, then we print `No value` to the console.

We are able to use optional binding to unwrap multiple optionals within the same optional binding line. For example, if we had three optionals named `optional1`, `optional2`, and `optional3`, we could use the following code to attempt to unwrap all the three at once:

```
if let tmp1 = optional1, let tmp2 = optional2, let tmp3 = optional3 {
}
```

If any of the three optionals are nil and fail to unwrap, the whole optional binding statement fails.

It is perfectly acceptable with optional binding to assign the value to a variable of the same name. The following code illustrates this:

```
if let myOptional = myOptional {
  print(myOptional)
} else {
  print("myOptional was nil")
}
```

One thing to note is that the `temp` variable is scoped only for the conditional block and cannot be used outside the conditional block. To illustrate the scope of the temporary variable, let's take a look at the following code:

```
var myOptional: String?
myOptional = "test"
if var tmp = myOptional {
    print("Inside:  \(tmp)")
}
// This next line will cause a compile time error
print("Outside: \(tmp)")
```

This code would not compile because the `tmp` variable is only valid within the conditional block and we are attempting to use it outside of the conditional block.

Using optional binding is a lot cleaner and easier than manually verifying that the optional has a value and then using forced unwrapping to retrieve the value of the optional.

Returning optionals from functions, methods, and subscripts

We can set the return type of a function or a method to an optional type. This allows us to return a nil (no value) from the function or method. To set the return type to an optional type, we will insert a question mark after the name of the type in the function or method declaration.

The following example shows us how we will return an optional from a function or method:

```
func getName(index: Int) -> String? {
    let names = ["Jon", "Kim", "Kailey", "Kara"]
    if index >= names.count || index < 0 {
        return nil
```

```
    }
else {
        return names[index]
    }
}
```

In the example, we defined the return type as an optional that can be either a string value or no value. Inside the function, we will return the name if the index is within the bounds of the array, or `nil` if it is outside the bounds of the array.

The following code shows how to call this function where the return value is an optional:

```
var name = getName(index: 2)
var name2 = getName(index: 5)
```

In the previous code, the `name` variable will contain `Kailey`, while the `name2` variable will contain `nil` (no value). Note that we do not have to define the variable as an optional (with a question mark) as Swift knows it is an optional type because the return type, defined by the function, is an optional.

We can also define a subscript that returns an optional type. We define a subscript as an optional in exactly the same way that we defined functions. Here is an example template of a subscript that returns an optional:

```
subscript(index: Int) -> String? {
    //some statements
}
```

With this definition, we are able to return a `nil` (no value) from our subscript.

Using optionals as a parameter in a function or method

We can also accept an optional as a parameter to a function or a method. This allows us to have the option of passing a nil (no value) into a function or method if required. The following example shows how to define an optional parameter for a function:

```
func optionalParam(myString: String?) {
  if let temp = myString {
    print("Contains value \(temp)")
  }
  else {
    print("Does not contain value")
  }
}
```

To define a parameter as an optional type, we use the question mark within the parameter definition. In this example, we use optional binding to check whether the optional contains a value or not. If it contains a value, we print `Contains value` to the console; otherwise, we print `Does not contain value`.

Optional types with tuples

We can define a whole tuple or any of the elements within a tuple as an optional. It is especially useful to use optionals with tuples when we return a tuple from a function or method. This allows us to return part (or all) of the tuples as nil. The following example shows how to define a tuple as an optional, and also how to define individual elements of a tuple as an optional type:

```
var tuple1: (one: String, two: Int)?
var tuple2: (one: String, two: Int?)
```

The first line defines the whole tuple as an optional type. The second line defines the second value within the tuple as an optional, while the first value is a non-optional.

Optional chaining

Optional binding allows us to unwrap one optional at a time, but what would happen if we had optional types embedded within other optional types? This would force us to have optional binding statements embedded within other optional binding statements. There is a better way to handle this by using optional chaining. Before we look at optional chaining, let's see how this would work with optional binding:

```
class Collar {
    var color: String
    init(color: String) {
        self.color = color
    }
}

class Pet {
    var name: String
    var collar: Collar?
    init(name: String) {
        self.name = name
    }
}

class Person {
```

```
        var name: String
        var pet: Pet?
        init(name: String) {
            self.name = name
        }
    }
```

In this example, we begin by defining a `Collar` class, which has one property defined. This property is named `color`, which is of the type `String`. We can see that the `color` property is not an optional; therefore, we can safely assume that it will always have a valid value.

Next, we define a `Pet` class that has two properties defined. These properties are named `name` and `collar`. The `name` property is of the `String` type, and the `collar` property is an optional that may contain an instance of the `Collar` type or no value.

Finally, we define the `Person` class that also has two properties. These properties are named `name` and `pet`. The `name` property is of the `String` type and the `pet` property is an optional that may contain an instance of the `Pet` type or no value.

For the examples that follow, let's use the following code to initialize the classes:

```
var jon = Person(name: "Jon")
var buddy = Pet(name: "Buddy")
jon.pet = buddy
var collar = Collar(color: "red")
buddy.collar = collar
```

Now, let's say that we want to get the color of the collar for a person's pet; however, the person may not have a pet (the `pet` property is nil) or the pet may not have a collar (the `collar` property is nil). We could use optional binding to drill down through each layer, as shown in the following example:

```
if let tmpPet = jon.pet, let tmpCollar = tmpPet.collar {
   print("The color of the collar is \(tmpCollar.color)")
   }
else {
   print("Cannot retrieve color")
}
```

While this example is perfectly valid, and would print out the message The color of the collar is red, the code is rather messy and hard to follow.

Optional chaining allows us to drill down through multiple optional type layers of properties, methods, and subscripts in one line of code. These layers can be chained together, and if any layer returns a nil, the entire chain gracefully fails and returns nil. If none of the values return nil, the last value of the chain is returned. Since the results of optional chaining may be a nil value, the results are always returned as an optional type, even if the final value we are retrieving is a non-optional type.

To specify optional chaining, we will place a question mark (?) after each of the optional values within the chain. The following example shows how to use optional chaining to make the preceding example much cleaner and easier to read:

```
if let color = jon.pet?.collar?.color {
    print("The color of the collar is \(color)")
} else {
    print("Cannot retrieve color")
}
```

In this example, we put a question mark after the `pet` and `collar` properties to signify that they are of the optional type, and if either value is `nil`, the whole chain will return `nil`. This code would also print out the message `The color of the collar is red`; however, it is much easier to read than the preceding example that used optional binding.

The nil coalescing operator

The nil coalescing operator is similar to the ternary operator that we discussed in `Chapter 2`, *Learning About Variables, Constants, Strings, and Operators* of this book. The ternary operator assigns a value to a variable, based on the evaluation of a comparison operator or a Boolean value. The nil coalescing operator unwraps an optional, and if it contains a value, it will return that value, or a default value if the optional is nil.

Let's look at a prototype for the nil coalescing operator:

```
optionalA ?? defaultValue
```

In this example, we demonstrate the nil coalescing operator when the optional contains a nil and also when it contains a value:

```
var defaultName = "Jon"

var optionalA: String?
var optionalB: String?

optionalB = "Buddy"
```

```
var nameA = optionalA ?? defaultName
var nameB = optionalB ?? defaultName
```

In this example, we begin by initializing our `defaultName` variable to `Jon`. We then define two optionals that are named `optionalA` and `optionalB`. The `optionalA` variable will be set to `nil` while the `optionalB` variable is set to `Buddy`.

The nil coalescing operator is used in the final two lines. Since the `optionalA` variable contains a `nil`, the `nameA` variable will be set to the value of the `defaultName` variable, which is `Jon`. The `nameB` variable will be set to the value of the `optionalB` variable since it contains a value.

Summary

While the concept of optional types, as used in the Swift language, might seem a little foreign at first, the more you use them, the more they will make sense. One of the biggest advantages with optional types is we get additional compile time checks that alert us if we forget to initialize non-optionals prior to using them.

The one thing to take away from this chapter is the concept of what optionals are. To reinforce this concept, let's review a couple of paragraphs from this chapter.

It is very important to understand that nil in Swift is very different than nil in Objective-C or other C-based languages. In Objective-C, nil is a pointer to a non-existent object; however, in Swift, nil is an absence of a value. Knowing this concept is very important in fully understanding optionals in Swift.

A variable defined as an optional can contain a valid value or it can have no value. We set a variable to a valueless state by assigning it Swift's special nil value. Optionals of any type can be set to nil, whereas in Objective-C, only objects can be set to nil.

The optional type is an enumeration with two possible values-`None` and `Some (T)`, where `T` is the associated value of the appropriate type. If we set the optional to `nil`, it will have a value of `None`, and if we set a value, the optional will have a value of `Some` with an associated value of the appropriate type. In `Chapter 2`, *Learning about Variables, Constants, Strings, and Operators*, we explained that an enum in Swift may have associated values. Associated values allow us to store additional information along with the enum's member value.

11
Working with Generics

My first experience with generics was back in 2004, when they were first introduced in the Java programming language. I can still remember picking up my copy of *The Java Programming Language, Fourth Edition*, which covered Java 5, and reading about Java's implementation of generics. Since then, I have used generics in a number of projects, not only in Java but in other languages as well. If you are familiar with generics in other languages, such as Java, the syntax that Swift uses will be familiar to you. Generics allow us to write very flexible and reusable code; however, just as with subscripts, we need to make sure that we use them properly and do not overuse them.

In this chapter, we will cover the following topics:

- An introduction to generics
- Creating and using generic functions
- Creating and using generic classes
- Using associated types with protocols

An introduction to generics

The concept of generics has been around for a while, so it should not be a new concept for developers coming from languages such as Java or C#. Swift's implementation of generics is very similar to that of these languages. For those developers coming from other languages, such as Objective-C, which do not have generics, they might seem a bit foreign at first, but once you start using them you will realize how powerful they are.

Generics allow us to write very flexible and reusable code that avoids duplication. With a type-safe language, such as Swift, we often need to write functions or types that are valid for multiple types. For example, we might need to write a function that swaps the values of two variables; however, we may use this function to swap two String types, two Int types, and two Double types. Without generics, we would need to write three separate functions; however, with generics, we can write one generic function to provide the swap functionality for multiple types. Generics allow us to tell a function or type: *I know Swift is a type-safe language, but I do not know the type that will be needed yet. I will give you a placeholder for now and will let you know what type to enforce later.*

In Swift, we have the ability to define both generic functions and generic types. Let's look at generic functions first.

Generic functions

Let's begin by examining the problem that generics try to solve, and then we will see how generics solve this problem. Let's say that we wanted to create functions that swap the values of two variables (as described in the first part of this chapter); however, for our application, we need to swap two Int types, two Double types, and two String types. Without generics, this would require us to write three separate functions. The following code shows what these functions could look like:

```
func swapInts (a: inout Int,b: inout Int) {
    let tmp = a
    a = b
    b = tmp
}

func swapDoubles(a: inout Double,b: inout Double) {
    let tmp = a
    a = b
    b = tmp
}

func swapStrings(a: inout String, b: inout String) {
    let tmp = a
    a = b
    b = tmp
}
```

With these three functions, we can swap the original values of two `Int` types, two `Double` types, and two `String` types. Now, let's say, as we develop our application further, we find out that we also need to swap the values of two `UInt32` types, two `Float` types, or even a couple of custom types. We might easily end up with eight or nine swap functions. The worst part is that each of these functions contains duplicate code. The only difference between these functions is that the parameter types change. While this solution does work, generics offer a much more elegant and simple solution that eliminates all of the duplicate code. Let's see how we would condense all three of the preceding functions into a single generic function:

```
func swap<T>(a: inout T, b: inout T) {
    let tmp = a
    a = b
    b = tmp
}
```

Let's look at how we defined the `swap()` function. The function itself looks pretty similar to a normal function, except for the capital `T`. The capital `T`, as used in the `swap()` function, is a placeholder type, and tells Swift that we will be defining the type later. When a type is defined, it will be used to replace all the placeholders.

To define a generic function, we include the placeholder type between two angular brackets (`<T>`) after the function's name. We can then use that placeholder type in place of any type definition within the parameter definitions, the return type, or the function itself. The important thing to keep in mind is once the placeholder is defined as a type, all the other placeholders assume that type. Therefore, any variable or constant defined with that placeholder must conform to that type.

There is nothing special about the capital `T`; we could use any valid identifier in place of `T`. The following definitions are perfectly valid:

```
func swap<G>(a: inout G, b: inout G) {
  //Statements
}

func swap<xyz>(a: inout xyz, b: inout xyz) {
  //Statements
}
```

In most documentation, generic placeholders are defined with either T (for type) or E (for element). For standard purposes, we will use T to define generic placeholders in this book. It is also good practice to use T to define a generic placeholder within our code so that the placeholder is easily recognized when we are looking at the code at a later time.

If we need to use multiple generic types, we can create multiple placeholders by separating them with commas. The following example shows how to define multiple placeholders for a single function:

```
func testGeneric<T,E>(a:T, b:E) {
}
```

In this example, we are defining two generic placeholders, T and E. In this case, we can set the T placeholder to one type and the E placeholder to a different type.

Let's look at how to call a generic function. The following code will swap two integers using the swap<T>(inout a: T, inout b: T) function:

```
var a = 5
var b = 10
swap(a: &a, b: &b)

print("a: \(a) b: \(b)")
```

If we run this code, the a: 10 b: 5 line will be printed to the console. We can see that we do not have to do anything special to call a generic function. The function infers the type from the first parameter and then sets all the remaining placeholders to that type. Now, if we need to swap the values of two strings, we will call the same function like this:

```
var c = "My String 1"
var d = "My String 2"
swap(a: &c, b: &d)
print("c: \(c) d: \(d)")
```

We can see that we call the function in exactly the same way as we called it when we wanted to swap two integers. One thing that we cannot do is pass two different types into the swap() function because we defined only one generic placeholder. If we attempt to run the following code, we will receive an error:

```
var a = 5
var c = "My String 1"
swap(a: &a, b: &c)
```

The error that we will receive is `cannot invoke 'swap' with an argument list of type '(inout Int, b: inout String`, which tells us that we are attempting to use a string value with an integer value when the function wants only one type. The reason the function is looking for an integer value is that the first parameter that we pass into the function is an integer value; therefore, all the generic types in the function became `Int` types.

Now, let's say we have the following function that has multiple generic types defined:

```
func testGeneric<T,E>(a:T, b:E) {
    print("\(a)  \(b)")
}
```

This function would accept parameters of different types; however, we would be unable to swap the values because the types are different. There are also other limitations on generics. For example, we may think that the following generic function would be valid; however, we would receive an error if we tried to implement it:

```
func genericEqual<T>(a: T, b: T) -> Bool{
    return a == b
}
```

The error that we receive is `binary operator '==' cannot be applied to two 'T' operands`. Since the type of the arguments is unknown at the time the code is compiled, Swift does not know if it is able to use the equal operator on the types; therefore, the error is thrown. We might think that this is a limit that will make generics hard to use; however, we have a way to tell Swift that we expect that the type, represented by the placeholder, will have certain functionality. This is done with type constraints.

A type constraint specifies that a generic type must inherit from a specific class or conform to a particular protocol. This allows us to use the methods or properties defined by the parent class or protocol within the generic function. Let's look at how to use type constraints by rewriting the `genericEqual()` function to use the comparable protocol:

```
func testGenericComparable<T: Comparable>(a: T, b: T) -> Bool{
    return a >= b
}
```

To specify the type constraint, we put the class or protocol constraint after the generic placeholder, where the generic placeholder and the constraint are separated by a colon. This new function works as we might expect, and it will compare the values of the two parameters and return `true` if they are equal or `false` if they are not.

We can declare multiple constraints just as we declare multiple generic types. The following example shows how to declare two generic types with different constraints:

```
func testFunction<T: MyClass, E: MyProtocol>(a: T, b: E) {
}
```

In this function, the type defined by the T placeholder must inherit from the MyClass class, and the type defined by the E placeholder must implement the MyProtocol protocol. Now that we have looked at generic functions, let's take a look at generic types.

Generic types

We have already had a general introduction to how generic types work when we looked at Swift arrays and dictionaries. A generic type is a class, structure, or enumeration that can work with any type, just like the way the Swift arrays and dictionaries work. As we recall, Swift arrays and dictionaries are written so that they can contain any type. The catch is that we cannot mix and match different types within an array or dictionary. When we create an instance of our generic type, we define the type that the instance will work with. After we define that type, we cannot change the type for that instance.

To demonstrate how to create a generic type, let's create a simple List class. This class will use a Swift array as the backend storage for the list, and will let us add items to the list or retrieve values from the list.

Let's begin by seeing how to define our generic list type:

```
class List<T> {
}
```

The preceding code defines the generic list type. We can see that we use the <T> tag to define a generic placeholder, just like we did when we defined a generic function. This T placeholder can then be used anywhere within the type instead of a concrete type definition.

To create an instance of this type, we need to define the type of items that our list will hold. The following examples show how to create instances of the generic list type for various types:

```
var stringList = List<String>()
var intList = List<Int>()
var customList = List<MyObject>()
```

The preceding example creates three instances of the `List` class. The `stringList` instance can be used with `String` types, the `intList` instance can be used with `Int` types, and the `customList` instance can be used with instances of the `MyObject` type.

We are not limited to only using generics with classes. We can also define structures and enumerations as generics. The following examples show how to define a generic structure and a generic enumeration:

```
struct GenericStruct<T> {
}

enum GenericEnum<T> {
}
```

The next step in our `List` class is to add the backend storage array. The items that are stored in this array need to be of the same type as we define when we initiate the class; therefore, we will use the `T` placeholder for the array's definition. The following code shows the `List` class with an array named `items`. The `items` array will be defined using the `T` placeholder, so it will hold the same types as we defined for the class:

```
class List<T> {
    var items = [T]()
}
```

This code defines our generic list type and uses `T` as the type placeholder. We can then use the `T` placeholder anywhere in the class to define the type of an item. That item will then be of the same type that we defined when we created the instance of the `List` class. Therefore, if we create an instance of the list type such as this `var stringList = List<String>()`, the items array will be an array of string instances. If we created an instance of the list type like this `var intList = List<Int>()`, the item array will be an array of integer instances.

Now we will need to add the `add()` method that will be used to add an item to the list. We will use the `T` placeholder within the method declaration to define that the item parameter will be of the same type as we declared when we initiated the class. Therefore, if we create an instance of the list type to use the `String` type, we would be required to use the `String` type as the parameter for the `add()` method. However, if we create an instance of the list type to use the `Int` type, we would be required to use the `Int` type as the parameter for the `add()` method.

Here is the code for the `add()` function:

```
func add(item: T) {
    items.append(item)
}
```

To create a standalone generic function, we add the `<T>` declaration after the function name to declare that it is a generic function; however, when we use a generic method within a generic type, we do not need the `<T>` declaration. Instead, all we need to do is to use the type that we defined in the class declaration. If we wanted to introduce another generic type, we could define it with the method declaration.

Now, let's add the `getItemAtIndex()` method that will return the item from the backend array at the specified index:

```
func getItemAtIndex(index: Int) -> T? {
    if items.count > index {
        return items[index]
    } else {
        return nil
    }
}
```

The `getItemAtIndex()` method accepts one argument that is the index of the item we want to retrieve. We then use the `T` placeholder to specify that our return type is an optional that might be of type `T` or might be `nil`. If the backend storage array contains an item at the specified index, we will return that item; otherwise, we return `nil`.

Now, let's look at our entire generic list class:

```
class List<T> {
    var items = [T]()
    func add(item: T) {
        items.append(item)
    }
    func getItemAtIndex(index: Int) -> T? {
        if items.count > index {
            return items[index]
        } else {
            return nil
        }
    }
}
```

As we can see, we initially define the generic `T` placeholder type in the class declaration. We then use this placeholder type within our class. In our `List` class, we use this placeholder in three places. We use it as the type for our items array, as the parameter type for our `add()` method, and as the associated value for the optional return type in the `getItemAtIndex()` method.

Now, let's look at how to use the `List` class. When we use a generic type, we define the type to be used within the class between angle brackets, such as: `<type>`. The following code shows how to use the `List` class to store `String` types:

```
var list = List<String>()
list.add(item: "Hello")
list.add(item: "World")
print(list.getItemAtIndex(index: 1)!)
```

In this code, we start off by creating an instance of the list type called `list` and set it to store `String` types. We then use the `add()` method twice to store two items in the list instance. Finally, we use the `getItemAtIndex()` method to retrieve the item at index number 1, which will display `Optional(World)` to the console.

We can also define our generic types with multiple placeholder types, similar to how we use multiple placeholders in our generic methods. To use multiple placeholder types, we would separate them with commas. The following example shows how to define multiple placeholder types:

```
class MyClass<T,E>{

}
```

We then create an instance of the `MyClass` type that uses the `String` and `Int` types, like this:

```
var mc = MyClass<String, Int>()
```

We can also use type constraints with generic types. Once again, using a type constraint for a generic type is exactly the same as using one with a generic function. The following code shows how to use a type constraint to ensure that the generic type conforms to the comparable protocol:

```
class MyClass<T: Comparable>{}
```

So far in this chapter, we have seen how to use placeholder types with functions and types. At times, it can be useful to declare one or more placeholder types in a protocol. These types are known as **associated types**.

Associated types

An associated type declares a placeholder name that can be used instead of a type within a protocol. The actual type to be used is not specified until the protocol is adopted. While creating generic functions and types, we used a very similar syntax. Defining associated types for a protocol, however, is very different. We specify an associated type using the `associatedtype` keyword.

Let's see how to use associated types when we define a protocol. In this example, we will define the `QueueProtocol` protocol that will define the capabilities that need to be implemented by the queue that implements it:

```
protocol QueueProtocol {
    associatedtype QueueType
    mutating func add(item: QueueType)
    mutating func getItem() -> QueueType?
    func count() -> Int
}
```

In this protocol, we define one associated type named `QueueType`. We then use this associated type twice within the protocol–once as the parameter type for the `add()` method and once when we define the return type of the `getItem()` method as an optional type that might return the associated type of `QueueType` or a nil.

Any type that implements the `QueueProtocol` protocol must be able to specify the type to use for the `QueueType` placeholder, and must also ensure that only items of that type are used where the protocol uses the `QueueType` placeholder.

Let's look at how to implement `QueueProtocol` in a non-generic class called `IntQueue`. This class will implement the `QueueProtocol` protocol using the `Int` type:

```
class IntQueue: QueueProtocol {
  var items = [Int]()
  func add(item: Int) {
    items.append(item)
  }
  func getItem() -> Int? {
    if items.count > 0 {
      return items.remove(at: 0)
    }
    else {
      return nil
    }
  }
  func count() -> Int {
```

```
        return items.count
    }
}
```

In the `IntQueue` class, we begin by defining our backend storage mechanism to be an array of `Int` types. We then implement each of the methods defined in the `QueueProtocol` protocol, replacing the `QueueType` placeholder defined in the protocol with the `Int` type. In the `add()` method, the parameter type is defined to be an `Int` type, and in the `getItem()` method, the return type is defined to be an optional that might return an `Int` type or no value.

We use the `IntQueue` class as we would use any other class. The following code shows this:

```
var intQ = IntQueue()
intQ.add(item: 2)
intQ.add(item: 4)
print(intQ.getItem()!)
intQ.add(item: 6)
```

We begin by creating an instance of the `IntQueue` class named `intQ`. We then call the `add()` method twice to add two values of the `Int` type to the `intQ` instance. We then retrieve the first item in the `intQ` instance by calling the `getItem()` method. This line will print the number `Optional(2)` to the console. The final line of code adds another integer type to the `intQ` instance.

In the preceding example, we implemented the `QueueProtocol` protocol in a non-generic way. This means that we replaced the placeholder types with an actual type (`QueueType` was replaced by the `Int` type). We can also implement the `QueueProtocol` protocol with a generic type. Let's see how to implement the `QueueProtocol` protocol in a generic type called `GenericQueue`:

```
class GenericQueue<T>: QueueProtocol {
    var items = [T]()
    func add(item: T) {
        items.append(item)
    }
    func getItem() -> T? {
        if items.count > 0 {
            return items.remove(at: 0)
        } else {
            return nil
        }
    }
    func count() -> Int {
        return items.count
```

```
    }
  }
```

As we can see, the GenericQueue implementation is very similar to the IntQueue implementation, except that we define the type to use as the generic placeholder T. We can then use the GenericQueue class as we would use any generic class. Let's take a look at how to use the GenericQueue class:

```
var intQ2 = GenericQueue<Int>()
intQ2.add(item: 2)
intQ2.add(item: 4)
print(intQ2.getItem()!)
intQ2.add(item: 6)
```

We begin by creating an instance of the GenericQueue class that will use the Int type. This instance is named intQ2. Next, we call the add() method twice to add two Int types to the intQ2 instance. We then retrieve the first Int type that was added using the getItem() method and print the value to the console. This line will print the number 2 to the console.

One of the things that we should avoid is using generics when we should be using protocols. This is, in my opinion, one of the most common misuses of generics in other languages. Let's take a look at an example so that we know what to avoid.

Let's say that we define a protocol called WidgetProtocol, which is as follows:

```
protocol WidgetProtocol {
    //Code
}
```

Now, let's say that we want to create a custom type (or function) that will use various implementations of the WidgetProtocol protocol. I have seen a couple of instances where developers have used generics with a type constraint to create custom types such as this:

```
class MyClass<T: WidgetProtocol> {
    var myProp: T?
    func myFunc(myVar: T) {
        //Code
    }
}
```

While this is a perfectly valid use of generics, it is recommended that we avoid implementations such as this. It is a lot cleaner and easier to read if we use `WidgetProtocol` without generics. For example, we can write a non-generic version of the `MyClass` type like this:

```
class MyClass {
    var myProp: WidgetProtocol?
    func myFunc(myVar: WidgetProtocol) {
    }
}
```

The second, non-generic version of the `MyClass` type is a lot easier to read and understand; therefore, this should be the preferable way to implement the class. However, there is nothing preventing us from using either implementation of the `MyClass` type.

Summary

Generic types can be incredibly useful, and they are also the basis of the Swift standard collection types (array and dictionary); however, as mentioned in the introduction to this chapter, we have to be careful to use them correctly.

We have seen a couple of examples in this chapter that show how generics can make our lives easier. The `swap()` function that was shown at the beginning of the chapter is a good use of a generic function because it allows us to swap the two values of any type we choose while only implementing the swap code once.

The generic list type is also a good example of how to make custom collection types that can be used to hold any type. The way we implemented the generic list type in this chapter is similar to how Swift implements the array and dictionary with generics.

12
Working with Closures

Today, most major programming languages have functionalities similar to what closures offer. Some of these implementations are really hard to use (Objective-C blocks), while others are easy (Java lambdas and C# delegates). I found that the functionality that closures provide is especially useful when developing frameworks. I have also used them extensively when communicating with remote services over a network connection. While blocks in Objective-C are incredibly useful (and I have used them quite a bit), their syntax used to declare a block was absolutely horrible. Luckily, when Apple was developing the Swift language, they made the syntax of closures much easier to use and understand.

In this chapter, we will cover the following topics:

- An introduction to closures
- Defining a closure
- Using a closure
- Several useful examples of closures
- How to avoid strong reference cycles with closures

An introduction to closures

Closures are self-contained blocks of code that can be passed around and used throughout our application. We can think of an `Int` type as a type that stores an integer, and a `String` type as a type that stores a string. In this context, a closure can be thought of as a type that contains a block of code. What this means is that we can assign closures to a variable, pass them as arguments to functions, and also return them from functions.

Closures have the ability to capture and store references to any variable or constant from the context in which they were defined. This is known as closing over the variables or constants, and the best thing is, for the most part, Swift will handle the memory management for us. The only exception is when we create a strong reference cycle, and we will look at how to resolve this in the *Creating strong reference cycles with closures* section of this chapter.

Closures in Swift are similar to blocks in Objective-C; however, closures in Swift are a lot easier to use and understand. Let's look at the syntax used to define a closure in Swift:

```
{
(parameters) -> return-type in
  statements
}
```

As we can see, the syntax used to create a closure looks very similar to the syntax we use to create functions in Swift, and, actually, in Swift, global and nested functions are closures. The biggest difference in the format between closures and functions is the in keyword. The in keyword is used in place of curly brackets to separate the definition of the closure's parameter and return types from the body of the closure.

There are many uses for closures, and we will go over a number of them later in this chapter, but first we need to understand the basics of closures. Let's start by looking at some very basic uses for closures, so that we can get a better understanding of what they are, how to define them, and how to use them.

Simple closures

We will begin by creating a very simple closure that does not accept any arguments and does not return a value. All it does is print Hello World to the console. Let's take a look at the following code:

```
let clos1 = {
  () -> Void in
  print("Hello World")
}
```

In this example, we create a closure and assign it to the constant clos1. Since there are no parameters defined between the parentheses, this closure will not accept any parameters. Also, the return type is defined as Void; therefore, this closure will not return any value. The body of the closure contains one line that prints Hello World to the console.

There are many ways to use closures; in this example, all we want to do is execute it. We execute this closure like this:

```
clos1()
```

When we execute the closure, we will see that `Hello World` is printed to the console. At this point, closures may not seem that useful, but as we get further along in this chapter, we will see how useful and powerful they can be.

Let's look at another example of a simple closure. This closure will accept one string parameter named `name`, but will once again not return a value. Within the body of the closure, we will print out a greeting to the name passed into the closure through the `name` parameter. Here is the code for this second closure:

```
let clos2 = {
  (name: String) -> Void in
  print("Hello \(name)")
}
```

The big difference between `clos2`, as defined in this example, and the previous `clos1` closure is that we define a single string parameter between the parentheses. As we can see, we define parameters for closures just like we define parameters for functions.

We can execute this closure in the same way in which we executed `clos1`. The following code shows how this is done:

```
clos2("Jon")
```

This example, when executed, will print the message `Hello Jon` to the console. Let's look at another way we can use the `clos2` closure.

Our original definition of closures stated that closures are self-contained blocks of code that can be passed around and used throughout our application code. What this tells us is that we can pass our closure from the context that it was created in to other parts of our code. Let's look at how to pass our `clos2` closure into a function. We will define a function that accepts our `clos2` closure like this:

```
func testClosure(handler:(String)->Void) {
  handler("Dasher")
}
```

We define the function just like we would any other function; however, in our parameter list, we define a parameter named `handler`, and the type defined for the handler parameter is `(String)->Void`. If we look closely, we can see that the `(String)->Void` definition of the `handler` parameter matches the parameter and return types that we defined for `clos2` closure. This means that we can pass the `clos2` closure into the function. Let's look at how to do this:

```
testClosure(handler: clos2)
```

We call the `testClosure()` function just like any other function and the closure that is being passed in looks like any other variable. Since the `clos2` closure executed in the `testClosure()` function, we will see the message, `Hello Dasher`, printed to the console when this code is executed.

As we will see a little later in this chapter, the ability to pass closures to functions is what makes closures so exciting and powerful.

As the final piece to the closure puzzle, let's look at how to return a value from a closure. The following example shows this:

```
let clos3 = {
    (name: String) -> String in
    return "Hello \(name)"
}
```

The definition of the `clos3` closure looks very similar to how we defined the `clos2` closure. The difference is that we changed the `Void` return type to a `String` type. Then, in the body of the closure, instead of printing the message to the console, we used the return statement to return the message. We can now execute the `clos3` closure just like the previous two closures, or pass the closure to a function like we did with the `clos2` closure. The following example shows how to execute `clos3` closure:

```
var message = clos3("Buddy")
```

After this line of code is executed, the message variable will contain the `Hello Buddy` string.

The previous three examples of closures demonstrate the format and how to define a typical closure. Those who are familiar with Objective-C can see that the format of closures in Swift is a lot cleaner and easier to use. The syntax for creating closures that we have shown so far in this chapter is pretty short; however, we can shorten it even more. In this next section, we will look at how to do this.

Shorthand syntax for closures

In this section, we will look at a couple of ways to shorten the definition of closures.

Using the shorthand syntax for closures is really a matter of personal preference. There are a lot of developers that like to make their code as small and compact as possible and they take great pride in doing so. However, at times, this can make code hard to read and understand for other developers.

The first shorthand syntax for closures that we are going to look at is one of the most popular and is the syntax we saw when we were using algorithms with arrays in Chapter 3, *Using Swift Collections and the Tuple Type*. This format is mainly used when we want to send a really small (usually one line) closure to a function, like we did with the algorithms for arrays. Before we look at this shorthand syntax, we need to write a function that will accept a closure as a parameter:

```
func testFunction(num: Int, handler:()->Void) {
   for _ in 0..<num {
handler()
   }
}
```

This function accepts two parameters-the first parameter is an integer named num, and the second parameter is a closure named handler that does not have any parameters and does not return any value. Within the function, we create a for loop that will use the num integer to define how many times it loops. Within the for loop, we call the handler closure that was passed into the function.

Now lets create a closure and pass it to the testFunction() like this:

```
let clos = {
    () -> Void in
    print("Hello from standard syntax")
}
testFunction(num: 5,handler: clos)
```

This code is very easy to read and understand; however, it does take five lines of code. Now, let's look at how to shorten this code by writing the closure inline within the function call:

```
testFunction(num: 5,handler: {print("Hello from Shorthand closure")})
```

In this example, we created the closure inline within the function call using the same syntax that we used with the algorithms for arrays. The closure is placed in between two curly brackets (`{ }`), which means the code to create our closure is `{print("Hello from Shorthand closure")}`. When this code is executed, it will print out the message, `Hello from Shorthand closure`, five times on the screen.

In `Chapter 3`, *Using Swift Collections and the Tuple Type*, we saw that we were able to pass parameters to the array algorithms using the `$0`, `$1`, `$2`, and so on parameters. Let's look at how to use parameters with this shorthand syntax. We will begin by creating a new function that will accept a closure with a single parameter. We will name this function `testFunction2`. The following example shows what the new `testFunction2` function does:

```
func testFunction2(num: Int, handler:(String)->Void) {
  for _ in 0..<num {
    handler("Me")
  }
}
```

In `testFunction2`, we define our closure like this: `(name: String)->Void`. This definition means that the closure accepts one parameter and does not return any value. Now, let's see how to use the same shorthand syntax to call this function:

```
testFunction2(num: 5,handler: {print("Hello from \($0)")})
```

The difference between this closure definition and the previous one is `$0`. The `$0` parameter is shorthand for the first parameter passed into the function. If we execute this code, it prints out the message, `Hello from Me`, five times.

Using the dollar sign (`$`) followed by a number with inline closures allows us to define the closure without having to create a parameter list in the definition. The number after the dollar sign defines the position of the parameter in the parameter list. Let's examine this format a bit more, because we are not limited to only using the dollar sign (`$`) and number shorthand format with inline closures. This shorthand syntax can also be used to shorten the closure definition by allowing us to leave the parameter names off. The following example demonstrates this:

```
let clos5: (String, String) ->Void = {
    print("\($0) \($1)")
}
```

In this example, our closure has two string parameters defined; however, we do not give them names. The parameters are defined like this: (String, String). We can then access the parameters within the body of the closure using $0 and $1. Also, note that closure definition is after the colon (:), using the same syntax that we use to define a variable type, rather than inside the curly brackets. When we use anonymous arguments, this is how we would define the closure. It will not be valid to define the closure such as this:

```
let clos5b = {
    (String, String) -> Void in
    print("\($0) \($1)")
}
```

In this example, we will receive the Anonymous closure arguments cannot be used inside a closure that has explicit arguments error.

We will use the clos5 closure like this:

```
clos5("Hello","Kara")
```

Since Hello is the first string in the parameter list, it is accessed with $0, and as Kara is the second string in the parameter list, it is accessed with $1. When we execute this code, we will see the message Hello Kara printed to the console.

This next example is used when the closure doesn't return any value. Rather than defining the return type as Void, we can use parentheses, as the following example shows:

```
let clos6: () -> () = {
    print("Howdy")
}
```

In this example, we define the closure as () -> (). This tells Swift that the closure does not accept any parameters and also does not return a value. We will execute this closure like this:

```
clos6()
```

 As a personal preference, I am not very fond of this shorthand syntax. I think the code is much easier to read when the void keyword is used rather than the parentheses.

We have one more shorthand closure example to demonstrate before we begin showing some really useful examples of closures. In this last example, we will demonstrate how we can return a value from the closure without the need to include the return keyword.

If the entire closure body consists of only a single statement, then we can omit the `return` keyword, and the results of the statement will be returned. Let's take a look at an example of this:

```
let clos7 = {
    (first: Int, second: Int) -> Int in
    first + second
}
```

In this example, the closure accepts two parameters of the `Int` type and will return an `Int` type. The only statement within the body of the closure adds the first parameter to the second parameter. However, if you notice, we do not include the `return` keyword before the addition statement. Swift will see that this is a single statement closure and will automatically return the results, just as if we put the `return` keyword before the addition statement. We do need to make sure the result type of our statement matches the return type of the closure. We would use this closure like this:

```
var result = clos7(1,2)
```

All of the examples that were shown in the previous two sections were designed to show how to define and use closures. On their own, these examples did not really show off the power of closures and they did not show how incredibly useful closures are. The remainder of this chapter is written to demonstrate the power and usefulness of closures in Swift.

Using closures with Swift's array algorithms

In Chapter 3, *Using Swift Collections and the Tuple Type*, we looked at several built-in algorithms that we could use with Swift's arrays. In that chapter, we briefly saw how to add simple rules to each of these algorithms with very basic closures. Now that we have a better understanding of closures, let's see how we can expand on these algorithms using more advanced closures.

In this section, we will primarily be using the map algorithm for consistency purposes; however, we can use the basic ideas demonstrated with any of the algorithms. We will start by defining an array to use:

```
let guests = ["Jon", "Kim", "Kailey", "Kara"]
```

This array contains a list of names and the array is named `guests`. This array will be used for all the examples in this section, except for the very last ones.

Now that we have our `guests` array, let's add a closure that will print a greeting to each of the names in the `guests` array:

```
guests.map({
    (name: String) -> Void in
    print("Hello \(name)")
})
```

Since the map algorithm applies the closure to each item of the array, this example will print out a greeting for each name within the `guests` array. After the first section in this chapter, we should have a pretty good understanding of how this closure works. Using the shorthand syntax that we saw in the last section, we could reduce the preceding example down to the following single line of code:

```
guests.map({print("Hello \($0)")})
```

This is one of the few times, in my opinion, where the shorthand syntax may be easier to read than the standard syntax.

Now, let's say that rather than printing the greeting to the console, we wanted to return a new array that contained the greetings. For this, we would have returned a string type from our closure, as shown in the following example:

```
var messages = guests.map({
    (name:String) -> String in
    return "Welcome \(name)"
})
```

When this code is executed, the `messages` array will contain a greeting to each of the names in the `guests` array while the `guests` array will remain unchanged.

The preceding examples in this section showed how to add a closure to the map algorithm inline. This would be good if we only had one closure that we wanted to use with the map algorithm, but what if we had more than one closure that we wanted to use, or if we wanted to use the closure multiple times or reuse them with different arrays? For this, we could assign the closure to a constant or variable and then pass in the closure, using its constant or variable name, as needed. Let's see how to do this. We will begin by defining two closures. One of the closures will print a greeting for each name in the `guests` array, and the other closure will print a goodbye message for each name in the `guests` array:

```
let greetGuest = {
    (name:String) -> Void in
    print("Hello guest named \(name)")
}
```

```
let sayGoodbye = {
  (name:String) -> Void in
    print("Goodbye \(name)")
}
```

Now that we have two closures, we can use them with the map algorithm as needed. The following code shows how to use these closures interchangeably with the guests array:

```
guests.map(greetGuest)
guests.map(sayGoodbye)
```

Whenever we use the greetGuest closure with the guests array, the greetings message is printed to the console, and whenever we use the sayGoodbye closure with the guests array, the goodbye message is printed to the console. If we had another array named guests2, we could use the same closures for that array, as shown in the following example:

```
guests.map(greetGuest)
guests2.map(greetGuest)
guests.map(sayGoodbye)
guests2.map(sayGoodbye)
```

All of the examples in this section so far have either printed a message to the console or returned a new array from the closure. We are not limited to such basic functionality in our closures. For example, we can filter the array within our closure, as shown in the following example:

```
let greetGuest2 = {
  (name:String) -> Void in
    if (name.hasPrefix("K")) {
      print("\(name) is on the guest list")
    } else {
    print("\(name) was not invited")
    }
}
```

In this example, we print out a different message depending on whether the name starts with the letter K or not.

As we mentioned earlier in the chapter, closures have the ability to capture and store references to any variable or constant from the context in which they were defined. Let's look at an example of this. Let's say that we have a function that contains the highest temperature for the last seven days at a given location, and this function accepts a closure as a parameter. This function will execute the closure on the array of temperature. The function can be written like this:

```
func temperatures(calculate:(Int)->Void) {
    let tempArray = [72,74,76,68,70,72,66]
    tempArray.map(calculate)

}
```

This function accepts a closure defined as `(Int)->Void`. We then use the map algorithm to execute this closure for each item of the `tempArray` array. The key to using a closure correctly in this situation is to understand that the `temperatures` function does not know or care what goes on inside the `calculate` closure. Also, be aware that the closure is also unable to update or change the items within the function's context, which means that the closure cannot change any other variable within the temperatures function; however, it can update variables in the context that it was created in.

Let's look at the function that we will create the closure in. We will name this function `testFunction`. Let's take a look at the following code:

```
func testFunction() {
    var total = 0
    var count = 0
    let addTemps = {
      (num: Int) -> Void in
      total += num
      count += 1
    }
    temperatures(calculate: addTemps)
    print("Total: \(total)")
    print("Count: \(count)")
    print("Average: \(total/count)")
}
```

In this function, we begin by defining two variables named `total` and `count`, where both variables are of the `Int` type. We then create a closure named `addTemps` that will be used to add all of the temperatures from the `temperatures` function together. The `addTemps` closure will also count how many temperatures there are in the array. To do this, the `addTemps` closure calculates the sum of each item in the array and keeps the total in the `total` variable that was defined at the beginning of the function. The `addTemps` closure also keeps track of the number of items in the array by incrementing the `count` variable for each item. Notice that neither the `total` nor `count` variables are defined within the closure; however, we are able to use them within the closure because they were defined in the same context as the closure.

We then call the `temperatures` function and pass it the `addTemps` closure. Finally, we print the total, count, and average temperature to the console. We would execute the `testFunction` like this:

```
testFunction()
```

When the `testFunction` is executed, we see the following output to the console:

```
Total: 498
Count: 7
Average: 71
```

As we can see from the output, the `addTemps` closure is able to update and use items that are defined within the context that it was created in, even when the closure is used in a different context.

Now that we have looked at using closures with the array map algorithm, let's look at using closures by themselves. We will also look at the ways we can clean up our code to make it easier to read and use.

Changing functionality

Closures also give us the ability to change the functionality of classes on the fly. We saw in `Chapter 11`, *Working with Generics*, that generics give us the ability to write functions that are valid for multiple types. With closures, we are able to write functions and classes whose functionality can change, based on the closure that is passed into it as a parameter. In this section, we will show how to write a function whose functionality can be changed with a closure.

Let's begin by defining a class that will be used to demonstrate how to swap out functionality. We will name this class TestClass:

```
class TestClass {
  typealias getNumClosure = ((Int, Int) -> Int)
  var numOne = 5
  var numTwo = 8
  var results = 0
  func getNum(handler: getNumClosure) -> Int {
    results = handler(numOne,numTwo)
    return results

  }
}
```

We begin this class by defining a type alias for our closure that is named getNumClosure. Any closure that is defined as a getNumClosure closure will take two integers and return an integer. Within this closure, we assume that it does something with the integers that we pass in to get the value to return, but it really doesn't have to. To be honest, this class doesn't really care what the closure does as long as it conforms to the getNumClosure type. Next, we define three integers that are named numOne, NumTwo, and results.

We also define a method named getNum(). This method accepts a closure that confirms the getNumClosure type as its only parameter. Within the getNum() method, we execute the closure by passing in the numOne and numTwo class variables, and the integer that is returned is put into the results class variable.

Now, let's look at several closures that conform to the getNumClosure type that we can use with the getNum() method:

```
var max: TestClass.getNumClosure = {
  if $0 > $1 {
    return $0
  } else {
    return $1
  }
}

var min: TestClass.getNumClosure = {
  if $0 < $1 {
    return $0
  } else {
    return $1
  }
}
```

```
var multiply: TestClass.getNumClosure = {
  return $0 * $1
}

var second: TestClass.getNumClosure = {
  return $1
}

var answer: TestClass.getNumClosure = {
  var tmp = $0 + $1
  return 42
}
```

In this code, we define five closures that conform to the getNumClosure type:

- max: This returns the maximum value of the two integers that are passed in
- min: This returns the minimum value of the two integers that are passed in
- multiply: This multiplies both the values that are passed in and returns the product
- second: This returns the second parameter that was passed in
- answer: This returns the answer to life, the universe, and everything

In the answer closure, we have an extra line that looks like it does not have a purpose: var tmp = $0 + $1. We do this purposely because the following code is not valid:

```
var answer: TestClass.getNumClosure = {
  return 42
}
```

This class gives us the error: contextual type for closure argument list expects 2 arguments, which cannot be implicitly ignored error. As we can see by the error, Swift does not think that our closure accepts any parameters unless we use $0 and $1 within the body of the closure. In the closure named second, Swifts assumes that there are two parameters because $1 specifies the second parameter.

We can now pass each one of these closures to the `getNum` method of our `TestClass` to change the functionality of the function to suit our needs. The following code illustrates this:

```
var myClass = TestClass()

myClass.getNum(handler: max)
myClass.getNum(handler: min)
myClass.getNum(handler: multiply)
myClass.getNum(handler: second)
myClass.getNum(handler: answer)
```

When this code is run, the following results will be returned from each closure:

- `max`: results = 8
- `min`: results = 5
- `multiply`: results = 40
- `second`: results = 8
- `answer`: results = 42

The last example we are going to show you in this chapter is one that is used a lot in frameworks, especially the ones that have a functionality that is designed to be run asynchronously.

Selecting a closure based on results

In the final example, we will pass two closures to a method, and then, depending on some logic, one, or possibly both, of the closures will be executed. Generally, one of the closures is called if the method was successfully executed and the other closure is called if the method failed.

Let's start off by creating a class that will contain a method that will accept two closures and then execute one of the closures based on the defined logic. We will name this class `TestClass`. Here is the code for the `TestClass` class:

```
class TestClass {
  typealias ResultsClosure = ((String) -> Void)

  func isGreater(numOne: Int, numTwo:Int, successHandler:
ResultsClosure, failureHandler: ResultsClosure) {
    if numOne > numTwo {
      successHandler("\(numOne) is greater than \(numTwo)")
```

```
  }
  else {
    failureHandler("\(numOne) is not greater than \(numTwo)")
  }

 }
}
```

We begin this class by creating a type alias that defines the closure that we will use for both the successful and failure closures. We will name this type alias `ResultsClosure`. This example also illustrates why we would use a type alias, rather than retyping the closure definition. It saves us a lot of typing and also prevents us from making mistakes. In this example, if we did not use a type alias, we would need to retype the closure definition four times, and if we needed to change the closure definition, we would need to change it in four spots. With the type alias, we only need to type the closure definition once and then use the alias throughout the remaining code.

We then create a method named `isGreater` that takes two integers as the first two parameters and then two closures as the next two parameters. The first closure is named `successHandler`, and the second closure is named `failureHandler`. Within the `isGreater` method, we check whether the first integer parameter is greater than the second one. If the first integer is greater, the `successHandler` closure is executed; otherwise, the `failureHandler` closure is executed.

Now, let's create two of our closures. The code for these two closures is as follows:

```
var success: TestClass.ResultsClosure = {
    print("Success: \($0)")
}

var failure: TestClass.ResultsClosure = {
    print("Failure: \($0)")
}
```

Note that both closures are defined as the `TestClass.ResultsClosure` type. In each closure, we simply print a message to the console to let us know which closure was executed. Normally, we would put some functionality in the closure.

We will then call the method with both the closures such as this:

```
var test = TestClass()
test.isGreater(numOne: 8, numTwo: 6, successHandler:success,
failureHandler:failure)
```

Note that in the method call, we are sending both the success closure and the failure closure. In this example, we will see the message, `Success: 8 is greater than 6`. If we reversed the numbers, we would see the message, `Failure: 6 is not greater than 8`. This use case is really good when we call asynchronous methods, such as loading data from a web service. If the web service call was successful, the success closure is called; otherwise, the failure closure is called.

One big advantage of using closures such as this is that the UI does not freeze while we wait for the web service call to complete. This also involves a concurrency piece, which we will be covering in `Chapter 14`, *Concurrency and Parallelism in Swift*, later in this book. As an example, try to retrieve data from a web service such as this:

```
var data = myWebClass.myWebServiceCall(someParameter)
```

Our UI would freeze while we wait for the response to come back, or we would have to make the call in a separate thread so that the UI would not hang. With closures, we pass the closures to the networking framework and rely on the framework to execute the appropriate closure when it is done. This does rely on the framework to implement concurrency correctly to make the calls asynchronously, but a decent framework should handle that for us.

Creating strong reference cycles with closures

Earlier in this chapter, we said, the best thing is, for the most part, Swift will handle the memory management for us. The *for the most part* section of the quote means that if everything is written in a standard way, Swift will handle the memory management of the closures for us. However, there are times where memory management fails us. Memory management will work correctly for all of the examples that we have seen in this chapter so far. It is possible to create a strong reference cycle that prevents Swift's memory management from working correctly. Let's look at what happens if we create a strong reference cycle with closures.

A strong reference cycle may happen if we assign a closure to a property of a class instance and within that closure, we capture the instance of the class. This capture occurs because we access a property of that particular instance using `self`, such as `self.someProperty`, or we assign self to a variable or constant, such as `let c = self`. By capturing a property of the instance, we are actually capturing the instance itself, thereby creating a strong reference cycle where the memory manager will not know when to release the instance. As a result, the memory will not be freed correctly.

Let's begin by creating a class that has a closure and an instance of the String type as its two properties. We will also create a type alias for the closure type in this class and define a deinit() method that prints a message to the console. The deinit() method is called when the class gets released and the memory is freed. We will know when the class gets released when the message from the deinit() method is printed to the console. This class will be named TestClassOne. Let's take a look at the following code:

```
class TestClassOne {
  typealias nameClosure = (() -> String)
  var name = "Jon"
  lazy var myClosure: nameClosure = {
    return self.name
  }
  deinit {
    print("TestClassOne deinitialized")
  }
}
```

Now, let's create a second class that will contain a method that accepts a closure that is of the nameClosure type that was defined in the TestClassOne class. This class will also have a deinit() method, so we can also see when it gets released. We will name this class TestClassTwo. Let's take a look at the following code:

```
class TestClassTwo {
  func closureExample(handler: TestClassOne.nameClosure) {
    print(handler())
  }
  deinit {
    print("TestClassTwo deinitialized")
  }
}
```

Now, let's see this code in action by creating instances of each class and then trying to manually release the instance by setting them to nil:

```
var testClassOne: TestClassOne? = TestClassOne()
var testClassTwo: TestClassTwo? = TestClassTwo()

testClassTwo?.closureExample(handler:testClassOne!.myClosure)
testClassOne = nil
print("testClassOne is gone")
testClassTwo = nil
print("testClassTwo is gone")
```

What we do in this code is create two optionals that may contain an instance of our two test classes or nil. We need to create these variables as optionals because we will be setting them to `nil` later in the code so that we can see whether the instances are released properly.

We then call the `closureExample()` method of the `TestClassTwo` instance and pass it the `myClosure` property from the `TestClassOne` instance. We now try to release the `TestClassOne` and `TestClassTwo` instances by setting them to `nil`. Keep in mind that when an instance of a class is released, it attempts to call the `deinit()` method of the class, if it exists. In our case, both classes have a `deinit()` method that prints a message to the console, so we know when the instances are actually released.

If we run this project, we will see the following messages printed to the console:

```
testClassOne is gone
TestClassTwo deinitialized
testClassTwo is gone
```

As we can see, we do attempt to release the `TestClassOne` instances, but the `deinit()` method of the class is never called, indicating that it was not actually released; however, the `TestClassTwo` instance was properly released because the `deinit()` method of that class was called.

To see how this is supposed to work without the strong reference cycle, change the `myClosure` closure to return a string type that is defined within the closure itself, as shown in the following code:

```
lazy var myClosure: nameClosure = {
  return "Just Me"
}
```

Now, if we run the project, we should see the following output:

```
TestClassOne deinitialized
testClassOne is gone
TestClassTwo deinitialized
testClassTwo is gone
```

This shows that the `deinit()` methods from both the `TestClassOne` and `TestClassTwo` instances were properly called, indicating that they were both released properly.

In the first example, we capture an instance of the `TestClassOne` class within the closure because we accessed a property of the `TestClassOne` class using `self.name`. This created a strong reference from the closure to the instance of the `TestClassOne` class, preventing memory management from releasing the instance.

Swift does provide a very easy and elegant way to resolve strong reference cycles in closures. We simply need to tell Swift not to create a strong reference by creating a capture list. A capture list defines the rules to use when capturing reference types within a closure. We can declare each reference to be a weak or unowned reference rather than a strong reference.

A `weak` keyword is used when there is the possibility that the reference will become nil during its lifetime; therefore, the type must be an optional. The `unowned` keyword is used when there is not a possibility of the reference becoming nil.

We define the capture list by pairing the `weak` or `unowned` keywords with a reference to a class instance. These pairings are written within square brackets (`[ ]`). Therefore, if we update the `myClosure` closure and define an `unowned` reference to `self`, we should eliminate the strong reference cycle. The following code shows what the new `myClosure` closure will look similar to:

```
lazy var myClosure: nameClosure =  {
  [unowned self] in
  return self.name
}
```

Notice the new line-`[unowned self] in`. This line says that we do not want to create a strong reference to the instance of `self`. If we run the project now, we should see the following output:

```
TestClassOne deinitialized
testClassOne is gone
TestClassTwo deinitialized
testClassTwo is gone
```

This shows that both the `TestClassOne` and `TestClassTwo` instances were properly released.

Summary

In this chapter, we saw that we can define a closure just like we can define an `Int` or `String` type. We can assign closures to a variable, pass them as an argument to functions, and also return them from functions.

Closures capture a store references to any constants or variables from the context in which the closure was defined. We have to be careful with this functionality to make sure that we do not create a strong reference cycle, which would lead to memory leaks in our applications.

Swift closures are very similar to blocks in Objective-C, but they have a much cleaner and eloquent syntax. This makes them a lot easier to use and understand.

Having a good understanding of closures is vital to mastering the Swift programming language and will make it easier to develop great applications that are easy to maintain. They are also essential for creating first class frameworks that are both easy to use and maintain.

The three use cases that we saw in this chapter are by no means the only three useful uses for closures. I can promise you that the more you use closures in Swift, the more uses you will find for them. Closures are definitely one of the most powerful and useful features of the Swift language, and Apple did a great job by implementing them in the language.

13
Using C Libraries with Swift

A large majority of my early development work was done in the C programming language, using the various C libraries that came with the system I was currently working on. These libraries provided a wealth of functionality that made my development life easier. To be honest, when I was using the C language as my primary development language, it was rare to write an application without linking to either a third-party library or using a system library. When Swift was initially released for the Linux platform, one of my first questions was how useful would it be without the ability to access these libraries because they provide so much functionality for the developer. Luckily, Apple has provided us with an easy way to link these libraries to our Swift applications.

In this chapter, you will learn the following:

- How to use C libraries with your Swift projects
- How to create system modules
- How to use the modules with your application
- How to use man pages

Swift developers coming from Apple's iOS and OS X environments are use to using Apple's frameworks that provide most of the functionality that they need. These frameworks provide the ability to build incredible GUI interfaces, access Bluetooth devices, and a wealth of other functionality.

It would be nice if Apple were able to provide similar frameworks for the Linux platform; however, that is not really feasible. The reason it is not feasible is that the Linux platform offers a wide variety of options for just about everything. It would be virtually impossible for Apple to provide frameworks that were compatible with all of these options, therefore Apple made it possible for Swift developers to link Linux's native C libraries to their Swift applications. This gives Swift developers access to all of the same libraries and functionality that Linux C developers have access to.

In this chapter, we will see how we can link native C libraries to our Swift application to give us access to functionality that is not provided by the Swift standard or core libraries. To do this, we will need to use the Swift Package Manager to manage our application's dependencies and builds. If you are not familiar with the Swift Package Manager, you can refer back to Chapter 1, *Taking the First Step with Swift*. To add C libraries to a Swift project, we need to begin by creating a module that defines the libraries.

Modules

A module in Swift is code that is distributed as a single unit that can then be imported into other modules using Swift's import keyword. Frameworks and applications are examples of modules. In this chapter, we are going to look at a special kind of module that can be used to map the C libraries we wish to import.

The Linux port of Swift comes with a predefined module named Glibc that contains most of the Linux standard library; however, there are numerous headers that have not been imported within this module. This module is similar to the Darwin module on Apple platforms. Let's start off by looking at the Glibc module, and then we will look at defining our own module to import a third-party C library.

To see what headers are defined in the Glibc module, we can look at the glibc.modulemap file that is located in the usr/lib/swift/linux/x86_64/ directory of our Swift installation. Don't worry if you do not fully understand the format of this file at this time; we will explain the format later in this chapter when we look at creating our own module. Right now, we just need to know that if we import the Glibc module into our code we will be including all of the headers that are defined in this file.

Let's look at an example that will show us how to import the Glibc module. In this example, we will create an extension to the array type that will randomly select an element from the array. We will use the random() function provided by the system to generate the random number for this extension. The following code shows the Array extension:

```
import Glibc

extension Array {

  func getRandomElement() -> Element {
     let index = Int(random() % self.count)
     return self[index]
  }
}
```

This example starts off with a single `import` statement that imports the `Glibc` framework. This import statement allows us to use the system libraries that are defined in the `Glibc` framework. If we tried to build the code without importing the `Glibc` framework, we would receive the following error:

```
/main.swift:6:19: error: use of unresolved identifier 'random'
let index = Int(random() % self.count)
```

What this error tells us is that the compiler does not know anything about the `random()` function. If we look at the man page for the `random()` function (you can access the man pages using the following command: `man random`), we see that we need to import the `stdlib.h` header if we want to use this function. If we then look at the headers that are imported in the `Glibc` framework, we will see that the `Glibc` framework does include the `stdlib.h` header. By importing the `Glibc` framework, we are essentially importing all of the header files defined within it; therefore, we are importing the `stdlib.h` header that defines the `random()` function. This allows us to use the `random()` function within our code.

If you are new to developing applications and utilities in the Linux environment, you will want to get familiar with Linux man pages to retrieve information about the system libraries and the functionality they provide. These man pages will give you a wealth of knowledge about the functions that you are using. We will discuss Linux man pages later in this chapter.

Earlier, we mentioned that the `Glibc` framework contains most of the Linux standard library, so what do we do if we want include headers that are not in the `Glibc` framework? These headers could be part of the Linux standard library that are not currently defined in the `Glibc` framework or libraries that are not part of the Linux standard library itself. Let's see how we can create custom modules that we can use to add other headers or third-party libraries to our applications. We will then see how we can use the functionality they provide within our application.

Creating a custom module

To create a custom module, we will begin by creating a directory to put all of its files in. This will be the module's main directory. Within this directory, we will need two files. The first is a file named `Package.swift`, and the second is named `module.modulemap`.

Within the `module.modulemap` file we will define the headers we want to import and the libraries that we wish to link to. The following sample shows how the `module.modulemap` file is formatted:

```
module CMyModule [system] {
    header "/usr/include/mylibheader.h"
    link "mylib"
    export *
}
```

The first line defines the name of the module. This name is what we will import in our Swift files. In this sample, the module's name is `CMyModule`. The next line defines the full path to the header file that we want to import. The third line is optional and tells the compiler that the functionality defined in the header can be found in the `mylib` library, so we will need to link it. If we do not need an external library, we can omit this line. The last line says to export all of the functionality.

The Swift Package Manager uses `git` and `git` tags to manage the packages and modules; therefore, once we have created both files, we will need to create a `Git` repository for the module. To do this, we run the following commands in the main directory for the module:

```
git init
git add .
git commit -m "Initial Import"
git tag 0.1.0
```

Before we explain how to use a module, let's go ahead and create the module needed for our examples.

Creating the Cpcap module

For our first example, we will be creating a utility that will list the default network device on the system the application is running on using the `pcap` library. For this utility, we will use the `pcap_lookupdev()` function from the `pcap` library. The man page for the `pcap_lookupdev()` function shows that we will need to import the `pcap/pcap.h` header file.

If you cannot pull up the `pcap_lookupdev` man page on your system, you might not have `libpcap-dev` installed. To install it using apt-get, run the following command:

```
sudo apt-get install libpcap-dev
```

To create the module, let's start off by creating the directory and files that we need:

```
mkdir Cpcap
cd Cpcap
touch Package.swift
touch module.modulemap
```

Now we will need to define the `pcap` headers in the `module.modulemap` file. To do this, we put the following code into `module.modulemap` file:

```
module Cpcap [system] {
module libpcap {
        header "/usr/include/pcap.h"
        link "pcap"
        export *
    }
}
```

Next, we need to add the following code to the `Package.swift` file to define our module:

```
import PackageDescription
let package = Package(
    name: "Cpcap"
)
```

Now we need to create the `Git` repository for the module by running the following commands in the module's main directory:

```
git init
git add .
git commit -m "Initial Import"
git tag 0.1.0
```

Our module has now been created and is ready to use.

Using the Cpcap module

Now that the module has been created, let's look at how we would use it in a project. The first thing we will need to do is to create a new project. The following commands will set up a new project named `pcapProject`:

```
mkdir pcapProject
cd pcapProject
swift package init
```

Now that the directory structure for our project has been created, we need to tell the compiler to use the newly created `Cpcap` module. To do this, we will need to add a dependency to the `Package.swift` file. The following code will define our application and also its dependency on the `Cpcap` module:

```
import PackageDescription
let package = Package(
    name: "pcapProject",
    dependencies: [.Package(url: "../Cpcap", majorVersion: 0, minor: 1)]
)
```

We add the dependency using the `dependencies` line. The `url` within the dependencies line defines the path to the module. This can be the filesystem path, as shown in our example, or an Internet URL to a GitHub repository. We can also define multiple dependencies by separating the packages with a comma, as shown here:

```
import PackageDescription
let package = Package(

    name: "exampleApp",
    dependencies: [.Package(url: "../modOne", majorVersion: 0, minor: 1),
    dependencies: [.Package(url: "../modTwo", majorVersion: 0, minor: 1)]
)
```

We can also define the minimum major and minor version numbers for the module. The major and minor version numbers for our module were defined using the `git tag` command.

We are now ready to use the libraries defined in the module within our application. The following code shows the `main.swift` file that uses the `pcap_lookupdev()` function. This file should be created in the `Sources` directory:

```
import Cpcap
import Glibc
var errbuf = UnsafeMutablePointer<Int8>.allocate(capacity:
Int(PCAP_ERRBUF_SIZE))

let dev = pcap_lookupdev(errbuf)

if let dev = dev {
    let devName = String(cString:dev)
    print("found \(devName)")
} else {
    print("Could not get dev")
}
```

In this code, we start off by importing both the `Glibc` and `Cpcap` modules. The `Cpcap` module is the module that we created earlier in this chapter, while the `Glibc` module contains most of the Linux standard library. When then declare an `UnsafeMutablePointer` of the `Int8` type.

The `UnsafeMutablePointer` type is a pointer to `pointee` objects. This type provides no automated memory management; therefore, we must allocate and free memory appropriately. Swift, whenever possible, avoids giving us direct access to memory with pointers, while C and C libraries use pointers to memory extensively. The `UnsafeMutablePointer` type allows us to use C libraries where we need to access memory with pointers. You will be using the `UnsafeMutablePointer` type a lot when working with C libraries.

Next, we call the `pcap_lookupdev()` function to retrieve the default `pcap` network device for our system. We then use optional binding to make sure we did not receive a nil value from the `pcap_lookupdev()` function.

The `pcap_lookupdev()` function returns a pointer to a `NUL-terminated arrays of characters`, which is also known as a C string; therefore, we use the `String(cString:)` initiator to convert this C string to a Swift string. Once we convert the device name to a Swift string, we then print it out.

We can now build our project by running the following command from the project's root directory, which contains the `Package.swift` file:

```
swift build
```

If we do not receive any errors, we will have an executable file named `pcapProject` (the same name as the project) in the `.build/debug/` directory. When can now run that file, and we should see some output similar to this:

```
Found eth0
```

This was a pretty good first example, and one that was pretty easy to understand, since the function we used returned a C string. For our next example, we will see how we can access the data from a linked list that is returned from a C function. It is very common, especially for system-level C libraries, to return a pointer to a linked list; therefore, it is important to understand how we would access the data stored in these lists.

For this example, we will also use the `pcap_findalldevs()` function from the `pcap` library. If you look at the man page for the `pcap_findalldevs()` function (`man pcap_findalldevs`), you will see that this function constructs a list of network devices that can be opened with `pcap_create()` and `pcap_activate()` or with `pcap_open_live()`.

The list that is returned is a linked list of the `pcap_if_t` type. The man page also gives us a list of properties in the `pcap_if_t` type. For our example, we are only interested in the `next` property (which points to the next item in the list) and the `name` property (which contains the name of the device).

Let's start off by creating a new project named `pcapAllDevs` using the following commands:

```
mkdir pcapAllDevs
cd pcapAllDevs
swift package init
```

Now we need to link the `Cpcap` module that we created earlier in this chapter to this new project. We do this by updating the projects `Package.swift` file to look such as this:

```
import PackageDescription
let package = Package(
    name: "pcapAllDevs",
    dependencies: [.Package(url: "../Cpcap", majorVersion: 0, minor: 1)]
)
```

Being able to link multiple projects to the same module is what makes modules so useful. This gives us the ability to configure a module once so that it includes everything we need for a certain type of project, and then link to that module whenever we need to. Now let's create the `main.swift` file in the Sources directory and put the following code in it:

```
import Cpcap
import Glibc

var errbuf = UnsafeMutablePointer<Int8>.allocate(
capacity:Int(PCAP_ERRBUF_SIZE))
var devs = UnsafeMutablePointer<UnsafeMutablePointer<pcap_if_t>?>.
allocate(capacity:1)

if (pcap_findalldevs(devs,errbuf) >= 0 ) {
   if var nDev = devs.pointee {
    var cont = true

    while (cont) {
        var devName = String(cString: nDev.pointee.name)
```

```
            print("Dev Name: \(devName)")
            if (nDev.pointee.next != nil) {
                nDev = nDev.pointee.next
            } else {
                cont = false
            }
        }
    }

    pcap_freealldevs(devs.pointee)
} else {
    print("Could not get devices")
}
```

This example starts off exactly like the last example: by importing the `Cpcap` and `Glibc` modules. We also create the `errbuf` variable of the `UnsafeMutablePointer<Int8>` type, just like in the last example.

Next, we create the `devs` variable of the `UnsafeMutablePointer<UnsafeMutablePointer<pcap_if_t>?>` type. This variable will contain the pointer to the first element in the linked list when the `pcap_findalldevs()` function returns. If the `pcap_findalldevs()` function fails, then the `UnsafeMutablePointer` will be nil, which is the reason we make it an optional.

On the `pcap_findalldevs` man page, we see that the `pcap_findalldevs()` function returns 0 if it was successful, or −1 if it failed; therefore, when we call the function, we check the return value to see if it was successful or not. If you are not familiar with Linux/Unix man pages, I cannot stress enough that you should get familiar with them. If you have any questions about how to use a particular function, the first place you should check is the man page.

We then use optional binding to retrieve the first element in the list and set the `cont` variable to true. The `cont` variable is used to tell the while loop when we have reached the end of the list and to exit the loop.

In the next line, the `nDev.pointee.name` code is used to retrieve the `name` element of the current `pcap_if_t` item pointed to by the `nDevUnsafeMutablePointer`. Since the name element is a C string, we use the `String(cString:)` initiator to convert it to a Swift string. We then print the device name to the console.

In the `pcap_if_t` structure, the `next` property points to the next element in the list. If we are at the end of the list, the `next` property is nil; therefore, in the next line we check to see if the `next` property is nil. If it is not nil, we set the nDev pointer to the next element in the list. If the `next` property is nil, we set the `cont` variable to false to stop the while loop.

Once we have looped through all of the elements in the list, we use the `pcap_freealldevs` function to free all of the elements of the list. If you look at the man page for the `pcap_findalldevs` function, you will see that the `pcap_freealldevs` function is mentioned as the function that will free all of the elements in the linked list. Keep in mind that the description of the `UnsafeMutablePointer` type tells us that there is no automated memory management for this type; therefore, we must allocate and free memory appropriately.

To build this project you would issue the following command from the project's root directory where the `Package.swift` file is located:

```
swift build
```

Linux man pages

In this chapter, we have made several reference to man pages. Man pages, which is short for manual pages, are how software is documented on Unix and Unix-like systems. You can find a wealth of information about applications, system calls, libraries, and even various abstract concepts. Understanding how to use man pages is an important concept for any Linux developer; therefore, let's look at how to use them by looking at the man page for the `pcap_findalldevs()` function. We will need to open a terminal prompt and use the following command:

```
man pcap_findalldevs
```

Once you run this command, you should see something similar to the following screenshot:

```
hoffmanjon@hoffmanjon-VirtualBox: ~/Dropbox/Books/Mastering Swift 3/Linux/Code/Cha
PCAP_FINDALLDEVS(3PCAP)                                        PCAP_FINDALLDEVS(3PCAP)

NAME
       pcap_findalldevs, pcap_freealldevs - get a list of capture devices, and
       free that list

SYNOPSIS
       #include <pcap/pcap.h>

       char errbuf[PCAP_ERRBUF_SIZE];

       int pcap_findalldevs(pcap_if_t **alldevsp, char *errbuf);
       void pcap_freealldevs(pcap_if_t *alldevs);

DESCRIPTION
       pcap_findalldevs() constructs a list of network  devices  that  can  be
       opened with pcap_create() and pcap_activate() or with pcap_open_live().
       (Note that there may be network devices that cannot be  opened  by  the
       process  calling pcap_findalldevs(), because, for example, that process
       does not have sufficient privileges to open them for capturing; if  so,
       those  devices  will not appear on the list.)  If pcap_findalldevs() suc-
       ceeds,  the pointer pointed to by alldevsp is set to point to the  first
       element  of the list, or to NULL if no devices were found (this is con-
       sidered success).  Each element of the list is of type  pcap_if_t,  and
       has the following members:

Manual page pcap_findalldevs(3pcap) line 1 (press h for help or q to quit)
```

To scroll through the page, you will use the up and down arrow keys, and to exit the page, simply press the *q* key. If you need help, press the *h* key. There are a number of other commands, but that will be enough to get you started. A man page may contain several sections, but almost all of them start with the NAME, SYNOPSIS, and DESCRIPTION sections. If you scroll through the page you will see that the pcap_findalldevs man page also includes RETURN and SEE ALSO sections.

The NAME section generally gives a list of what is covered by this man page, with a brief description. You can see that that this man page covers both the pcap_findalldevs and the pcap_freealldevs functions. It also tells us that these functions will get a list of capture devices and frees the list.

The SYNOPSIS section shows us how to use the functions and also what we need to use them. For the pcap_findalldevs and the pcap_freealldevs functions, this man page tells us that we need to include the pcap/pcap.h header. If you recall, we included that header in our Cpcap module at the beginning of this chapter. This section also shows us how to use the pcap_findalldevs and the pcap_freealldevs functions. The hardest part of being a Swift Linux developer is converting these function calls from the C language to the Swift language.

The next section is the DESCRIPTION section. This section gives a detailed description of the functions. For this particular man page, it also tells us what elements make up the pcap_if_t structure, which is returned by the pcap_findalldevs function. If this was the first time you have used a function, I would recommend taking the time to read the description section in its entirety, because it usually contains useful information about the function.

The RETURN section gives us information about what is returned from the function. This is the section that told us that a 0 was returned if the function was successful, or a −1 if the function failed.

The SEE ALSO section gives us a list of other man pages related to this one.

If you are going to be working with C libraries with your Swift projects, the man pages are going to be one of your main resources.

Summary

In this chapter, we saw how we to create a custom module to import C libraries and headers into our Swift projects. Understanding how to use C libraries in our Swift projects gives us the ability to include any Linux and third-party C libraries in our Swift projects.

We also saw how to use the Linux man pages to get information about C functions. If you have a question about a C function, the first place you should look is the man pages.

14
Concurrency and Parallelism in Swift

When I first started learning Objective-C, I already had a good understanding of concurrency and multitasking with my background in other languages, such as C and Java. This background made it very easy for me to create multithreaded applications using threads in Objective-C. Then, Apple changed everything when they released **Grand Central Dispatch** (**GCD**) with OS X 10.6 and iOS 4. At first, I went into denial: there was no way GCD could manage my application's threads better than I could. Then I entered the anger phase: GCD was hard to use and understand. Next was the bargaining phase: maybe I can use GCD with my threading code, so I could still control how the threading worked. Then there was the depression phase: maybe GCD does handle threading better than I can. Finally, I entered the wow phase: this GCD thing is really easy to use and works amazingly well. After using GCD on Apple platforms for so long, I was very happy to hear that Apple was bringing it to the Linux platform with Swift.

In this chapter, we will cover the following topics:

- Basics of concurrency and parallelism
- How to use GCD to create and manage concurrent dispatch queues
- How to use GCD to create and manage serial dispatch queues
- How to use various GCD functions to add tasks to the dispatch queues

Concurrency and parallelism

Concurrency is the concept of multiple tasks starting, running, and completing within the same time period. This does not necessarily mean that the tasks are executing simultaneously. In fact, in order for tasks to be run simultaneously, our application needs to be running on a multicore or multiprocessor system. Concurrency allows us to share the processor or cores with multiple tasks; however, a single core can only execute one task at a given time.

Parallelism is the concept of two or more tasks running simultaneously. Since each core of our processor can only execute one task at a time, the number of tasks executing simultaneously is limited to the number of cores within our processors and the number of processors that we have. As an example, if we have a four-core processor, then we are limited to running four tasks simultaneously. Today's processors can execute tasks so quickly that it may appear that larger tasks are executing simultaneously. However, within the system, the larger tasks are actually taking turns executing subtasks on the cores.

In order to understand the difference between concurrency and parallelism, let's look at how a juggler juggles balls. If you watch a juggler, it seems they are catching and throwing multiple balls at any given time; however, a closer look reveals that they are, in fact, only catching and throwing one ball at a time. The other balls are in the air waiting to be caught and thrown. If we want to be able to catch and throw multiple balls simultaneously, we need to have multiple jugglers.

This example is really good because we can think of jugglers as the cores of a processer. A system with a single core processor (one juggler), regardless of how it seems, can only execute one task (catching and throwing one ball) at a time. If we want to execute more than one task at a time, we need to use a multicore processor (more than one juggler).

Back in the old days, when all processors were single-core, the only way to have a system that executed tasks simultaneously was to have multiple processors in the system. This also required specialized software to take advantage of the multiple processors. In today's world, just about every device has a processor that has multiple cores.

Traditionally, the way applications added concurrency was to create multiple threads; however, this model does not scale well to an arbitrary number of cores. The biggest problem with using threads was that our applications ran on a variety of systems (and processors), and in order to optimize our code, we needed to know how many cores/processors could be efficiently used at a given time, which is usually not known at the time of development.

In order to solve this problem, many operating systems, including iOS and OS X, started relying on asynchronous functions. These functions are often used to initiate tasks that could possibly take a long time to complete, such as making an HTTP request or writing data to disk. An asynchronous function typically starts the long-running task and then returns prior to the task completion. Usually, this task runs in the background and uses a callback function (such as a closure in Swift) when the task completes.

These asynchronous functions work well for the tasks that the OS provides them for, but what if we need to create our own asynchronous functions and do not want to manage the threads ourselves? For this, Apple provides GCD with Swift 3 on the Linux platform. GCD is a low-level C-based API that allows specific tasks to be queued up for execution and schedules the execution on any of the available processor cores. Let's look at GCD and how we can use it.

GCD

Prior to Swift 3, using GCD felt like writing low-level C code. The API was a little cumbersome and sometimes hard to understand because it did not use any of the Swift language design features. This all changed with Swift 3, because Apple took up the task of rewriting the API so it would meet the Swift 3 API guidelines.

GCD provides what is known as dispatch queues to manage submitted tasks. The queues manage these submitted tasks and execute them in a **first-in, first-out** (**FIFO**) order. This ensures that the tasks are started in the order they were submitted.

A task is simply some work that our application needs to perform. As examples, we can create tasks that perform simple calculations, read/write data to disk, make an HTTP request, or anything else that our application needs to do. We define these tasks by placing the code inside either a function or a closure and adding it to a dispatch queue.

GCD provides three types of queue:

- **Serial queues**: Tasks in a serial queue (also known as a **private queue**) are executed one at a time in the order they were submitted. Each task is started only after the preceding task is completed. Serial queues are often used to synchronize access to specific resources because we are guaranteed that no two tasks in a serial queue will ever run simultaneously. Therefore, if the only way to access the specific resource is through the tasks in the serial queue, then no two tasks will attempt to access the resource at the same time or out of order.

- **Concurrent queues**: Tasks in a concurrent queue (also known as a **global dispatch queue**) execute concurrently; however, the tasks are still started in the order that they were added to the queue. The exact number of tasks that can be executing at any given instance is variable and is dependent on the system's current conditions and resources. The decision on when to start a task is up to GCD and is not something that we can control within our application.
- **Main dispatch queue**: The main dispatch queue is a globally available serial queue that executes tasks on the application's main thread. Since tasks put into the main dispatch queue run on the main thread, it is usually called from a background queue when some background processing has finished and the user interface needs to be updated.

Dispatch queues offer a number of advantages over traditional threads. The first and foremost advantage is that, with dispatch queues, the system handles the creation and management of threads rather than the application itself. The system can scale the number of threads dynamically based on the overall available resources of the system and the current system conditions. This means that dispatch queues can manage the threads with greater efficiency than we could.

Another advantage of dispatch queues is that we are able to control the order in which our tasks are started. With serial queues, not only do we control the order in which tasks are started, but also ensure that one task does not start before the preceding one is complete. With traditional threads, this can be very cumbersome and brittle to implement, but with dispatch queues, as we will see later in this chapter, it is quite easy.

Helper functions

Before we look at how to use dispatch queues, let's create a couple of helper functions that will help us demonstrate how the various types of queue work. The first function will simply perform some basic calculations and then return a value. Here is the code for this function, which is named doCalc():

```
func doCalc() {
  var x=100
  var y = x*x
  _ = y/x
}
```

The other function, which is named `performCalculation()`, accepts two parameters. One is an integer named `iterations`, and the other is a string named `tag`. The `performCalculation()` function calls the `doCalc()` function repeatedly until it calls the function the same number of times as defined by the iterations parameter. We also use the `CFAbsoluteTimeGetCurrent()` function to calculate the elapsed time it took to perform all of the iterations and then print the elapsed time with the `tag` string to the console. This will let us know when the function completes and how long it took to complete it. Here is the code for this function:

```
func performCalculation(_ iterations: Int, tag: String) {
  let start = CFAbsoluteTimeGetCurrent()
  for _ in 0 ..< iterations {
    doCalc()
  }
  let end = CFAbsoluteTimeGetCurrent()
  print("time for \(tag):  \(end-start)")
}
```

You will need to import the `Foundation` and `Glibc` libraries.

These functions will be used together to keep our queues busy, so we can see how they work. Let's begin by looking at how we would create a dispatch queue.

Creating queues

We use the `DispatchQueue` initializer to create a new dispatch queue. The following code shows how to create a new dispatch queue:

```
let concurrentQueue = DispatchQueue(label: "cqueue.hoffman.jon",
attributes: .concurrent)
let serialQueue = DispatchQueue(label: "squeue.hoffman.jon")
```

The first line creates a concurrent queue with the label of `cqueue.hoffman.jon`, while the second line creates a serial queue with the label of `squeue.hoffman.jon`. You will need to import the Dispatch library to use the dispatch queues.

The `DispatchQueue` initializer takes the following parameters:

- `label`: This is a string label that is attached to the queue to uniquely identify it in debugging tools, such as instruments and crash reports. It is recommended that we use a reverse DNS naming convention. This parameter is optional and can be nil.

- `attributes`: This specifies the type of queue to make. This can be `DISPATCH_QUEUE_SERIAL`, `DISPATCH_QUEUE_CONCURRENT`, or nil. If this parameter is nil, a serial queue is created.

 Some programming languages use the reverse DNS naming convention to name certain components. This convention is based on a registered domain name that is reversed. As an example, if we worked for company that had a `mycompany.com` domain name with a product called widget, the reverse DNS name will be `com.mycompany.widget`.

Creating and using a concurrent queue

A concurrent queue will start the tasks in the FIFO order; however, the tasks will execute concurrently and therefore they may finish in any order. Let's see how to create and use a concurrent queue. The following line creates the concurrent queue that we will be using for this section:

```
let cqueue = DispatchQueue(label: "cqueue.hoffman.jon", attributes:
.concurrent)
```

This line will create a new dispatch queue that we will name `cqueue`. This queue has a label of `cqueue.hoffman.jon`. Now let's see how we would use our concurrent queue by using the `performCalculation()` function to perform some calculations:

```
let c = { performCalculation(1000, tag: "async1")}
cqueue.async(execute: c)
```

In the preceding code, we created a closure, which represents our task, that simply calls the `performCalculation()` function, requesting that it runs through `1000` iterations of the `doCalc()` function. Finally, we use the `async(execute:)` method of our queue to execute it. This code will execute the task in a concurrent dispatch queue, which is separate from the main thread.

While the preceding example works perfectly, we can actually shorten the code a little bit. The next example shows that we do not need to create a separate closure as we did in the preceding example; we can also submit the task to execute like this:

```
cqueue.async {
  performCalculation(1000, tag: "async1")
}
```

This shorthand version is how we usually submit small code blocks to our queues. If we have larger tasks, or tasks that we need to submit multiple times, we will generally want to create a closure and submit the closure to the queue, as we showed in the first example.

Let's see how the concurrent queue actually works by adding several items to the queue and looking at the order and time in which they return. The following code will add three tasks to the queue. Each task will call the `performCalculation()` function with various iteration counts. Remember that the `performCalculation()` function will execute the calculation routine continuously until it is executed the number of times defined by the iteration count passed in. Therefore, the larger the iteration count we pass into the `performCalculation()` function, the longer it should take to execute. Let's take a look at the following code:

```
cqueue.async {
  performCalculation(10000000, tag: "async1")
}

cqueue.async {
  performCalculation(1000, tag: "async2")
}

cqueue.async {
  performCalculation(100000, tag: "async3")
}
```

Since we are running the tasks in a dispatch queue, the application may exit prior to the tasks finishing. To prevent the application from exiting, you can put in the following code, which will cause the application to wait for the user to press *Enter* before exiting:

```
print("press enter to exit")
let _ = readLine(strippingNewline: true)
```

Notice that each of the functions is called with a different value in the `tag` parameter. Since the `performCalculation()` function prints out the `tag` variable with the elapsed time, we can see the order in which the tasks complete and the time it took to execute. If we execute the preceding code, we should see results similar to this:

```
time for async2:  0.000200986862182617
time for async3:  0.00800204277038574
time for async1:  0.461670994758606
```

The elapsed time will vary from one run to the next, and from system to system.

Since the queues function in the FIFO order, the task that had the tag of `async1` was executed first. However, as we can see from the results, it was the last task to finish. Since this is a concurrent queue, if it is possible (if the system has the available resources), the blocks of code will execute concurrently. This is why the tasks with the `async2` and `async3` tags completed prior to the task that had the `async1` tag, even though the execution of the `async1` task began before the other two.

Now, let's see how a serial queue executes tasks.

Creating and using a serial queue

A serial queue functions a little differently from a concurrent queue. A serial queue will only execute one task at a time and will wait for one task to complete before starting the next one. This queue, like the concurrent dispatch queue, follows a FIFO order. The following line of code will create a serial queue that we will be using for this section:

```
let squeue = DispatchQueue(label: "squeue.hoffman.jon")
```

Now let's see how we would use the serial queue by using the `performCalculation()` function to perform some calculations:

```
let s = { performCalculation(1000, tag: "sync1")}
squeue.async (execute: s)
```

In the preceding code, we created a closure, which represents our task, that simply calls the `performCalculation()` function, requesting that it runs through `1000` iterations of the `doCalc()` function. Finally, we use the `async(execute:)` method of our queue to execute it. This code will execute the task in a serial dispatch queue, which is separate from the main thread. As we can see from this code, we use the serial queue exactly like we use the concurrent queue.

We could shorten this code a little bit, just like we did with the concurrent queue. The next example shows how we would do this with a serial queue:

```
squeue.async {
  performCalculation(1000, tag: "sync2")
}
```

Let's see how the serial queues works by adding several items to the queue and looking at the order in which they complete. The following code will add three tasks, which will call the `performCalculation()` function with various iteration counts, to the queue:

```
squeue.async {
  performCalculation(100000, tag: "sync1")
}
```

```
squeue.async {
  performCalculation(1000, tag: "sync2")
}

squeue.async {
  performCalculation(100000, tag: "sync3")
}
```

Just like with the concurrent queue example, we call the `performCalculation()` function with various iteration counts and different values in the `tag` parameter. Since the `performCalculation()` function prints out the `tag` string with the elapsed time, we can see the order that the tasks complete in and the time it takes to execute. If we execute this code, we should see results similar to this:

```
time for sync1:   0.00648999214172363
time for sync2:   0.00009602308273315
time for sync3:   0.00515800714492798
```

 The elapsed time will vary from one run to the next, and from system to system.

Unlike with concurrent queues, we can see that the tasks were completed in the same order that they were submitted in, even though the `sync2` and `sync3` tasks took considerably less time to complete. This demonstrates that a serial queue only executes one task at a time and that the queue waits for each task to be completed before starting the next one.

In the previous examples, we used the `async` method to execute the code blocks. We could also use the `sync` method.

async versus sync

In the previous examples we used the `async` method to execute the code blocks. When we use the `async` method, the call will not block the current thread. This means that the method returns and the code block is executed asynchronously.

Rather than using the `async` method, we could use the `sync` method to execute the code blocks. The sync method will block the current thread, which means it will not return until the execution of the code has completed. Generally, we use the `async` method, but there are use cases where the `sync` method is useful. This is usually when we have a separate thread and we want that thread to wait for some work to finish.

Executing code on the main queue function

The `DispatchQueue.main.async(execute:)` function will execute code on the application's main queue. We generally use this function when we want to update our code from another thread or queue.

The main queue is automatically created for the main thread when the application starts. This main queue is a serial queue; therefore, items in this queue are executed one at a time, in the order in which they were submitted. We will generally want to avoid using this queue unless we need to update the user interface from a background thread.

The following code example shows how to use this function:

```
DispatchQueue.main.async {
//perform task on the main thread.
}
```

There will be times when we need to execute tasks after a delay. If we were using a threading model, we would need to create a new thread, perform some sort of delay or sleep function, and execute our task. With GCD, we can use the `asyncAfter` method.

Using asyncAfter

The `asyncAfter` function will execute a block of code asynchronously after a given delay. This is very useful when we need to pause the execution of our code. The following code sample shows how to use the `asyncAfter` function:

```
let queue2 = DispatchQueue(label: "squeue.hoffman.jon")
let delayInSeconds = 2.0
let pTime = DispatchTime.now() + Double(Int64(delayInSeconds *
Double(1000000))) / Double(1000000)
queue2.asyncAfter(deadline: pTime) {
    print("Times Up")")
}
```

In this code, we begin by creating a serial dispatch queue. We then create an instance of the `DispatchTime` type and calculate the time to execute the block of code based on the current time. We then use the `asyncAfter` function to execute the code block after the delay.

Summary

Before we consider adding concurrency to our application, we should make sure that we understand why we are adding it and ask ourselves whether it is necessary. While concurrency can make our application more responsive by offloading work from our main application thread to a background thread, it also adds extra complexity to our code and overhead to our application. I have even seen numerous applications, in various languages, which actually run better after we have pulled out some of the concurrency code. This is because the concurrency was not well thought out or planned. With this in mind, it is always a good idea to think and talk about concurrency while we are discussing the application's expected behavior.

At the start of this chapter, we had a discussion about running tasks concurrently compared to running tasks in parallel. We also discussed the hardware limitation that limits how many tasks can run in parallel on a given device. Having a good understanding of those concepts is very important for understanding how and when to add concurrency to our projects.

While we are able to use native threads with Swift, as we do with C applications, I would recommend taking looking at GCD instead.

15
Swifts Core Libraries

I was really excited when Apple announced that they were going to release a version of Swift for Linux. This meant I could use Swift for my Linux and embedded development, as well as my Mac OS and iOS development. When Apple first released Swift 2.2 for Linux I was very excited, but I was also a little disappointed because I could not read/write files, access network services, or use libdispatch (GCD) on Linux like I could on Apple's platforms. With the release of Swift 3, Apple has corrected this with the release of the Swift's core libraries.

In this chapter, you will learn about the following topics:

- What are the Swift core libraries
- How to use Apple's URL loading system
- How to use the Formatter classes
- How to use the FileManager class

The Swift core libraries are written to provide a rich set of APIs that are consistent across the various platforms that Swift supports. By using these libraries, developers will be able to write code that will be portable to all platforms that Swift supports. These libraries provide a higher level of functionality than the Swift standard library.

The core libraries provide functionality in a number of areas, such as the following:

- Networking
- Unit testing
- Scheduling and execution of work (libdispatch)
- Property lists, JSON parsing, and XML parsing
- Support for dates, times, and calendar calculations
- Abstraction of OS-specific behavior
- Interaction with the filesystem
- User preferences

We are unable to cover all of the core libraries in this single chapter; however, we will look at some of the more useful one. We will start off by looking at Apple's URL loading system, which is used for network development.

Apple's URL loading system

Apple's URL loading system is a framework of classes available to interact with URLs. We can use these classes to communicate with services that use standard Internet protocols. The classes that we will be using in this section to connect to and retrieve information from REST services are as follows:

- `URLSession`: This is the main session object.
- `URLSessionConfiguration`: This is used to configure the behavior of the `URLSession` object.
- `URLSessionTask`: This is a base class to handle the data being retrieved from the URL. Apple provides three concrete subclasses of the `URLSessionTask` class.
- `URL`: This is an object that represents the URL to connect to.
- `URLRequest`: This class contains information about the request that we are making and is used by the `URLSessionTask` service to make the request.
- `HTTPURLResponse`: This class contains the response to our request.

Now, let's look at each of these classes a little more in depth so that we have a basic understanding of what each does.

URLSession

An URLSession object provides an API for interacting with various protocols, such as HTTP and HTTPS. The session object, which is an instance of the URLSession, manages this interaction. These session objects are highly configurable, which allows us to control how our requests are made and how we handle the data that is returned.

Like most networking API, URLSession is asynchronous. This means that we have to provide a way to return the response from the service back to the code that needs it. The most popular way to return the results from a session is to pass a completion handler block (closure) to the session. This completion handler is then called when the service successfully responds or we receive an error. All of the examples in this chapter use completion handlers to process the data that is returned from the services.

URLSessionConfiguration

The URLSessionConfiguration class defines the behavior and policies to use when using the URLSession object to connect to a URL. When using the URLSession object, we usually create an URLSessionConfiguration instance first because an instance of this class is required when we create an instance of the URLSession class.

The URLSessionConfiguration class defines three session types:

- **Default session configuration**: Manages the upload and download tasks with default configurations
- **Ephemeral session configuration**: This configuration behaves similarly to the default session configuration, except that it does not cache anything to disk
- **Background session configuration**: This session allows for uploads and downloads to be performed, even when the app is running in the background

It is important to note that we should make sure that we configure the URLSessionConfiguration object appropriately before we use it to create an instance of the URLSession class. When the session object is created, it creates a copy of the configuration object that we provide. Any changes made to the configuration object once the session object is created are ignored by the session. If we need to make changes to the configuration, we must create another instance of the URLSession class.

URLSessionTask

The URLSession service uses an instance of the URLSessionTask class to make the call to the service that we are connecting to. The URLSessionTask class is a base class, and Apple has provided three concrete subclasses that we can use:

- URLSessionDataTask: This returns the response, in memory, directly to the application as one or more Data objects. This is the task that we generally use most often.
- URLSessionDownloadTask: This writes the response directly to a temporary file.
- URLSessionUploadTask: This is used for making requests that require a request body, such as a POST or PUT request.

It is important to note that a task will not send the request to the service until we call the resume() method.

URL

The URL object represents the URL that we are going to connect to. The URL class is not limited to URLs that represent remote servers, but it can also be used to represent a local file on disk. In this chapter, we will be using the URL class exclusively to represent the URL of the remote service that we are connecting to.

URLRequest

We use the URLRequest class to encapsulate our URL and the request properties. It is important to understand that the URLRequest class is used to encapsulate the necessary information to make our request, but it does not make the actual request. To make the request, we use instances of the URLSession and URLSessionTask classes.

HTTPURLResponse

The HTTPURLResponse class is a subclass of the URLResponse class that encapsulates the metadata associated with the response to a URL request. The HTTPURLResponse class provides methods for accessing specific information associated with an HTTP response. Specifically, this class allows us to access the HTTP header fields and the response status codes.

We briefly covered a number of classes in this section and it may not be clear how they all actually fit together; however, once you see the examples a little further in this chapter, it will become much clearer. Before we go into our examples, let's take a quick look at the type of service that we will be connecting to.

REST web services

REST has become one of the most important technologies for stateless communications between devices. Due to the lightweight and stateless nature of the REST-based services, its importance is likely to continue to grow as more devices are connected to the Internet.

REST is an architecture style for designing networked applications. The idea behind REST is that instead of using complex mechanisms, such as **Simple Object Access Protocol** (**SOAP**) or **Common Object Request Broker Architecture** (**CORBA**), to communicate between devices, we use simple HTTP requests. While, in theory, REST is not dependent on the Internet protocols, it is almost always implemented using them. Therefore, when we are accessing REST services, we are almost always interacting with web servers in the same way that our web browsers interact with these servers.

REST web services use the HTTP POST, GET, PUT, or DELETE methods. If we think about a standard **Create/Read/Update/Delete** (**CRUD**) application, we would use a POST request to create or update data, a GET request to read data, and a DELETE request to delete data.

When we type a URL into our browser's address bar and hit *Enter*, we are generally making a GET request to the server and asking it to send us the web page associated with that URL. When we fill out a web form and click the submit button, we are generally making a POST request to the server. We then include the parameters from the web form in the body of our POST request.

Now, let's look at how to make an HTTP GET request using Apple's networking API.

Making an HTTP GET request

In this example, we will make a GET request to Apple's iTunes search API to get a list of items related to the search term Jimmy Buffett. Since we are retrieving data from the service, by REST standards, we should use a GET request to retrieve the data.

While the REST standard is to use GET requests to retrieve data from a service, there is nothing stopping a developer of a web service from using a GET request to create or update a data object. It is not recommended to use a GET request in this manner, but just be aware that there are services out there that do not adhere to the REST standards.

The following code makes a request to Apple's iTunes search API and then prints the results to the console:

```
public typealias dataFromURLCompletionClosure = (URLResponse?, Data?) ->
Void
public func sendGetRequest (
    _ handler: @escaping dataFromURLCompletionClosure) {

    let sessionConfiguration = URLSessionConfiguration.default;
    let urlString =
        "https://itunes.apple.com/search?term=jimmy+buffett"
    if let encodeString =
        urlString.addingPercentEncoding(
            withAllowedCharacters: CharacterSet.urlQueryAllowed),
        let url = URL(string: encodeString) {
        var request = URLRequest(url:url)
        request.httpMethod = "GET"
        let urlSession = URLSession(
            configuration:sessionConfiguration, delegate: nil,
delegateQueue: nil)

        let sessionTask = urlSession.dataTask(with: request) {
            (data, response, error) in
            handler(response, data)
        }
        sessionTask.resume()
    }
}
```

We start off by creating a type alias named `DataFromURLCompletionClosure`. The `DataFromURLCompletionClosure` type will be used for both the GET and POST examples of this chapter. If you are not familiar with using a `typealias` object to define a closure type, please refer to `Chapter 12`, *Working with Closures*, for more information.

We then create a function named `sendGetRequest()` that will be used to make the GET request to Apple's iTunes API. This function accepts one argument named handler, which is a closure that conforms to the `DataFromURLCompletionClosure` type. The handler closure will be used to return the results from the request.

Starting with Swift 3, the default for closure arguments to functions is not escaping, which means that, by default, the closures argument cannot escape the function body. A closure is considered to escape a function when that closure, which is passed as an argument to the function, is called after the function returns. Since the closure will be called after the function returns, we use the `@escaping` attribute before the parameter type to indicate it is allowed to escape.

Within our `sendGetRequest()` method, we begin by creating an instance of the `URLSessionConfiguration` class using the default settings. If we need to, we can modify the session configuration properties after we create it, but in this example, the default configuration is what we want.

After we create our session configuration, we create the URL string. This is the URL of the service we are connecting to. With a GET request, we put our parameters in the URL itself. In this specific example, `https://itunes.apple.com/search` is the URL of the web service. We then follow the web service URL with a question mark (?), which indicates that the rest of the URL string consists of parameters for the web service.

The parameters take the form of key/value pairs, which means that each parameter has a key and a value. The key and value of a parameter, in a URL, are separated by an equals sign (=). In our example, the key is `term` and the value is `jimmy+buffett`. Next, we run the URL string that we just created through the `addingPercentEncoding()` method to make sure our URL string is encoded properly. We use the `CharacterSet.urlQueryAllowed` character set with this method to ensure we have a valid URL string.

Next, we use the URL string that we just built to create an `URL` instance named `url`. Since we are making a GET request, this `URL` instance will represent both the location of the web service and the parameters that we are sending to it.

We create an instance of the `URLRequest` class using the `URL` instance that we just created. In this example, we set the `HTTPMethod` property; however, we can also set other properties such as the timeout interval or add items to our HTTP header.

Now, we use the `sessionConfiguration` constant that we created at the beginning of the `sendGetRequest()` function to create an instance of the `URLSession` class. The `URLSession` class provides the API that we will use to connect to Apple's iTunes search API. In this example, we use the `dataTask(with:)` method of the `URLSession` instance to return an instance of the `URLSessionDataTask` type named `sessionTask`.

The `sessionTask` instance is what makes the request to the iTunes search API. When we receive the response from the service, we use the handler callback to return both the `URLResponse` object and the `Data` object. The `URLResponse` contains information about the response, and the `Data` instance contains the body of the response.

Finally, we call the `resume()` method of the `URLSessionDataTask` instance to make the request to the web service. Remember, as we mentioned earlier, a `URLSessionTask` instance will not send the request to the service until we call the `resume()` method.

Now, let's look at how we would call the `sendGetRequest()` function. The first thing we need to do is to create a closure that will be passed to the `sendGetRequest()` function and called when the response from the web service is received. In this example, we will simply print the response to the console. Here is the code:

```
let printResultsClosure: dataFromURLCompletionClosure = {
    if let data = $1 {
        let sString = String(data: data,
                encoding: String.Encoding(rawValue:
                String.Encoding.utf8.rawValue))
        print(sString)
    } else {
        print("Data is nil")
    }
}
```

We define this closure, named `printResultsClosure`, to be an instance of the `dataFromURLCompletionClosure` type. Within the closure, we unwrap the first parameter and set the value to a constant named `data`. If the first parameter is not nil, we convert the data constant to an instance of the `String` class, which is then printed to the console.

Now, let's call the `sendGetRequest()` method with the following code:

```
let aConnect = HttpConnect()
aConnect.sendGetRequest(printResultsClosure)
```

This code creates an instance of the `HttpConnect` class and then calls the `sendGetRequest()` method, passing the `printResultsClosure` closure as the only parameter. If we run this code while we are connected to the Internet, we will receive a JSON response that contains a list of items related to Jimmy Buffett on iTunes.

Now that we have seen how to make a simple HTTP GET request, let's look at how we would make an HTTP POST request to a web service.

Making an HTTP POST request

Since Apple's iTunes, APIs use GET requests to retrieve data. In this section, we will use the free `http://httpbin.org` service to show you how to make a POST request. The POST service that `http://httpbin.org` provides can be found at `http://httpbin.org/post`. This service will echo back the parameters that it receives so that we can verify that our request was made properly.

When we make a POST request, we generally have some data that we want to send or post to the server. This data takes the form of key/value pairs. These pairs are separated by an ampersand (&) symbol, and each key is separated from its value by an equals sign (=). As an example, let's say that we want to submit the following data to our service:

```
firstname: Jon
lastname: Hoffman
age: 47 years
```

The body of the POST request would take the following format:

```
firstname=Jon&lastname=Hoffman&age=47
```

Once we have the data in the proper format, we will then use the `dataUsingEncoding()` method, as we did with the GET request, to properly encode the POST data.

Since the data going to the server is in the key/value format, the most appropriate way to store this data, prior to sending it to the service, is with a `Dictionary` object. With this in mind, we will need to create a method that will take a `Dictionary` object and return a `String` object that can be used for the POST request. The following code will do that:

```
private func dictionaryToQueryString(_ dict: [String : String]) -> String {
    var parts = [String]()
    for (key, value) in dict {
        let part : String = key + "=" + value
        parts.append(part);
    }
    return parts.joined(separator: "&")
}
```

This function loops through each key/value pair of the `Dictionary` object and creates a `String` object that contains the key and the value separated by the equals sign (=). We then use the `joinWithSeperator()` function to join each item in the array, separated by the specified sting. In our case, we want to separate each string with the ampersand symbol (&). We then return this newly created string to the code that called it.

Now, let's create the `sendPostRequest()` function that will send the POST request to the `http://httpbin.org` post service. We will see a lot of similarities between this `sendPostRequest()` function and the `sendGetRequest()` function, which we showed you in the *Making an HTTP GET request* section. Let's take a look at the following code:

```
public typealias dataFromURLCompletionClosure = (URLResponse?, Data?) ->
Void

public func sendPostRequest(_ handler: @escaping
dataFromURLCompletionClosure) {
```

```
let sessionConfiguration =
URLSessionConfiguration.default
let urlString = "http://httpbin.org/post"
if let encodeString =
    urlString.addingPercentEncoding(
        withAllowedCharacters: CharacterSet.urlQueryAllowed),
    let url = URL(string: encodeString) {
    var request = URLRequest(url:url)
    request.httpMethod = "POST"
    let params = dictionaryToQueryString(["One":"1 and 1",
        "Two":"2 and 2"])
    request.httpBody = params.data(
        using: String.Encoding.utf8, allowLossyConversion: true)
    let urlSession = URLSession(
        configuration:sessionConfiguration, delegate: nil,
            delegateQueue: nil)
    let sessionTask = urlSession.dataTask(with: request) {
        (data, response, error) in handler(response, data)
    }
    sessionTask.resume()
}
}
```

This code is very similar to the `sendGetRequest()` function that we saw earlier in this section. The two main differences are that the `httpMethod` of the `URLRequest` is set to `POST` rather than `GET` and how we set the parameters. In this function we set the `httpBody` property of the `URLRequest` instance to the parameters we are submitting.

Now that we have seen how to use the URL loading system, let's look at how we can use Formatters.

Formatter

Formatter is an abstract class that declares an interface for an object that creates, converts or validates a human-readable form of some data. The types that subclass the `Formatter` class are generally used when we want to take a particular object, such as an instance of the `Date` class, and present the value in a form that the user of our application can understand.

Apple has provided several concrete implementations of the `Formatter` class and in this section we will look at two of them. It is important to remember that the formatters that Apple provides will provide the proper format for the default locale of the device the application is running on.

We will start off by looking at the `DateFormatter` type.

DateFormatter

The `DateFormatter` class is a subclass of the `Formatter` abstract class that can be used to convert a `Date` object into a human readable string. It can also be used to convert a `String` representation of a date into a `Date` object. We will look at both of these use cases in this section. Let's begin by seeing how we could covert a `Date` object into a human readable string.

The `DateFormatter` type has five predefined styles that we can use when we are converting a `Date` object to a human readable string. The following chart shows what the five styles look like for an en-US locale:

DateFormatter style	Date	Time
.none	No format	No format
.short	12/25/16	6:00 AM
.medium	Dec 25, 2016	6:00:00 AM
.long	December 25, 2016	6:00:00 AM EST
.full	Sunday December 25, 2016	6:00:00 AM EST

The following code shows how we would use the predefined `DateFormatter` styles:

```
let now = Date()

let formatter = DateFormatter()
formatter.dateStyle = .medium
formatter.timeStyle = .medium

let dateStr = formatter.string(from: now)
 print(dateStr)
```

We use the `string(from:)` method to convert the `now` date to a human-readable string. In this example, for the en-US locale, the `dateStr` constant would contain text similar to `Oct 22, 2016, 4:57 PM`".

There are numerous times when the predefined styles do not meet our needs. For those times, we can define our own styles using a custom format string. This string is a series of characters that the `DateFormatter` type knows are stand-ins for the values we want to show. The `DateFormatter` instance will replace these stand-ins with the appropriate values. The following table shows some of the formatting values that we can use to format our `Date` objects:

Stand-in format	Description	Example output
Yy	Two-digit year	16, 14, 04
Yyyy	Four-digit year	2016, 2014, 2004
MM	Two-digit month	06, 08, 12
MMM	Three-letter month	Jul, Aug, Dec
MMMM	Full month name	July, August
Dd	Two-digit day	10, 11, 30
EEE	Three-letter day	Mon, Sat, Sun
EEEE	Full day	Monday, Sunday
A	Period of day	AM, PM
Hh	Two-digit hour	02, 03, 04
HH	Two-digit hour for 24-hour clock	11, 14, 16
Mm	Two-digit minute	30, 35, 45
Ss	Two-digit seconds	30, 35, 45

The following code shows how we would use these custom formatters:

```
let now = Date()
let formatter2 = DateFormatter()
formatter2.dateFormat = "YYYY-MM-dd HH:mm:ss"

let dateStr2 = formatter2.string(from: now)
  print(dateStr2)
```

We use the `string(from:)` method to convert the `now` date to a human-readable string. In this example, for the en-US locale, the `dateStr2` constant would contain text similar to `2016-08-19 19:03:23`.

Now let's look at how we would take a formatted date string and convert it into a `Date` object. We will use the same format string that we used in our last example:

```
formatter2.dateFormat = "YYYY-MM-dd HH:mm:ss"

let dateStr3 = "2016-08-19 16:32:02"
let date = formatter2.date(from: dateStr3)
 print(date)
```

In this example , we took the human-readable date string and converted it into a `Date` object using the `date(from:)` method. If the format of the human-readable date string does not match the format specified in the `DateFormatter` instance, the conversion will fail and return nil.

Now let's take a look at the `NumberFormatter` type.

NumberFormatter

The `NumberFormatter` class is a subclass of the `Formatter` abstract class, which can be used to convert a number into a human-readable string with a specified format. This formatter is especially useful when we want to display a currency string, especially since it will convert the string to the proper currency of the locale.

Let's begin by looking at how we would convert a number into a currency string:

```
let formatter1 = NumberFormatter()
formatter1.numberStyle = .currency
let num1 = formatter1.string(from: 23.99)
```

In the previous code, we define our number style to be `.currency`, which tells our formatter that we want to convert our number to a currency string. We then use the `string(from:)` method to convert the number to a string. In this example, for the en-US locale, the `num1` constant would contain the string `$23.99`.

Now let's see how we can spell out a number using the `NumberFormatter` type. The following code will take a number and spell out the number:

```
let formatter3 = NumberFormatter()
formatter3.numberStyle = .spellOut
let num3 = formatter3.string(from: 2015)
```

In this example, we set the `numberStyle` property to the `.spellout` style. This style will spell out the number. For this example, the `num3` constant will contain the string `two thousand fifteen`.

Now let's look at how we can manipulate the filesystem using the `FileManager` class.

FileManager

The filesystem is a complex topic, and how we manipulate it within our applications is generally specific to the operating system that our application is running on. This can be an issue when we are trying to port code from one operating system to another. Apple has addressed this issue by putting the `FileManager` object in the core libraries. The `FileManager` object lets us examine and make changes to the filesystem in a uniform manner across all the operating systems that Swift supports.

The `FileManager` class provides us with a shared instance that we can use. This instance should be suitable for most of our filesystem-related tasks. We can access this shared instance using the `default` property.

When we use the `FileManager` object, we can provide paths as either an instance of the `URL` or `String` types. In this section all of our paths will be `String` types for consistency purposes.

Let's start off by seeing how we could list the contents of a directory using the `FileManager` object. The following code shows how to do this:

```
let fileManager = FileManager.default

do {
    let path = "/home/hoffmanjon/"
    let dirContents = try fileManager.contentsOfDirectory(atPath: path)
    for item in dirContents {
        print(item);
    }
} catch let error {
    print("Failed reading contents of directory: \(error)")
}
```

Replace the `/home/hoffmanjon` path with the path to your `home` directory

We start off by getting the shared instance of the `FileManager` object using the default property. We will use this same shared instance for all of our examples in this section rather than redefining it for each example. Next, we define our path and use it with the `contentsOfDirectory(atPath:)` method. This method returns an array of `String` types that contains the names of the items in the path. We use a `for` loop to list these items.

Next, let's look at how we would create a directory using the file manager. The following code shows how to do this:

```
do {
    let path = "/hoffman/hoffmanjon/masteringswift/test/dir"
    try fileManager.createDirectory(atPath: path,
    withIntermediateDirectories: true)
} catch let error {
    print("Failed creating directory, \(error) ")
}
```

In this example, we use the `createDirectory(atPath: withIntermediateDirectories:)` method to create the directory. When we set the `withIntermediateDirectories` parameter to true, this method will create any parent directories that are missing. The operation will fail if any parent directories are missing when this parameter is set to false. The file manager also has a method that will let us move an item. Let's see how to do this:

```
do {
    let pathOrig = "/home/hoffmanjon/masteringswift2/"
    let pathNew = "/home/hoffmanjon/masteringswift3/"
    try fileManager.moveItem(atPath: pathOrig, toPath: pathNew)
} catch let error {
    print("Failed moving directory, \(error) ")
}
```

To move an item, we use the `moveItem(atPath: toPath:)` method. Just like the copy example we just saw, the move method can be used for both files and directories. If the path specifies a directory, then the entire directory structure below that path will be moved. Now let's see how we can delete an item from the filesystem:

```
do {
    let path = "/home/hoffmanjon/masteringswift/"
    try fileManager.removeItem(atPath: path)
} catch let error {
    print("Failed Removing directory, \(error) ")
}
```

In this example, we use the `removeItem(atPath:)` method to remove the item from the filesystem. A word of warning: once you delete something, it is gone and there is no getting it back.

Next, let's look at how we can read permission for items in our filesystem. For this, we will need to create a file named `test.file` that our path will point to:

```
let path = "/home/hoffmanjon/masteringswift3/test.file"
if fileManager.fileExists(atPath: path) {
    let isReadable = fileManager.isReadableFile(atPath: path)
    let isWriteable = fileManager.isWritableFile(atPath: path)
    let isExecutable = fileManager.isExecutableFile(atPath: path)
    print("can read \(isReadable)")
    print("can write \(isWriteable)")
    print("can execute \(isExecutable)")
}
```

In this example, we used three different methods to read the filesystem permissions for the filesystem item. These methods are as follows:

- `isReadableFile(atPath:)`: true if the file is readable
- `isWritableFile(atPath:)`: true if the file is writable
- `isExecutableFile(atPath:)`: true if the file is executable

In this section, we covered a number of filesystem-related functions. There are some additional functions that were not covered because they have not been implemented in the Linux version of Swift as of Swift 3.0.1 Preview 3, but should be implemented soon. Two methods that are very useful are the `copyItem(atPath: toPath:)` and the `isDeletableFile(atPath:)` functions.

Summary

In this chapter, we looked at some of the libraries that make up the Swift core libraries. While these libraries are only a small portion of the libraries that make up the Swift core libraries, they are arguably some of the most useful libraries. To explore the other libraries, you can refer to Apple's GitHub page:
`https://github.com/apple/swift-corelibs-foundation`.

16
Swift on Single Board Computers

This is probably my favorite chapter to write. I am not only a software developer, but I am also very familiar with hardware and one of my favorite hobbies is building robots. I have been building robots for a couple of years now and I have used several different single board computers as the brains. These single board computers have included the BeagleBone Black, Next Thing C.H.I.P, Raspberry Pi and several Arduino models. When I first started using the single board computers for my robotics projects, I used an assortment of languages such as JavaScript, Python and C, but when it was announced that iachieved.it built the Swift language for the ARM platform I started experimenting using Swift for these projects. I think that you will find, as I did, that Swift is an excellent language for any type of project on the single board computers, but it is especially good for robotics projects.

In this chapter, we will cover the following topics:

- What is a single board computer
- How to get Swift on the BeagleBone Black
- What are expansion headers on Single board computers
- How to use Swift to interact with external sensors and devices
- How to use Swift to build an autonomous robot

A **single board computer** (**SBC**) is a complete computer built on a single circuit board that includes the microprocessor(s), RAM and I/O. These computers have several purposes including educational purposes, as well as serving as controllers for embedded systems or as development environments.

The main difference between personal computers and SBCs is that SBCs do not rely on expansion slots for peripherals. Most SBCs do, however include USB ports that allow us to add peripherals such as mice, keyboards, and Bluetooth adapters.

A single board configuration can greatly reduce the cost of a system by eliminating the need for items such as connectors and bus circuitry that are needed for communication between different components. It can also greatly reduces the overall size of the system because all of the components are integrated together.

Some examples of SBCs are the BeagleBone Black, Raspberry Pi and the Next Thing C.H.I.P. In this chapter, we will be looking at how we can use Swift on my favorite SBC, which is the BeagleBone Black. While we may be focusing on the BeagleBone Black, I have also used Swift on the Raspberry Pi and the Next Thing C.H.I.P. Lets start off by examining the BeagleBone Black so we understand what we can do with it.

 This book is about Swift development. While we talk about the hardware in this chapter, the primary emphasis is on the software development side. If you do not have a basic understanding of electronics and how to connect components we would recommend additional reading on these subjects prior to performing the projects in this chapter.

The BeagleBone Black

The BeagleBone Black, which was originally released in April of 2013, is a credit card size single board computer that features the Sitara AM335x Cortex-A8 processor running at 1GHZ with 512 Meg of RAM and 4 GB of eMMC memory. The current version of the BeagleBone Black is the Rev C version that was released in May of 2014.

The BeagleBone Black is a true open-source computing platform where both the hardware and software are open-source. All design material for the BeagleBone Black is easily accessible from the Beagleboard's Wiki page (`http://elinux.org/Beagleboard:BeagleBoneBlack`). This material allows you to build your own board either by using the design as is or by making modifications to the design. You can also choose to purchase the board, as I did, from outlets like Amazon.

The latest supported Linux image for the BeagleBone Black, as of the writing of this book, is Debian 8.4. This is the image that is used for all development in this chapter. You can find the latest images on the BeagleBoard.org site (`https://beagleboard.org/latest-images`).

The BeagleBone Black features two expansion headers that provide extensive I/O capabilities. These expansion headers are used to interact with items such as motors, LEDs, buttons and other sensors. The I/O capabilities are where, in my opinion, the BeagleBone Black really excels, because you can connect so many different items to it at once. In this chapter we will see how we can use Swift to interact with various external sensors and also how to build a very basic autonomous robot.

The following two images of the BeagleBone Black highlight some of its main hardware features. The first image is the top view and the second image is the bottom view.

Top view:

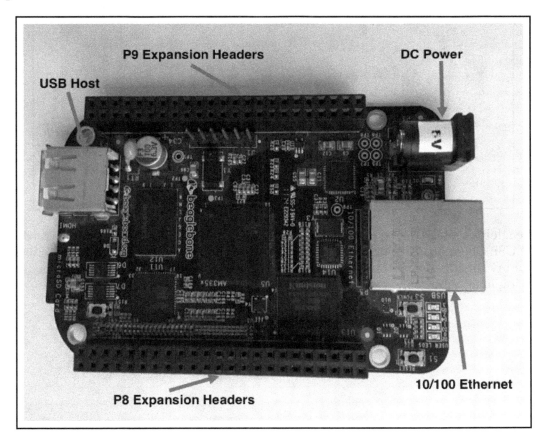

Bottom view:

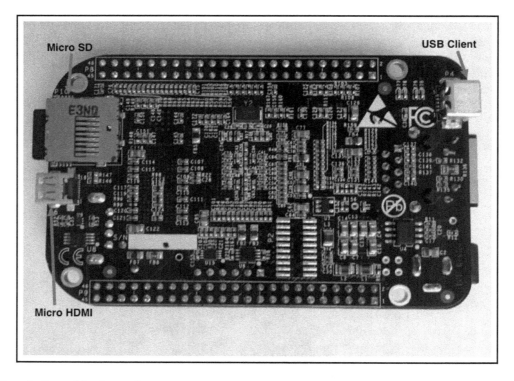

The BeagleBone black can be powered by the 5V DC Connector on the top of the board or by the USB Client on the bottom of the board. I generally power the board by the USB client and for my robotic projects I use external battery packs that are made to charge phones. The following image shows the types of battery packs I use.

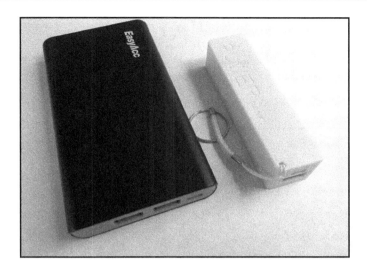

The Micro SD card can be used as a system drive that the device can boot off of. The USB host allows you to add additional peripherals like keyboards, mice, and Bluetooth adapters.

As I mentioned earlier, the expansion headers are what sets the BeagleBone Black apart from other SBCs, like the Raspberry Pi, because it contains more pins and it also contains multiple analog and PWM pins with the GPIO pins. Let's take a closer look at these expansion headers.

BeagleBone Black's expansion headers

The BeagleBone Black comes with two expansion headers labeled P8 and P9. These expansion headers are used to connect external devices and sensors to the BeagleBone Black. These devices and sensors can be items such as temperature sensors to read the current temperature, motors to move a robot around the room or a GPS sensor that will tell the computer where it is in the world. With these external devices, we can interact with or monitor the outside world.

The expansion headers proved a wealth of I/O capabilities. The different pins on the expansion headers provide different types of I/O. In this introductory chapter, we will be focusing on the digital GPIO and analog pins. We will also see how the expansion headers can provide power and ground for the external devices.

The following charts show the various pins and the functionality they provide:

		P8							P9			
		Pin	PIN						Pin	PIN		
	DGND	1	2	DGND				DGND	1	2	DGND	
	GPIO_38	3	4	GPIO_39				VDD_3V3	3	4	VDD_3V3	
	GPIO_34	5	6	GPIO_35				VDD_5V	5	6	VDD_5V	
Timer4	GPIO_66	7	8	GPIO_67	Timer7			SYS_5V	7	8	SYS_5V	
Timer5	GPIO_69	9	10	GPIO_68	Timer6			PWR_BUT	9	10	SYS_RESET	
	GPIO_45	11	12	GPIO_44				GPIO_30	11	12	GPIO_60	
EHRPWM2B	GPIO_23	13	14	GPIO_26				GPIO_31	13	14	GPIO_40	EHRPWM1A
	GPIO_47	15	16	GPIO_46				GPIO_48	15	16	GPIO_51	EHRPWM1B
	GPIO_27	17	18	GPIO_65				GPIO_4	17	18	GPIO_5	
EHRPWM2A	GPIO_22	19	20	GPIO_63				I2C2_SCL	19	20	I2C2_SDA	
	GPIO_62	21	22	GPIO_37			EHRPWM0B	GPIO_3	21	22	GPIO_2	EHRPWM0A
	GPIO_36	23	24	GPIO_33				GPIO_49	23	24	GPIO_15	
	GPIO_32	25	26	GPIO_61				FPIO_117	25	26	SPIO_14	
	GPIO_86	27	28	GPIO_88				GPIO_125	27	28	GPIO_123	
	GPIO_87	29	30	GPIO_89				GPIO_121	29	30	GPIO_122	
	GPIO_10	31	32	GPIO_11				GPIO_120	31	32	VDD_ADC	
	GPIO_9	33	34	GPIO_81				AIN4	33	34	GNDA_ADC	
	GPIO_8	35	36	GPIO_80				AIN6	35	36	AIN5	
	GPIO_78	37	38	GPIO_79				AIN2	37	38	AIN3	
	GPIO_76	39	40	GPIO_77				AIN0	39	40	AIN1	
	GPIO_74	41	42	GPIO_75				GPIO_20	41	42	GPIO_7	ECAPPWM0
	GPIO_72	43	44	GPIO_73				DGND	43	44	DGND	
	GPIO_70	45	46	GPIO_71				DGND	45	46	DGND	

The pins with the light green background are **General Purpose Input Output (GPIO)** that function as the digital I/O. The pins with the light blue background are the **analog** pins and the ones with the yellow background are the **PWM** pins. As you probably noticed, some of the pins can be configured for different types.

We will be looking at the functionality of the pins as we go through this chapter and you can refer back to this image to see what the various pins do and where a particular pin is located. To use Swift as our development language, the first thing we need to do is to install it.

Installing Swift

The Swift port for the ARM platform is built and maintained on the iachieved.it site (`http://dev.iachieved.it/iachievedit/swift/`). iAchieved.it LLC is a group of independent software developers and one of the projects the group works on is this Swift port. At the time this book is being written, the installation process for Swift 3 is a manual process, but hopefully we will eventually be able to install it using the `apt-get` package manager. Since the installation process is changing, the current installation process is documented on the SwiftyBones 3 GitHub page here: `https://github.com/hoffmanjon/SwiftyBones3`. This page will be updated as the installation process changes.

SwiftyBones3

SwiftyBones3 is a Swift 3 framework for interacting with the GPIO, PWM and analog pins on the BeagleBone Black. This framework makes it very easy to interact with these pins and is the framework we will be working with in this chapter. While SwiftyBones is written for the BeagleBone Black, if you are using another board like the Raspberry Pi you can use the very good SwiftyGPIO framework: `https://github.com/uraimo/SwiftyGPIO`.

The reason that we have chosen to use the SwiftyBones framework over the SwiftyGPIO is that the SwiftyBones framework offers support for the analog and PWM pins as well as the GPIO pins. The analog and PWM pins are very useful when interacting with various sensors. SwiftyBones also comes with a build script that will help you build projects with multiple files since the Swift package manager is not installed, at this time, with the ARM version of Swift.

The instructions for installing SwiftyBones are on the SwiftyBones GitHub page `https://github.com/hoffmanjon/SwiftyBones3`.

The SwiftyBones packages contains four directories which are:

- **Images**: Images needed for this README like the SwiftyBones logo
- **Sources**: The SwiftyBones source files
- **swiftybuild**: The swiftybuild script to help you compile your Swift projects
- **Examples**: Example projects to help you get started with SwiftyBones

The `Images` directory can be ignored because it contains the images needed for the `Readme.md` file. The `Examples` directory contains some very good examples of how to use the SwiftyBones framework. The `Sources` directory contains the source files for the SwiftyBones framework that you will want to include with your project. Let's take a look at the files and directories in the `Sources` directory.

Sources directory

The `Sources` directory contains the Swift source files that make up the SwiftyBones framework and the SwiftyBones components framework. The four files that make up the SwiftyBones framework are:

- `SwiftyBonesCommon.swift`: This file contains common code that is required for interacting with PWM, analog and digital GPIO pins
- `SwiftyBonesDigitalGPIO.swift`: This file contains the code for interacting with the digital GPIO pins
- `SwiftyBonesAnalog.swift`: This file contains the code for interacting with the Analog IN pins
- `SwiftyBonesPWM.swift`: This file contains the code for interacting with the PWM pins

SwiftyBones is designed to be modular, so you only need to include the files that contain the functionality you need. The only file that is required for all projects that uses the SwiftyBones framework is the `SwiftyBonesCommon.swift` file, because the other files rely on it. This means, as an example, if we are only going to use the GPIO pins in a particular project then we only need to include the `SwiftyBonesCommon.swift` and `SwiftyBonesDigitalGPIO.swift` files in the project. If we are going to use the GPIO and analog pins in a project, as we do with the autonomous robot later in this chapter, then we need to include the `SwiftyBonesCommon.swift`, `SwiftyBonesAnalog.swift`, and `SwiftyBonesDigitalGPIO.swift` files

The `SwiftyBones_Components` directory, located in the `Sources` directory, contains a collection of types that make it easy to interact with specific components. These types encapsulate the logic needed to interact with specific sensors. For example, if we wanted to use the **tmp36** temperature sensor then we would include the `SBTmp36.swift`and `ComponentsCommon.swift` files from the component library with the necessary SwiftyBones source files. Then, within our code, we could create an instance of the `SBTmp36` type and read current temperature in either Celsius or Fahrenheit using the `getTempCelsius()` or `getTempFahrenheit()` methods from the `SBTmp36` type.

SwiftyBones also comes with a script that makes it easy to compile projects with multiple source files. Before we start creating our projects lets look at what this script does and how it can help us.

SwiftyBuild

SwiftyBones is built in a modular way with multiple files, which means we will need to compile all necessary files within our project. It would very quickly become annoying compiling our projects like this:

```
swiftc -o myexec main.swift tempSensor.swift
SwiftyBonesCommon.swift SwiftyBonesDigitalGPIO.swift
```

With this in mind, SwiftyBones comes with a script that would search the current directory and all subdirectories for any files that has the `.swift` extension. This script will then build a swift compiler command that compiles all of the swift files that it found into a single executable. The script is named `swiftybuild.sh`. This script takes a single optional command line argument that would be the name of the executable file if everything successfully compiles. You would use this script like this:

```
./swiftybuild.sh
or
./swiftybuild.sh myexec
```

The output from the first command would be an executable file named `main` if everything compiled successfully. The second command would generate an executable named `myexec` if everything compiled successfully.

Now lets see how we can use SwiftyBones in some sample projects. Lets start off by seeing how we can blink an LED using the `SBDigitalGPIO` type.

Blinking an LED with the SBDigitalGPIO type

Before we do any programming we will need to collect the hardware components needed for this project and connect them together. For this project you will need the following components:

- 100 ohm resistor
- 3mm or 5mm LED
- Breadboard

- Jumper wire
- BeagleBone Black

The following fritzing diagram shows how we would wire the components for this project:

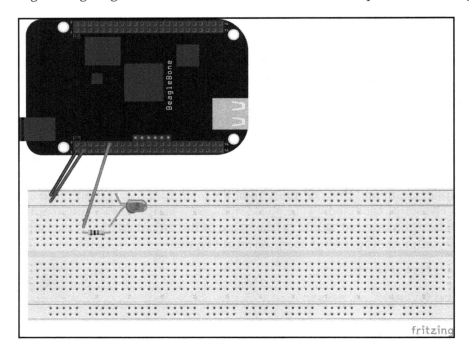

We will start off by using a black jumper wire to connect pin 1 of the P9 expansion header, which is ground, to the ground rail on the breadboard. Then, use a red jumper wire to connect pin 3 of the P9 expansion header, which is 3.3V, to the power rail on the breadboard. When we wire electronic components, we use red wires to indicate power and black wires to indicate ground.

For this circuit we will want to connect the cathode end of the LED (the shorter leg of the LED) to the ground rail and the anode end of the LED to one end of the 100 ohm resistor. We then run a third jumper wire from pin 12 of the P9 expansion header, which has an ID of GPIO60, to the other end of the resistor. We don't actually use the power rail in this example but it is good practice to connect both the power and ground rails of the breadboard when stating a project.

Make sure you have the circuit connected as shown in the fritzing images prior to powering up the BeagleBone Black. An incorrectly wired circuit can damage your BeagleBone Black. Trust me when I say that it is always a good idea to double-check your wiring before powering everything up.

Once the circuit is correctly wired, we can power on the BeagleBone Black and begin writing the application that will blink the LED. We will begin by creating a new directory that will contain the source code for our application. We will start off by copying the `SwiftyBonesCommon.swift` and `SwiftyBonesDigitalGPIO.swift` files into the newly created directory. If we want to use the `swiftybuild.sh` script, we would also need to copy that script to directory as well.

We will now create a file named `main.swift` in the newly created directory and put the following code in it:

```
import Glibc

if let led = SBDigitalGPIO(id: "gpio60", direction: .OUT){
  while(true) {
    if let oldValue = led.getValue() {
        var newValue = (oldValue == DigitalGPIOValue.HIGH) ?
            DigitalGPIOValue.LOW : DigitalGPIOValue.HIGH
        led.setValue(value: newValue)
        usleep(150000)
    }
  }
} else {
  print("Error init pin")
}
```

As with all code in this chapter, we start off by importing the `Glibc` module. We then create an instance of the `SBDigitalGPIO` type, using the `SBDigitalGPIO(id:direction:)` initializer, and assign it to the `led` constant. Since the initializer is a failable initializer, we use optional binding to ensure the instance is not nil. The `SBDigitalGPIO` initializer takes the ID of the pin we wish to connect to and the direction of the pin. The direction we are using, for this example, is `.OUT` because we will need to read from and write to the pin. We would use `.IN` if we only needed to read the value.

We use the `getValue()` method to read the current value of the pin. This will return an optional which is either `nil` or a `DigitalGPIOValue` value. The `DigitalGPIOValue` value can be either `.HIGH` or `.LOW` depending on if the pin is at a high state or a low state.

We then use the ternary operator to reverse the value by checking to see if the current value of the pin is .HIGH and if so we set the newValue variable to .LOW otherwise we set it to .HIGH. We then use the newValue variable with the setValue(value:) method to set the new value for the led pin. This blinks the LED on and off. Finally, we use the usleep() function to pause before looping back.

The digital GPIO pins on the BeagleBone Black can be in a high state which is 3.3V or a low state which is 0V. These pins are really good for turning things on and off, or detecting if something is on or off similar to what we did for the LED in this example. The SBDigitalGPIO type is designed to make it very easy to interact with the digital GPIO pins.

The SBDigitalGPIO type is included in the SwiftyBonesDitialGPIO.swift file and has two initializers. In the last example we saw the most common initializer but we can also use the SBDigitalGPIO(header:pin:direction:) initializer. In this initializer we would set the expansion header (.P8 or .P9) and the pin number instead of using the GPIO ID. As we saw in this example we use the getValue() and setValue(value:) methods to read from and write to the pin.

Using the digital GPIO is the most common way to interact with sensors and other devices but there are times when we need to read a range of values, like when we use a distance sensor. For this we can use the analog pins. Let's see how we would use an analog pin with the SBAnalog type.

TMP36 temperature sensor with the SBAnalog type

For this project we will read the analog input from a TMP36 temperature sensor and calculate the current temperature based on the voltage. For this project we will need the following components:

- TMP36 temperature sensor
- Breadboard
- Jumper wire
- BeagleBone Black

The following fritzing diagram shows how we would wire the components for this project:

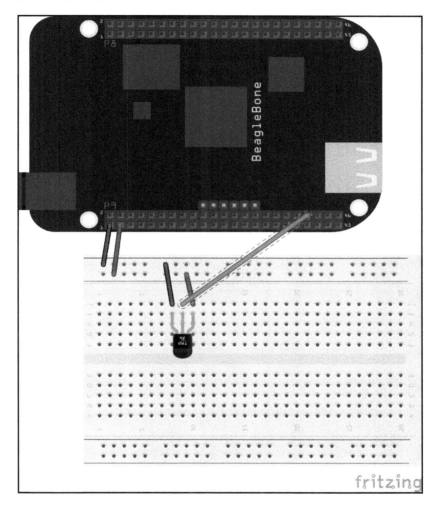

As with the previous example, we will start off by using a black jumper wire to connect pin 1 of the P9 expansion header, which is ground, to the ground rail on the breadboard. Next, use a red jumper wire to connect pin 3 of the P9 expansion header, which is 3.3V, to the power rail on the breadboard.

The TMP36 temperature sensor has three legs, one for voltage in, one for ground and one for voltage out. The following image shows these three legs:

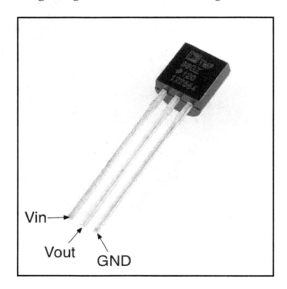

In our example we will connect the Vout pin on the TMP36 sensor to the AIN1 pin on the BeagleBone Black which is pin 40 on the P9 expansion header. We also need to connect power and ground to the sensor as shown in the wiring diagram.

 Once again, make sure you have the circuit connected as shown in the fritzing images prior to powering up the Beaglebone Black. An incorrectly wired circuit can damage your BeagleBone Black.

Once the circuit is correctly wired, we can power on the BeagleBone Black and begin writing the application to read the temperature. Just like the previous project we will want to create a new directory that will contain the source files for our project. For this project we will need to include the `SwiftyBonesCommon.swift` and `SwiftyBoneAnalog.swift` files.

After we create the directory for our project and copy the SwiftyBones files to it we will create a file named `main.swift` file and put the following code into it:

```
import Glibc

if let tmp36 = SBAnalog(id: "AIN1") {
    while(true) {
        if let value = tmp36.getValue() {
            let milliVolts = (value / 4096.0) * 1800.0
            let celsius = (milliVolts - 500.0) / 10.0
            let fahrenheit = (celsius * 9.0 / 5.0) + 32.0

            print("celsius:  \(celsius)")
            print("Fahrenheit:  \(fahrenheit)")

            usleep(150000)
        }
    }
}
```

In this code we begin by creating an instance of the `SBAnalog` type, using the `SBAnalog(id:)` initializer, and assign that instance to the `tmp36` variable. This initializer takes the ID of the pin we wish to connect to. We then use the `getValue()` method of the `SBAnalog` type to read the value from the TMP36 temperature sensor and calculate the temperature.

Since the Analog IN pins on the BeagleBone Black are input only pins, there is no `setValue()` method with the `SBAnalog` type.

As with the `SBDigitalGPIO` type, the `SBAnalog` type has a second initializer that accepts the expansion header and pin number rather than the Analog ID. We would use this initializer like this:

```
SBAnalog(header: .P9, pin: 40)
```

The analog pins are very useful when we have a sensor like the TMP36 temperature sensor or a distance sensor that has a range of values.

Now that we have seen how to use the `SBDigitalGPIO` and `SBAnalog` types, let's use these to do something pretty cool like building a very basic autonomous robot.

Autonomous robot

An autonomous robot is a robot that performs a task with no human intervention. The autonomous robot that we are going to create in this section will be an obstacle avoidance robot that will move around a room and detect when an object is in front of it and turn.

For this project we will need the following components:

- **Two DC motors and wheels**: We are using the smart car motors that you can find on Amazon or eBay pretty cheaply. If you search for *smart car motor*, you will find the yellow motors and wheels as shown in the parts image:

- **Motor controller**: We are using the L9110s H-Bridge controller.

- **Range finders**: We are using the MaxSonar EZ1 Range finder.

- **BeagleBone Board**: We are using the BeagleBone Black, but the BeagleBone Green should work with little to no modifications.
- **Battery holder**: We are using a 9V battery, but a 4xAA battery holder will work just as well.
- **Resistors**: Two 1K resistors and two 3.3K resistors for the MaxSonar range finder. If you are using different range finders, you may not need these.
- **One swivel castor wheel**: The robot will only have two wheels, therefore we use the castor wheel to balance the robot.
- **Miscellaneous**: Jumper wires, breadboards, and body for the robot.
- **3mm screws and nuts**: These are used to attach the component holders to the chassis.

 By doing a search on Amazon, we can find many different robot chassis and frames. Most of these will work great for your robot projects and some even come with motors and/or motor controllers. When you first start building robots, it is a good idea to get chassis where the parts are designed to work together. For the robot in this chapter, the chassis was printed using a 3D printer. The downloadable code for this book contains the STL files so you can print your own parts.

When building robots, it is usually a good idea to break the whole project into smaller projects or blocks. We then get each of these smaller projects working before moving on to the next one. This keeps us from getting overwhelmed with everything we want our robots to do. If I am building a robot that has motors and wheels I usually try to get these working first. The following image shows how the motors and wheels are connected to the bottom of the lower chassis:

The lower tray is designed so we can connect the smart car motors directly to the tray. We also attached the swivel castor wheel for balancing.

When we designed the chassis for this robot we put in a number of 3mm slots in the trays. This allows us to connect additional parts to the robot. Once you start building robots, having the ability to add additional components is important because we always think of new things for our robot to do.

The next image, which shows the top of the lower chassis, shows how we would attach the L9110s holder (with the L9110s motor controller) to the lower tray:

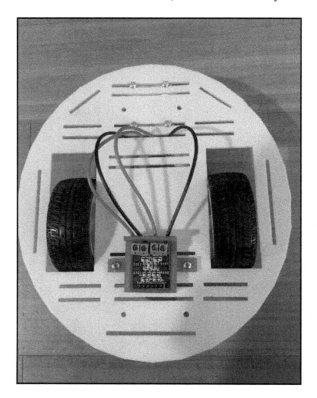

When we designed the L9110s holder, we put two 3mm holes on either side of the holder. This allows us to connect the holder to the lower tray using 3mm screws and nuts.

We connect a DC motor to the motor controller using two wires. In the previous projects the red and black wires represented positive and ground connections, however, with DC motors is does not matter which way you connect the wires. Connecting one wire to positive voltage and the other to ground will spin the motor in one direction. If you reverse the connections the motor will spin in the opposite direction. The red and black wires were used because that is what comes with the motors.

The following diagram shows how we would connect the BeagleBone Black to the L9110s motor controller and the motor controller to the DC motors:

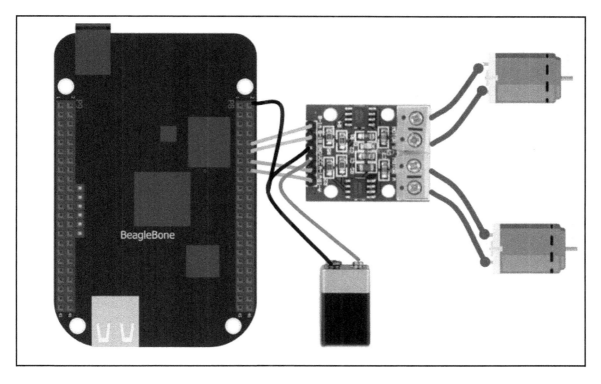

In this image we can see that we connected the DC motors directly to the L9110s motor controller. We are also connecting pins 10, 12, 14 and 16 of the P8 expansion header to the L9110s motor controller. We will explain how these pins are used to control the motors when we look at the code for the robot.

We also connect the battery directly to the L9110s motor controller. The image shows that we are running the ground wire to pin 1 of the P8 expansion header that is listed as digital ground (DGND). We show this connection because we should have a common ground for our components however what we actually want to do is to run a single ground connection to the ground rail on a breadboard and then connect the ground for all of our components to that breadboard's ground rail. This ensures a common ground for our components.

Now that we have our motors, motor controller and BeagleBone Black connected, lets test them to ensure everything is connected correctly. To do this we will need to create a new project and add the `SwiftyBonesCommon.swift`, `SwiftBonesDigitalGPIO.swift`, `SwiftyBonesAnalog.swift`, and `swiftybuild.sh` files to it.

It is usually a good idea to keep the code that controls the different components of our robot in a separate file from the robot's logic. This will allow us to very easily create different versions of our robot that has different logic. With that in mind, we will create a new type for the code that controls the components and name it Mastering Swift Bot (`MSBot`). In this type, we will need a private instance of the `SBDigitalGPIO` type for each connection to the motor controller. We will also need to create an initializer that will initialize these instances. The following code shows how we will write this:

```
import Glibc

struct MSBot {
  private let rMotor1: SBDigitalGPIO
  private let rMotor2: SBDigitalGPIO
  private let lMotor1: SBDigitalGPIO
  private let lMotor2: SBDigitalGPIO

  init?() {
    if let rMotor1 = SBDigitalGPIO(id:"gpio68", direction: .OUT),
       let rMotor2 = SBDigitalGPIO(id:"gpio44", direction: .OUT),
       let lMotor1 = SBDigitalGPIO(id:"gpio26", direction: .OUT),
       let lMotor2 = SBDigitalGPIO(id:"gpio46", direction: .OUT),
    {
      self.rMotor1 = rMotor1
      self.rMotor2 = rMotor2
      self.lMotor1 = lMotor1
      self.lMotor2 = lMotor2
    } else {
      return nil
    }
  }
}
```

Notice that the initializer is a failable initializer. If any of the `SBDigitalGPIO` instances fail to initialize then the `MSBot` type will fail to initialize. Also notice that we have two instances of the `SBDigitalGPIO` for each motor. The `rMotor1` and `rMotor2` instances are for the right motor and the `lMotor1` and `lMotor2` is for the left motor.

To make the motor spin, we need to bring one of the instances high and one low. For example, if we set rMotor1 high and rMotor2 low the motor will spin in one direction. If we reversed this, and set rMotor1 low and rMotor2 high, then the motor will spin in the opposite direction. If rMotor1 and rMotor2 were set the same (both high or both low) then the motor will stop spinning. With this in mind we can create methods to move the robot forward or backwards, to stop the robot, or to turn the robot. These methods are shown in the following code:

```
func stop() {
    _ = rMotor1.setValue(value: .LOW)
    _ = rMotor2.setValue(value: .LOW)
    _ = lMotor1.setValue(value: .LOW)
    _ = lMotor2.setValue(value: .LOW)
}

func forward() {
    _ = rMotor1.setValue(value: .HIGH)
    _ = rMotor2.setValue(value: .LOW)
    _ = lMotor1.setValue(value: .HIGH)
    _ = lMotor2.setValue(value: .LOW)
}

func reverse() {
    _ = rMotor1.setValue(value: .LOW)
    _ = rMotor2.setValue(value: .HIGH)
    _ = lMotor1.setValue(value: .LOW)
    _ = lMotor2.setValue(value: .HIGH)
}

func left() {
    _ = rMotor1.setValue(value: .LOW)
    _ = rMotor2.setValue(value: .HIGH)
    _ = lMotor1.setValue(value: .HIGH)
    _ = lMotor2.setValue(value: .LOW)
}

func right() {
    _ = rMotor1.setValue(value: .HIGH)
    _ = rMotor2.setValue(value: .LOW)
    _ = lMotor1.setValue(value: .LOW)
    _ = lMotor2.setValue(value: .HIGH)
}
```

In these methods, all we are doing is setting the digital pins either high or low. Don't worry too much about which pins are high and which are low at this point. The odds are, the first time we wire the robot and write our code, the wiring and the code will not match. This means when we call the `forward()` method for the first time, both motors many not spin in the same direction. Our main concern is making sure that the logic is correct. For example, for the `stop()` method all of the pins set either high or low.

Now that we have the code to initialize the robot and move it around, let's test it out. To test the code that controls the motors of a robot, I usually put the robot on a block similar to what mechanics do with cars. The following image demonstrates this:

Now let's test the motors and the controller code. Create the `main.swift` file and put the following code in it:

```
import Glibc

if let bot = MSBot() {
   bot.forward()
   usleep(2500000)
   bot.left()
   usleep(2500000)
   bot.right()
   usleep(2500000)
   bot.stop()
}
```

Now let's compile the project and run it. If everything is wired correctly, the robot motors will spin in the forward direction, then in the direction to turn the robot left, then to turn the robot right and finally the motors will stop. If the motors spin in the wrong direction, simply reverse the wires going in to the motor controller from the motor and then rerun the test.

Now that we have the motors configured correctly, it is time to add the MaxSonar EZ1 range finders. The following image shows how we would wire the range finders to the BeagleBone Black:

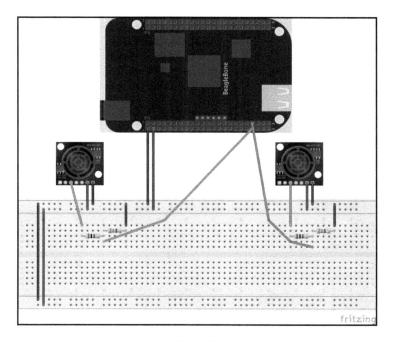

To connect the MaxSonar EZ1 sensor to the BeagleBone Black we connect a 1K ohm resistor to the analog voltage output pin on the MaxSonar. Then, connect a 3.3K ohm resistor in series with the 1K ohm resistor and tie the 3.3K ohm resistor to ground. Finally, we connect the analog pin from the BeagleBone Black in series with the two resistors as shown in the diagram. We will want to connect the sensor for the right side of the robot to AIN0 (P9 Expansion Header pin 39) and the sensor for the left side of the robot to AIN1 (P9 Expansion Header pin 40) on the BeagleBone Black.

Now we need to add the code that will read the range sensors. Add the following two properties to the MSBot type:

```
private let rRange: SBAnalog
private let lRange: SBAnalog
```

Now we need to initialize these properties in the initializer. The new initializer for the MSBot should look like this:

```
init?() {
    if let rMotor1 = SBDigitalGPIO(id:"gpio68", direction: .OUT),
       let rMotor2 = SBDigitalGPIO(id:"gpio44", direction: .OUT),
       let lMotor1 = SBDigitalGPIO(id:"gpio26", direction: .OUT),
       let lMotor2 = SBDigitalGPIO(id:"gpio46", direction: .OUT),
       let rRange = SBAnalog(id:"AIN0"),
       let lRange = SBAnalog(id:"AIN1")
    {
        self.rMotor1 = rMotor1
        self.rMotor2 = rMotor2
        self.lMotor1 = lMotor1
        self.lMotor2 = lMotor2
        self.rRange = rRange
        self.lRange = lRange
    } else {
        return nil
    }
}
```

We are now initializing the motor controller's digital GPIO pins and the range finder's analog pins. Finally, we will add a method to read the right range finder and another one to read the left range finder:

```swift
func leftRange() -> Double {
    if let rawValue = lRange.getValue() {
      let mv = (Double(rawValue) / 4096.0) * 1.80
      return mv/0.002148
    } else {
      return 0.0
    }
}

func rightRange() -> Double {
    if let rawValue = rRange.getValue() {
      let mv = (Double(rawValue) / 4096.0) * 1.80
      return mv/0.002148
    } else {
      return 0.0
    }
}
```

 I am using 2.148mV/in in this code. The datasheets state that we should get 6.4mV/in; however, every test I have done, on multiple MaxSonar range finders, has shown that the 2.148mV/in is accurate. If you are getting different results when you test your range finders, try adjusting this value.

Just like the motor controller, once we connect the range finders and write the code to control them, we will want to test it. Let's erase the old `main.swift` file and create a new one with the following code in it:

```swift
import Glibc

if let bot = MSBot() {
  while(true) {
    let rightRange = bot.rightRange()
    let leftRange = bot.leftRange()
    print("\(leftRange) .. \(rightRange)")
    usleep(250000)
  }
}
```

Now compile and run the project. As the ranges are being printed to the console, put an object in front of the range finders and see what distances are being printed out. The range finder should tell you pretty accurately what the range is to the object. Once the range finders are working properly, we are ready to write the code for our robot, but first let's see what the finished robot looks like if you were to print out the pieces from the downloadable code. This first image shows what the front of the robot looks like:

This next image shows what the back of the robot looks like:

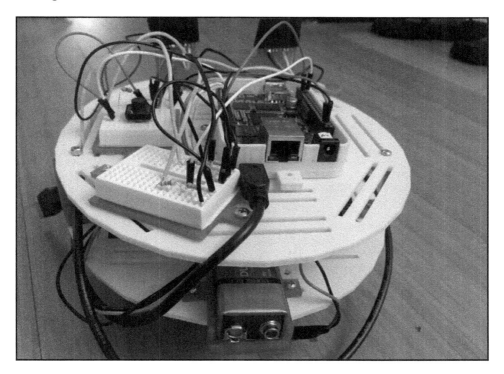

Let's create a new `main.swift` file that will contain the logic for our robot. We will start off by importing the `Glibc` module and creating an enumeration that defines the states our robot can be in. The enumeration is defined like this:

```
enum BotState {
    case STOPPED
    case FORWARD
    case REVERSE
    case TURNINGLEFT
    case TURNINGRIGHT
}
```

Next we will want to create a constant that defines how close an object has to be to trigger our robot to turn. We will use `18` inches in this example:

```
private let RANGE_CHECK = 18.0
```

We will need a variable to keep track of the current state of our robot. This can be done as shown in the following code:

```
var botState = BotState.STOPPED
```

Now we can create the logic for the robot:

```
if let bot = MSBot() {
  while(true) {

    let rightRange = bot.rightRange()
    let leftRange = bot.leftRange()

    if leftRange < RANGE_CHECK || rightRange < RANGE_CHECK {
      if leftRange < rightRange && botState != .TURNINGLEFT {
        bot.right()
        botState = .TURNINGRIGHT
      } else if rightRange < leftRange &&
          botState != .TURNINGRIGHT {
        bot.left()
        botState = .TURNINGLEFT
      } else if leftRange == rightRange &&
          botState != .TURNINGLEFT {
        bot.right()
        botState = .TURNINGRIGHT
      }
    } else if botState != .FORWARD {
      bot.forward()
      botState = .FORWARD
    }
    if botState == .FORWARD {
      usleep(25000)
    } else {
      usleep(50000)
    }
  }
}
```

In this code, we begin by creating an instance of the MSBot type and start a forever loop that will run until the process is stopped. Once we are in the loop, the first thing we do is to read both range finders and then check if either of the range finders have an object close enough to trigger a turn.

If there is an object close enough to trigger a turn, we check to see if the object is closer to the left side, the right side or is the same distance. Whichever side of the robot is closer to the object we turn in the opposite direction unless we are already turning. If we are already turning we continue to turn in the current direction.

If we do not have an object close enough to trigger a turn, we then check to see if the state of the robot is not .FORWARD. If the robot is not currently going in the forward direction we then tell it to go forward.

Finally the robot pauses for a split second and then loops back to go though the process again. Now, if we compile the project and let our robot go, it will move around the room avoiding the obstacles that it detects. Be careful, as the robot will not detect obstacles that are not at the height of MaxSonar range finders (ones that are too low) or cliffs. Definitely keep your new robot away from cliffs.

Summary

This was a very brief introduction to what you can do with Swift and the BeagleBone Black. There are so many different sensors that can be purchased; you are only limited by your imagination and creativity. While there are numerous tutorials that show how we can use JavaScript, Python and C to develop applications for the SBC, I have found that Swift is an excellent language for these boards as well.

17
Swift Formatting and Style Guide

Throughout my development experience, every time I learned a new programming language, there was usually some mention of how code for that language should be written and formatted. Early in my development career (which was a long time ago), these recommendations were very basic formatting recommendations, such as how to indent your code, or something like having one statement per line. It really wasn't until the last 10 to 12 years that I started to see complex and detailed formatting and style guides for different programming languages. Today, you will be hard pressed to find a development shop with more than two or three developers that does not have style/formatting guides for each language that they use. Even companies that do not create their own style guides generally refer back to some standard guide published by other companies, such as Google, Oracle, or Microsoft. These style guides help teams to write consistent and easy-to-maintain code.

What is a programming style guide?

Coding styles are very personal and every developer has his or her own preferred style. These styles can vary from language to language, person to person, and also change over time. The personal nature of coding styles can make it difficult to have a consistent and readable code base when numerous individuals are contributing to the code.

While most developers might have their own preferred styles, the recommended or preferred style between languages can vary. As an example, in C#, when we name a method or function, it is preferred to use camel case with the first letter being capitalized. While in most other languages, such as C, Objective-C, and Java, it is also recommended that we use camel case, but it is recommended that we make the first letter lower case.

The best applications are coded properly, and by properly we do not just mean that they function correctly but also that they are easy to maintain and the code is easy to read. It is hard for large projects and companies with a large number of developers to have code that is easy to maintain and read if every developer uses their own coding style. This is why companies and projects with multiple developers usually adopt programming style guides for each language that they use.

A programming style guide defines a set of rules and guidelines that a developer should follow while writing applications with a specific language within a project or company. These style guides can differ greatly between companies or projects and reflect how that company or project expects code to be written. These guides can also change over time. It is important to follow these style guides to maintain a consistent code base.

A lot of developers do not like the idea of being told how they should write code, and argue that as long as their code functions correctly, why should it matter how they format their code? I liken this to a basketball team. If all of the players come in believing that how they want to play is correct and believe that the team is better when they are doing their own thing, then that team is probably going to lose the majority of their games. It is impossible for a basketball team (or any sports team, for that matter) to win the majority of their games unless they are working together. It is up to the coach to make sure that everyone is working together and executing the same game plan, just like it is up to the team leader of the development project to make sure all the developers are writing code according to the adopted style guide.

Your style guide

The style guide that we define in this book is just a guide. It reflects the author's opinion on how Swift code should be written and is meant to be a good starting point for creating your own style guide. If you really like this guide and adopt it as it is, great. If there are parts that you do not agree with and you change them within your guide, that is great as well. The appropriate style for you and your team is the one that you and your team feel comfortable with, and it may or may not be different from the guide in this book. We should also point out that Swift is a very young language and people are still trying to figure out the appropriate style to use with Swift; therefore, what is recommended today may be frowned upon tomorrow. Don't be afraid to adjust your style guide as needed.

One thing that is noticeable in the style guide within this chapter, and most good style guides, is that there is very little explanation about why each item is preferred or not preferred. A style guide should give enough details so that the reader understands the preferred and non-preferred methods for each item, but should also be small and compact enough to make it easy and quick to read.

If a developer has questions about why a particular method is preferred, he or she should escalate that concern up to the development group. With that in mind, let's get started with the guide.

Do not use semicolons at the end of statements

Unlike a lot of languages, Swift does not require semicolons at the end of statements. Therefore, we should not use them. Let's take a look at the following code:

```
//Preferred Method
var name = "Jon"
print(name)

//Non-preferred Method
var name = "Jon";
print(name);
```

Do not use parentheses for conditional statements

Unlike a lot of languages, parentheses are not required around conditional statements; therefore, we should avoid using them unless they are needed for clarification. Let's take a look at the following code:

```
//Preferred Method
if speed == 300000000 {
    print("Speed of light")
}

//Non-Preferred Method
if (speed == 300000000) {
    print("Speed of light")
}
```

Naming

We should always use descriptive names with camel case for customer types, methods, variables, constants, and so on. Let's look at some general naming rules.

Custom types

Custom types should have a descriptive name that describes what the type is for. The name should begin with a capital letter and be in camel case. Here are examples of proper names and non-proper names based on our style guide:

```
// Proper Naming Convention
BaseballTeam
LaptopComputer
//Non-Proper Naming Convention
baseballTeam         //Starts with a lowercase letter
Laptop_Computer      //Uses an underscore
```

Functions and methods

Function names should be descriptive, describing the function or method. They should begin with a lowercase letter and be in camel case. Here are some examples of proper and non-proper names:

```
//Proper Naming Convention
getCityName
playSound

//
//Non-Proper Naming Convention
get_city_name        //All lowercase and has an underscore
PlaySound            //Begins with an upper case letter
```

Constants and variables

Constants and variables should have a descriptive name. They should begin with a lowercase letter and should also be in camel case. The only exception is when the constant is global; in that case, the name of the constant should contain all uppercase characters with the words separated by underscores. I have seen numerous guides that frown on having all uppercase names, but I personally like them for constants in the global scope because they stand out as globally, not locally, scoped. Here are some examples of proper and non-proper names:

```
//Proper Names
playerName
driveSize
PLAYERS_ON_A_TEAM    //Only for globally scoped constants

//Non-Proper Names
```

```
PlayerName              //Starts with uppercase letter
drive_size              //Has underscore in name
```

Indenting

The indenting width in Xcode, by default, is defined as four spaces, and the tab width is also defined as four spaces. We should use this default for Swift with Linux as well.

We should also add an extra blank line between functions/methods. We should also use a blank line to separate the functionality within a function or method. That being said, using many blank lines within a function or method might signify that we should break the function into multiple functions.

Comments

We should use comments as needed to explain how and why our code is written. We should use block comments before custom types and functions. We should use the double slashes to comment code in line. Here is an example of how to write comments:

```
/**
 * This is a block comment that should be used
 * to explain a class or function
 */
public class EmployeeClass {
  // This is an inline comment with double slashes
  var firstName = ""
  var lastName = ""

  /**
  Use Block comments for functions

  :parm: paramName  use this tag for parameters
  :returns:  explain what is returned
  */
  func getFullName() -> String {
    return firstName + " " + lastName
  }
}
```

When we are commenting methods, we should also use the documentation tags that will generate documentation in Xcode, as shown in the preceding example. At a minimum, we should use the following tags if they apply to our method:

- parameter: This is used for parameters

- `returns`: This is used for what is returned
- `throws`: This is used to document errors that may be thrown

Even though we are developing code for the Linux platform and we do not use Xcode on Linux, we should still use Xcode commit tags for consistency purposes.

Using the self keyword

Since Swift does not require us to use the `self` keyword when accessing properties or invoking methods of an object, we should avoid using it unless we need to distinguish between an instance property and local variables. Here is an example of when you should use the `self` keyword:

```
public class EmployeeClass {
  var firstName = ""
  var lastName = ""
  func setName(firstName: String, lastName: String) {
    self.firstName = firstName
    self.lastName = lastName
  }
}
```

Here is an example of when not to use the `self` keyword:

```
public class EmployeeClass {
    var firstName = ""
    var lastName = ""
    func getFullName() -> String {
        return self.firstName + " " + self.lastName
    }
}
```

Constants and variables

The difference between constants and variables is that the value of a constant never changes, whereas the value of a variable may change. Wherever possible, we should define constants rather than variables.

One of the easiest ways of doing this is to define everything as a constant, by default, and then change the definition to a variable only after you reach a point in your code that requires you to change it. In Swift, you will get a warning if you define a variable and then never change the value within your code.

Optional types

Only use optional types when absolutely necessary. If there is no absolute need for a nil value to be assigned to a variable, we should not define it as an optional.

Use optional binding

We should avoid forced unwrapping of optionals, as there is rarely any need to do this. We should prefer optional binding or optional chaining for force unwrapping.

The following examples show the preferred and non-preferred methods where the `myOptional` variable is defined as an optional:

```
//Preferred Method Optional Binding
if let value = myOptional {
  // code if myOptional is not nil
} else {
  // code if myOptional is nil
}

//Non-Preferred Method
if myOptional != nil {
  // code if myOptional is not nil
} else {
  //  code if myOptional is nil
}
```

If there is more than one optional that we need to unwrap, we should include them on the same line rather than unwrapping them on separate lines provided our business logic does not require separate paths if the unwrapping fails. The following examples show the preferred and non-preferred methods:

```
//Preferred Method Optional Binding
if let value1 = myOptional1, let value2 = myOptional2 {
  // code if myOptional1 and myOptional2 is not nil
} else {
  // code if myOptional1 and myOptional2 is nil
}

//Non-Preferred Method Optional Binding
if let value1 = myOptional1 {
    if let value2 = myOptional2 {
        // code if myOptional is not nil
    } else {
     // code if myOptional2 is nil
    }
```

```
} else {
  // code if myOptional1 is nil
}
```

Use optional chaining over optional binding for multiple unwrapping

When we need to unwrap multiple layers, we should use optional chaining over multiple optional binding statements. The following example shows the preferred and non-preferred methods:

```
//Preferred Method
if let color = jon.pet?.collar?.color {
    print("The color of the collar is \(color)")
} else {
    print("Cannot retrieve color")
}

//Non-Preferred Method
if let tmpPet = jon.pet, tmpCollar = tmpPet.collar {
    print("The color of the collar is \(tmpCollar.color)")
} else {
    print("Cannot retrieve color")
}
```

Use type inference

Rather than defining the variable types, we should let Swift infer the type. The only time we should define the variable or constant type is when we are not giving it a value while defining it. Let's take a look at the following code:

```
//Preferred method
var myVar = "String Type"  //Infers a String type
var myNum = 2.25           //Infers a Double type

//Non-Preferred method
var myVar: String = "String Type"
var myNum: Double = 2.25
```

Use shorthand declaration for collections

When declaring native Swift collection types, we should use the shorthand syntax and, unless absolutely necessary, we should initialize the collection. The following example shows the preferred and non-preferred methods:

```
//Preferred Method
var myDictionary: [String: String] = [:]
var strArray: [String] = []
var strOptional: String?

//
//Non-Preferred Method
var myDictionary: Dictionary<String,String>
var strArray: Array<String>
var strOptional: Optional<String>
```

Use switch rather than multiple if statements

Wherever possible, we should prefer to use a single `switch` statement over multiple `if` statements. The following example shows the preferred and non-preferred methods:

```
//Preferred Method
let speed = 300000000
switch speed {
case 300000000:
    print("Speed of light")
case 340:
    print("Speed of sound")
default:
    print("Unknown speed")
}

//Non-preferred Method
let speed = 300000000
if speed == 300000000 {
    print("Speed of light")
} else if speed == 340 {
    print("Speed of sound")
} else {
    print("Unknown speed")
}
```

Don't leave commented-out code in your application

If we comment out a block of code while we attempt to replace it, once we are comfortable with the changes, we should remove the code that we commented out. Having large blocks of code commented out can make the code base messy and harder to follow.

Summary

When we are developing an application in a team environment, it is important to have a well-defined coding style that everyone on the team adheres to. This allows us to have a code base that is easy to read and maintain.

If a style guide remains static for too long, it means that it is probably not keeping up with the latest changes within the language. What is too long is different for each language. For example, with the C language, too long will be defined in years, since the language is very stable; however, with Swift, the language is so new and changes are coming pretty often, thus too long can probably be defined as a couple of months.

It is recommended that we keep our style guides in a version control system so that we can refer to the older versions if need be. This allows us to pull out older versions of the style guide and refer back to them when we are looking at older code.

18
Adopting Design Patterns in Swift

While the first publication of the Gang of Four's *Design Patterns: Elements of Reusable Object-Oriented Software* was released in October 1994, I have only been paying attention to design patterns for the past nine or ten years. Similar to most experienced developers, when I first started reading about design patterns, I recognized a lot of them because I had already been using them without realizing what they were. I would have to say that in the past nine or ten years, since I first read about design patterns, I have not written a serious application without using at least one of the Gang of Four's design patterns. I will tell you that I am definitely not a design pattern zealot, and if I get into a conversation about design patterns, there are usually only a couple of them that I can name without having to look them up. However, what I do remember are the concepts behind the major patterns and the problems they are designed to solve. This way, when I encounter one of these problems, I can look up the appropriate pattern and apply it. So remember, as you go through this chapter, to take the time to understand the major concepts behind the design patterns rather than trying to memorize the patterns themselves.

In this chapter, we will take a look at the following topics:

- What design patterns are
- What types of patterns make up the creational, structural, and behavioral categories of design patterns
- How to implement the builder and singleton creational patterns in Swift
- How to implement the bridge, façade, and proxy structural patterns in Swift
- How to implement the strategy and commandbehavioral patterns in Swift

What are design patterns?

Every experienced developer has a set of informal strategies that shape how he or she designs and writes applications. These strategies are shaped by the experiences of developers and the obstacles they have had to overcome in previous projects. While these developers might swear by their own strategies, it does not mean that their strategies have been fully vetted. The use of these strategies can also introduce inconsistent implementations among different projects and developers.

While the concept of design patterns dates back to the mid 80s, they did not gain popularity until the Gang of Four released their book *Design Patterns: Elements of Reusable Object-Oriented Software*, published in 1994. The book's authors, *Erich Gamma, Richard Helm, Ralph Johnson*, and *John Vlissides* (also known as the Gang of Four), discuss the pitfalls of object-oriented programming and describe 23 classic software design patterns. These 23 patterns are broken up into three categories: creational, structural, and behavioral.

A design pattern identifies common software development problems and provides a strategy to deal with them. These strategies have been proven, over the years, to be an effective solution for the problems they are intended to solve. Using these patterns can greatly speed up our development process because they provide us with solutions that have already been proven to solve several common software development problems.

Another advantage that we gain when we use design patterns is consistent code that is easy to maintain, because when we look at our code months or years from now, we will recognize the patterns and understand what the code does. If we properly document our code and the design pattern we are implementing, it will also help other developers understand what our code is doing.

The two main philosophies behind design patterns are code reuse and flexibility. As a software architect, it is essential that we build reusability and flexibility into our code. This allows us to easily maintain our code in the future and makes it easier for our applications to expand to meet future requirements because we all know how quickly the requirements change.

While there is a lot to like about design patterns and they are extremely beneficial for both developers and architects, they are not the solution for world hunger that some developers make them out to be. Sometime in your development career, you will probably meet a developer or an architect who thinks that design patterns are immutable laws. These developers usually try to force the use of design patterns even when they are not necessary. A good rule of thumb is to make sure that you have a problem that needs to be fixed before you try to fix it.

Design patterns are starting points for avoiding and solving common programming problems. We can think of each design pattern as a recipe and we can tinker and adjust it to meet our particular tastes; however, we usually do not stray too far from the original recipe because we may mess it up.

There are also times when we do not have the recipe of a certain dish that we want to make, just like there are times when there isn't a design pattern to solve the problem we face. In such cases, we can use our knowledge of design patterns and their underlying philosophy to come up with an effective solution for our problem.

Design patterns are split into three categories. They are as follows:

- **Creational patterns**: Creational patterns support the creation of objects
- **Structural patterns**: Structural patterns concern types and object compositions
- **Behavioral patterns**: Behavioral patterns deal with communication between types

While the Gang of Four defined over 20 design patterns, we are only going to look at examples of some of the more popular patterns in this chapter. Let's start off by looking at creational patterns.

 Design patterns were originally defined for object-oriented programming. In this chapter, where possible, we will focus on implementing the patterns in a more protocol-oriented way. Therefore, the examples in this chapter may look a little different from examples in other design pattern books, but the underlying philosophy of the solutions will be the same.

Creational patterns

Creational patterns are design patterns that deal with how an object is created. These patterns create objects in a manner suitable for particular situations.

There are two basic ideas behind creational patterns. The first is encapsulating the knowledge of which concrete types should be created, and the second is hiding how the instances of these types are created.

The following are the five well-known patterns that are a part of the creational pattern category:

- **Abstract factory pattern**: This provides an interface for creating related objects without specifying the concrete type
- **Builder pattern**: This separates the construction of a complex object from its representation, so the same process can be used to create similar types
- **Factory method pattern**: This creates objects without exposing the underlying logic of how the object (or which type of object) is created
- **Prototype pattern**: This creates an object by cloning an existing one
- **Singleton pattern**: This allows one (and only one) instance of a class for the lifetime of an application

In this chapter, we are going to look at examples regarding how to implement the builder and singleton patterns in Swift. Let's start off by looking at one of the most controversial, and possibly the most overused, design patterns: the singleton pattern.

The singleton design pattern

The use of the singleton pattern is a fairly controversial subject in certain corners of the development community. One of the main reasons for this is that the singleton pattern is probably the most overused and misused pattern. Another reason why this pattern is controversial is that the singleton pattern introduces a global state into an application, which provides the ability to change the object at any point within the application. The singleton pattern can also introduce hidden dependencies and tight compiling. My personal opinion is that if the singleton pattern is used correctly, there is nothing wrong with using it. However, we do need to be careful not to misuse it.

The singleton pattern restricts the instantiation of a class to a single instance for the complete life of an application. This pattern is very effective when we need exactly one object to coordinate actions within our application. An example of a good use of a singleton is if our application communicates with a remote device over Bluetooth and we also want to maintain that connection throughout our application. Some would say that we could pass the instance of the connection class from one page to the next, which is essentially what a singleton is. In my opinion, the singleton pattern, in this instance, is a much cleaner solution because with the singleton pattern, any page that needs the connection can get it without forcing every page to maintain the instance. This also allows us to maintain the connection without having to reconnect each time we go to another page.

Understanding the problem

The problem the singleton pattern is designed to address is when we need one, and only one, instance of a type for the lifetime of our application. The singleton pattern is usually used when we need centralized management of an internal or external resource and a single global point of access. Another popular use of the singleton pattern is when we want to consolidate a set of related activities that are needed throughout our application, and do not maintain a state, in one place.

In `Chapter 5`, *Classes and Structures*, we used the singleton pattern in the text validation example because we only needed one instance of our text validation types throughout the lifetime of our application. In that example, we used the singleton pattern for our text validation types because we wanted to create a single instance of the types that could then be used by all the components of the application without requiring us to create new instances of the types. These text validation types did not have a state that could be changed. They only had methods that performed the validation on the text and constants that defined how to validate the text. While some may disagree with me, I believe types such as these are excellent candidates for the singleton pattern because there is no reason to create multiple instances of these types.

Understanding the solution

There are several ways to implement the singleton pattern in Swift. The way it is presented here uses class constants that were introduced in version 1.2 of Swift. With this method, a single instance of the class is created the first time we access the class constant. We will then use the class constant to gain access to this instance throughout the lifetime of our application. We will also create a private initializer that will prevent external code from creating additional instances of the class.

 Note that we use the word class in this description and not type. The reason for this is that the singleton pattern can only be implemented with reference types.

Implementing the singleton pattern

Let's take a look at how we can implement the singleton pattern with Swift. The following code example shows how to create a singleton class:

```
class MySingleton {
    static let sharedInstance = MySingleton()
    var number = 0

    private init() {}

}
```

We can see that within the MySingleton class, we created a static constant named sharedInstance that contains an instance of the MySingleton class. A static constant can be called without having to instantiate the class. Since we declared the sharedInstance static constant, only one instance will exist throughout the life cycle of the application, thereby creating the singleton pattern.

We also created the private initiator, which will restrict other code from creating another instance of the MySingleton class.

Now let's take a look at how this pattern works. The MySingleton pattern has another property named number, which is of the Int type. We will monitor how this property changes as we use the sharedInstance property to create multiple variables of the MySingleton type, as shown in the following code:

```
var singleA = MySingleton.sharedInstance
var singleB = MySingleton.sharedInstance
var singleC = MySingleton.sharedInstance

singleB.number = 2

print(singleA.number)
print(singleB.number)
print(singleC.number)

singleC.number = 3

print(singleA.number)
print(singleB.number)
print(singleC.number)
```

In this example, we used the `sharedInstance` property to create three variables of the `MySingleton` type. We initially set the `number` property of the second `MySingleton` variable (`singleB`) to 2. When we printed out the value of the `number` property for `singleA`, `singleB`, and `singleC`, we saw that the `number` property for all three equals 2. We then changed the value of the `number` property of the third `MySingleton` variable (`singleC`) to the number 3. When we printed out the value of the `number` property again, we saw that all three now have a value of 3. Therefore, when we change the value of the `number` property, in any of the instances, the values of all three change because each variable points to the same instance.

In this example, we implemented the singleton pattern using a reference (class) type because we wanted to ensure that only one instance of the type existed throughout our application. If we implemented this pattern with a value type, such as a structure or an enumeration, we would run the risk of there being multiple instances of our type. If you recall, each time we pass an instance of a value type, we are actually passing a copy of that instance, which means that if we implemented the singleton pattern with a value type, each time we called the `sharedInstance` property, we would receive a new copy, which would effectively break the singleton pattern.

The singleton pattern can be very useful when we need to maintain the state of an object throughout our application; however, be careful not to overuse it. The singleton pattern should not be used unless there is a specific requirement (*requirement* is the key word here) for having one, and only one, instance of our class throughout the life cycle of our application. If we are using the singleton pattern simply for convenience, then we are probably misusing it.

Keep in mind that while Apple recommends that we prefer value types to reference types, there are still plenty of examples, such as the singleton pattern, where we need to use reference types. When we continuously tell ourselves to prefer value types to reference types, it can be very easy to forget that there are times when a reference type is needed. Don't forget to use reference types with this pattern.

Now, let's take a look at the builder design pattern.

The builder design pattern

The builder pattern helps us with the creation of complex objects and enforces the process of how these objects are created. With this pattern, we generally separate the creation logic from the complex type and put it in another type. This allows us to use the same construction process to create different representations of the type.

Understanding the problem

The problem that the builder problem is designed to address arises when an instance of a type requires a large number of configurable values. We could set the configuration options when we create instances of the class, but that can cause issues if the options are not set correctly or we do not know the proper values for all of the options. Another issue is the amount of code that might be needed to set all of the configurable options each time we create an instance of our types.

Understanding the solution

The builder pattern solves this problem by introducing an intermediary, known as a builder type. This builder type contains most if not all of the information necessary to create an instance of the original complex type.

There are two methods that we can use to implement the builder pattern. The first method is to have multiple builder types, where each builder type contains the information to configure the original complex object in a specific way. In the second method, we implement the builder pattern with a single builder type that sets all of the configurable options to a default value, and then we could change the values as needed.

In this section, we will look at both ways to use the builder pattern in because it is important to understand how each works.

Implementing the builder pattern

Before we see how to the builder pattern, let's take a look at how to create a complex structure without the builder pattern and the problem we run into.

The following code creates a structure named `BurgerOld` and does not use the builder pattern:

```
structBurgerOld {
  var name: String
  var patties: Int
  var bacon: Bool
  var cheese: Bool
  var pickles: Bool
  var ketchup: Bool
  var mustard: Bool
  var lettuce: Bool
  var tomato: Bool

    init(name: String, patties: Int, bacon: Bool, cheese: Bool, pickles:
Bool,ketchup: Bool,mustard: Bool,lettuce: Bool,tomato: Bool) {
        self.name = name
        self.patties = patties
        self.bacon = bacon
        self.cheese = cheese
        self.pickles = pickles
        self.ketchup = ketchup
        self.mustard = mustard
        self.lettuce = lettuce
        self.tomato = tomato
    }
}
```

In the `BurgerOld` structure, we have several properties that define the condiments on the burger and also the name of the burger accordingly. Since we need to know which items are on the burgers and which items aren't, when we create an instance of the `BurgerOld` structure, the initializer requires us to define each item. This can lead to some complex initializations throughout our application, not to mention that if we had more than one standard burger (bacon cheeseburger, cheeseburger, hamburger, and so on), we would need to make sure that each was defined correctly. Let's take a look at how to create instances of the `BurgerOld` class:

```
// Create Hamburger
var burgerOld = BurgerOld(name: "Hamburger", patties: 1, bacon:     false,
cheese: false, pickles: false, ketchup: false, mustard:        false,
lettuce: false, tomato: false)

// Create Cheeseburger
var burgerOld = BurgerOld(name: "Cheeseburger", patties: 1, bacon:
false, cheese: true, pickles: false, ketchup: false, mustard:        false,
lettuce: false, tomato: false)
```

As we can see, creating instances of the `BurgerOld` type requires a lot of code. Now, let's look at a better way to do this. In this example, we will see how to use multiple builder types, where each type will define the condiments that are on a particular burger. We will begin by creating a `BurgerBuilder` protocol, which will have the following code in it:

```
protocol BurgerBuilder {
    var name: String {get}
    var patties: Int {get}
    var bacon: Bool {get}
    var cheese: Bool {get}
    var pickles: Bool {get}
    var ketchup: Bool {get}
    var mustard: Bool {get}
    var lettuce: Bool {get}
    var tomato: Bool {get}
}
```

This protocol simply defines the nine properties that will be required for any type that implements this protocol. Now, let's create two structures that implement this protocol with the `HamburgerBuilder` and `CheeseBurgerBuilder` structures:

```
struct HamBurgerBuilder: BurgerBuilder {
    let name = "Burger"
    let patties = 1
    let bacon = false
    let cheese = false
    let pickles = true
    let ketchup = true
    let mustard = true
    let lettuce = false
    let tomato = false
}

struct CheeseBurgerBuilder: BurgerBuilder {
    let name = "CheeseBurger"
    let patties = 1
    let bacon = false
    let cheese = true
    let pickles = true
    let ketchup = true
    let mustard = true
    let lettuce = false
    let tomato = false
}
```

In both the `HamburgerBuilder` and `CheeseBurgerBuilder` structures, all we are doing is defining the values for each of the required properties. In more complex types, we might need to initialize additional resources.

Now, let's take a look at our `Burger` structure, which will use instances of the `BurgerBuilder` protocol to create instances of itself. The following code shows this new `Burger` type:

```
structBurger {
  var name: String
  var patties: Int
  var bacon: Bool
  var cheese: Bool
  var pickles: Bool
  var ketchup: Bool
  var mustard: Bool
  var lettuce: Bool
  var tomato: Bool

  init(builder: BurgerBuilder) {
    self.name = builder.name
    self.patties = builder.patties
    self.bacon = builder.bacon
    self.cheese = builder.cheese
    self.pickles = builder.pickles
    self.ketchup = builder.ketchup
    self.mustard = builder.mustard
    self.lettuce = builder.lettuce
    self.tomato = builder.tomato
  }

  func showBurger() {
    print("Name:     \(name)")
    print("Patties: \(patties)")
    print("Bacon:    \(bacon)")
    print("Cheese:  \(cheese)")
    print("Pickles: \(pickles)")
    print("Ketchup: \(ketchup)")
    print("Mustard: \(mustard)")
    print("Lettuce: \(lettuce)")
    print("Tomato:  \(tomato)")
  }
}
```

The difference between this `Burger` structure and the `BurgerOld` structure shown earlier is the initializer. In the previous `BurgerOld` structure, the initializer took nine arguments-one for each constant defined in the structure. In the new `Burger` structure, the initializer takes one argument, which is an instance of a type that conforms to the `BurgerBuilder` protocol. This new initializer allows us to create instances of the `Burger` class similar to this:

```
// Create Hamburger
var myBurger = Burger(builder: HamBurgerBuilder())
myBurger.showBurger()
// Create Cheeseburger without tomatos
var myCheeseBurgerBuilder = CheeseBurgerBuilder()
var myCheeseBurger = Burger(builder: myCheeseBurgerBuilder)
// Lets addtomatos
myCheeseBurger.tomato = true
myCheeseBurger.showBurger()
```

If we compare how we create instances of the new `Burger` structure with the earlier `BurgerOld` structure, we can see that it is much easier to create instances of the `Burger` structure. We also know that we are correctly setting the property values for each type of burger because the values are set directly in the builder classes.

As we mentioned earlier, there is a second method that we can use to implement the builder pattern. Rather than having multiple builder types, we can have a single builder type that sets all of the configurable options to a default value; then we would change the values as needed. I use this implementation method a lot when I am updating older code because it is easy to integrate it with preexisting code.

For this implementation, we will create a single `BurgerBuilder` structure. This `BurgerBuilder` structure will be used to create instances of the `BurgerOld` structure and will, by default, set all of the ingredients to their default values. The `BurgerBuilder` structure also gives us the ability to change the ingredients that will go on the burger prior to creating instances of the `BurgerOld` structure. We create the `BurgerBuilder` structure, such as this:

```
struct BurgerBuilder {
  var name = "Burger"
  var patties = 1
  var bacon = false
  var cheese = false
  var pickles = true
  var ketchup = true
  var mustard = true
  var lettuce = false
  var tomato = false
```

```
mutatingfunc setPatties(choice: Int) {self.patties = choice}
mutatingfunc setBacon(choice: Bool) {self.bacon = choice}
mutatingfunc setCheese(choice: Bool) {self.cheese = choice}
mutatingfunc setPickles(choice: Bool) {self.pickles = choice}
mutatingfunc setKetchup(choice: Bool) {self.ketchup = choice}
mutatingfunc setMustard(choice: Bool) {self.mustard = choice}
mutatingfunc setLettuce(choice: Bool) {self.lettuce = choice}
mutatingfunc setTomato(choice: Bool) {self.tomato = choice}

    func buildBurgerOld(name: String) -> BurgerOld {
            return BurgerOld(name: name, patties: self.patties,
            bacon: self.bacon, cheese: self.cheese,
            pickles: self.pickles, ketchup: self.ketchup,
            mustard: self.mustard, lettuce: self.lettuce,
            tomato: self.tomato)
    }
}
```

In the `BurgerBuilder` structure, we define nine properties (ingredients) for our burger and then create a setter method for each of the properties except the `name` property. We also create one method named `buildBurgerOld()`, which will create an instance of the `BurgerOld` structure based on the values of the properties for the `BurgerBuilder` instance. We use the `BurgerBuilder` structure:

```
var burgerBuilder = BurgerBuilder()
burgerBuilder.setCheese(choice: true)
burgerBuilder.setBacon(choice: true)
var jonBurger = burgerBuilder.buildBurgerOld(name: "Jon's Burger")
```

In this example, we create an instance of the `BurgerBuilder` structure. We then use the `setCheese()` and `setBacon()` methods to add cheese and bacon to our burger. Finally, we call the `buildBurgerOld()` method to create the instance of the `Burger` structure.

As we can see, both methods that were used to implement the builder pattern greatly simplify the creation of our complex type. Both methods also ensured that our instances were properly configured with default values. If you find yourself creating instances of types with very long and complex initialization commands, I would recommend that you look at the builder pattern to see whether you can use it to simplify the initialization.

Now, let's take a look at structural design patterns.

Structural design patterns

Structural design patterns describe how types can be combined to form larger structures. These larger structures can generally be easier to work with and hide a lot of the complexity of the individual types. Most patterns in the structural pattern category involve connections between objects.

There are seven well-known patterns that are part of the structural design pattern type. They are as follows:

- **Adapter**: This allows types with incompatible interfaces to work together
- **Bridge**: This is used to separate the abstract elements of a type from the implementation so the two can vary
- **Composite**: This allows us to treat a group of objects as a single object
- **Decorator**: This lets us add or override behavior in an existing method of an object
- **Façade**: This provides a simplified interface for a larger and more complex body of code
- **Flyweight**: This allows us to reduce the resources needed to create and use a large number of similar objects
- **Proxy**: This is a type acting as an interface for another class or classes

In this chapter, we are going to look at examples of how to use the bridge, façade, and proxy patterns in Swift. Now, let's start looking at the bridge pattern.

The bridge pattern

The bridge pattern decouples the abstraction from the implementation so that they can both vary independently. The bridge pattern can also be thought of as a two-layer abstraction.

Understanding the problem

The bridge pattern is designed to solve a couple of problems, but the one we are going to focus on here tends to arise over time as new requirements come in with new features. At some point, as these new requirements and features come in, we will need to change how the features interact. Usually, this will eventually require us to refactor our code.

In object-oriented programming, this is known as an *exploding class hierarchy*, but it can also happen in protocol-oriented programming.

Understanding the solution

The bridge pattern solves this problem by taking the interacting features and separating the functionality specific to each feature from the functionality that is shared between them. A bridge type can then be created that will encapsulate the shared functionality, bringing them together.

Implementing the bridge pattern

To demonstrate how we would use the bridge pattern, we will create two features. The first feature is a message feature that will store and prepare a message that we wish to send out. The second feature is the sender feature, which will send the message through a specific channel, such as e-mail or SMS.

Let's start off by creating two protocols named `MessageProtocol` and `SenderProtocol`. `MessageProtocol` will define the requirements for types that are used to create messages. `SenderProtocol` will be used to define the requirements for types that are used to send the messages through specific channels. The following code shows how we would define these two protocols:

```
protocol MessageProtocol {
    var messageString: String {get set}
    init(messageString: String)
    func prepareMessage()
}

protocol SenderProtocol {
    func sendMessage(message: MessageProtocol)
}
```

The `MessageProtocol` protocol defines one stored property of the `String` type, named `messageString`. This property will contain the text of the message and cannot be nil. We also define one initiator and a method named `prepareMessage()`. The initiator will be used to set the `messageString` property and anything else required by the message type. The `prepareMessage()` method will be used to prepare the message prior to sending it. This method can be used to encrypt the message, add formatting, or do anything else to the message prior to sending it.

The `SenderProtocol` protocol defines a method named `sendMessage()`. This method will send the message through the channel defined by conforming types. In this function, we will need to ensure that the `prepareMessage()` method from the message type is called prior to sending the message.

Now let's see how we would define two types that would conform to the `MessageProtocol` protocol:

```
class PlainTextMessage: MessageProtocol {
    var messageString: String
    required init(messageString: String) {
        self.messageString = messageString
    }
    func prepareMessage() {
        //  Nothing to do
    }
}

class DESEncryptedMessage: MessageProtocol {
    var messageString: String
    required init(messageString: String) {
        self.messageString = messageString
    }
    func prepareMessage() {
    // Encrypt message here
        self.messageString = "DES: " + self.messageString
    }
}
```

Each of these types contains the required functionality to conform to the `MessageProtocol` protocol. The only real difference between these types is in the `prepareMessage()` methods. In the `PlainTextMessage` class, the `prepareMessage()` method is empty because we do not need to do anything to the message prior to sending it. The `prepareMessage()` method of the `DESEncryptionMessage` class would normally contain the logic to encrypt the message, but for our example, we will just prepend a `DES` tag to the beginning of the message, letting us know that this method was called.

Now let's create two types that will conform to the `SenderProtocol` protocol. These types would typically handle sending the message through a specific channel; however, in our example, we will simply print a message to the console:

```
class EmailSender: SenderProtocol {
  func sendMessage(message: MessageProtocol) {
  print("Sending through E-Mail:")
  print("\(message.messageString)")
    }
```

```
    }

class SMSSender: SenderProtocol {
    func sendMessage(message: MessageProtocol) {
        print("Sending through SMS:")
        print("\(message.messageString)")
        }
    }
```

Both the `EmailSender` and the `SMSSender` types conform to the `SenderProtocol` protocol by implementing the `sendMessage()` function.

We could now use these two features, as shown in the following code:

```
var myMessage = PlainTextMessage(messageString: "Plain Text Message")
myMessage.prepareMessage()
var sender = SMSSender()
sender.sendMessage(message: myMessage)
```

This would work great, and we could add code similar to this anywhere we needed to create and send a message. Let's say that one day in the near future, we get a requirement to add new functionality that would verify the message prior to sending it to make sure it meets the requirements of the channel we are sending the message through. To do this, we will start off by changing the `SenderProtocol` protocol to add the verification functionality. The new sender protocol would look like this:

```
protocol SenderProtocol {
    var message: MessageProtocol? {getset}
    func sendMessage()
    func verifyMessage()
}
```

To the `SenderProtocol` protocol, we added a method named `verifyMessage()` and also added a property named `message`. We also changed the definition of the `sendMessage()` method. The original `SenderProtocol` protocol was designed to simply send the message, but now we need to verify the message prior to calling the `sendMessage()` function; therefore, we couldn't simply pass the message to it like we did in the previous definition.

Now, we will need to change the types that conform to the `SenderProtocol` protocol to make them conform to this new protocol. The following code shows how we would make these changes:

```
class EmailSender: SenderProtocol {
    var message: MessageProtocol?
    func sendMessage() {
        print("Sending through E-Mail:")
```

```
      print("\(message!.messageString)")
      }
   func verifyMessage() {
     print("Verifying E-Mail message")
      }
}

class SMSSender: SenderProtocol {
   var message: MessageProtocol?
   func sendMessage() {
     print("Sending through SMS:")
     print("\(message!.messageString)")
      }
   func verifyMessage() {
     print("Verifying SMS message")
      }
}
```

With the changes that we made to the types that conform to the `SenderProtocol` protocol, we will need to change how our code uses these types. The following example shows how we would now use them:

```
var myMessage = PlainTextMessage(messageString: "Plain Text Message")
myMessage.prepareMessage()
var sender = SMSSender()
sender.message = myMessage
sender.verifyMessage()
sender.sendMessage()
```

These changes are not that hard to make; however, without the bridge pattern, we would need to refactor our entire code base and make the change everywhere that we are sending messages. The bridge pattern tells us that when we have two hierarchies that interact together closely, we should put this interaction logic into a bridge type that will encapsulate the logic in one spot. This way, when we receive new requirements or enhancements, we can make the change in one spot, thereby limiting the refactoring that we have to do. We could make a bridge type for our message and sender hierarchies, as shown in the following example:

```
struct MessageingBridge {
staticfunc sendMessage(message: MessageProtocol, sender: SenderProtocol) {
     var sender = sender
     message.prepareMessage()
     sender.message = message
     sender.verifyMessage()
     sender.sendMessage()
      }
}
```

The logic of how our messaging and sender hierarchies interact is now encapsulated in the `MessagingBridge` structure. Now when the logic needs to change, we will only need to make the change to this one structure rather than having to refactor our entire code base.

The bridge pattern is a very good pattern to remember and use. There have been (and still are) times that I have regretted not using the bridge pattern in my code because, as we all know, requirements change frequently, and being able to make the changes in one spot rather than throughout the code base can save us a lot of time in the future.

Now, let's take a look at the next pattern in the structural category: the façade pattern.

The façade pattern

The façade pattern provides a simplified interface to a larger and more complex body of code. This allows us to make our libraries easier to use and understand by hiding some of the complexities. It also allows us to combine multiple APIs into a single, easier to use API, which is what we will see in our example.

Understanding the problem

The façade pattern is often used when we have a complex system that has a large number of independent APIs that are designed to work together. Sometimes, it is hard to tell where we should use the façade pattern during our initial application design. The reason for this is that we normally try to simplify our initial API design; however, over time and as requirements change and new features are added, our APIs become more and more complex and then it becomes pretty evident where we should have used the façade pattern. A good rule to use is that if you have several APIs that are working closely together to perform a task, you should think about using the façade pattern.

Understanding the solution

The main idea of the façade pattern is to hide the complexity of our APIs behind a simple interface. This offers us several advantages, with the most obvious being that it simplifies how we interact with the APIs. It also promotes loose coupling, which allows our APIs to change as requirements change, without the need to refactor all of the code that uses them.

Implementing the façade pattern

To demonstrate the façade pattern, we will create three APIs: `HotelBooking`, `FlightBooking`, and `RentalCarBooks`. These APIs will be used to search for and book hotels, flights, and rental cars for trips. While we could very easily call each of the APIs individually in our code, we are going to create a `TravelFacade` structure that will allow us to access the functionality of the APIs in single calls.

We will begin by defining the three APIs. Each of the APIs will need a data storage class that will store the information about the hotel, flight, or rental car. We will start off by implementing the hotel API:

```
struct Hotel {
    //Information about hotel room
}

struct HotelBooking {
    static func getHotelNameForDates(to: NSDate, from: NSDate) ->
      [Hotel]? {
        let hotels = [Hotel]()
        //logic to get hotels
        return hotels
    }

    static func bookHotel(hotel: Hotel) {
        // logic to reserve hotel room
    }
}
```

The hotel API consists of `Hotel` and `HotelBooking` structures. The `Hotel` structure will be used to store the information about a hotel room; the `HotelBooking` structure will be used to search for a hotel room and also to book the room for our trip. The flight and rental car APIs are very similar to the hotel API. The following code shows both of these APIs:

```
struct Flight {
    //Information about flights
}

struct FlightBooking {
    static func getFlightNameForDates(to: NSDate, from: NSDate) ->
      [Flight]? {
        let flights = [Flight]()
        //logic to get flights
        return flights
    }
```

```
        static func bookFlight(flight: Flight) {
            // logic to reserve flight
        }
    }


    struct RentalCar {
        //Information about rental cars
    }

    struct RentalCarBooking {
        static func getRentalCarNameForDates(to: NSDate, from: NSDate)
          -> [RentalCar]? {
            let cars = [RentalCar]()
            //logic to get flights
            return cars
        }

        static func bookRentalCar(rentalCar: RentalCar) {
            // logic to reserve rental car
          }
    }
```

In each of these APIs, we have a structure that is used to store information and a structure that is used to provide the search or booking functionality. In our initial design, it would have been very easy to call these individual APIs within our application; however, as we all know, requirements tend to change, which causes our APIs to change over time. By using the façade pattern here, we are able to hide how we implement the APIs; therefore, if we need to change how the APIs work in the future, we will only need to update the façade type rather than refactor all of our code. This makes our code easier to maintain and update in the future. Now let's take a look at how we will implement the façade pattern, by creating a TravelFacade class:

```
    class TravelFacade {

        var hotels: [Hotel]?
        var flights: [Flight]?
        var cars: [RentalCar]?

        init(to: NSDate, from: NSDate) {
            hotels = HotelBooking.getHotelNameForDates(to: to, from: from)
            flights = FlightBooking.getFlightNameForDates(to: to, from:
                from)
            cars = RentalCarBooking.getRentalCarNameForDates(to: to, from:
                from)
        }
```

```
    func bookTrip(hotel: Hotel, flight: Flight, rentalCar:
      RentalCar) {
        HotelBooking.bookHotel(hotel: hotel)
        FlightBooking.bookFlight(flight: flight)
        RentalCarBooking.bookRentalCar(rentalCar: rentalCar)
    }
}
```

The `TravelFacade` class contains the functionality to search the three APIs and also book a hotel, flight, and rental car. We can now use the `TravelFacade` class to search for and book hotels, flights, and rental cars without having to directly access the individual APIs.

As was mentioned at the start of this chapter, it is not always obvious where we should use the façade pattern in our initial design. A good rule to follow is that if we have several APIs that are working together to perform a task, we should think about using the façade pattern.

Now, let's take a look at our last structural pattern, which is the proxy design pattern.

The proxy design pattern

In the proxy design pattern, there is one type acting as an interface for another type or API. This wrapper class, which is the proxy, can then add functionality to the object, make the object available over a network, or restrict access to the object.

Understanding the problem

We can use the proxy pattern to solve a number of problems, but I find that I mainly use this pattern to solve two problems.

The first problem that I use the proxy pattern to solve is when I want to create a layer of abstraction between a single API and my code. The API could be a local or remote API, but I usually use this pattern to put an abstraction layer between my code and a remote service. This will allow changes to the remote API without the need to refactor large portions of our code.

The second problem that I use the proxy pattern to solve is when I need to make changes to an API but I do not have the code or there is already a dependency on the API elsewhere in the application.

Understanding the solution

To solve these problems, the proxy pattern tells us that we should create a type that will act as an interface for interacting with the other type or API. In our example, we will see how to use the proxy pattern to add functionality to an existing type.

Implementing the proxy pattern

In this section, we will look at an example of the proxy pattern by creating a `House` class that we can add multiple floor plans to, where each floor plan represents a different story of the house. Let's begin by creating a `FloorPlanProtocol` protocol:

```
protocol FloorPlanProtocol {
  var bedRooms: Int {get set}
  var utilityRooms: Int {get set}
  var bathRooms: Int {get set}
  var kitchen: Int {get set}
  var livingRooms: Int {get set}
}
```

In the `FloorPlanProtocol` protocol, we define five properties that will represent the number of rooms contained in each floor plan. Now, let's create an implementation of the `FloorPlanProtocol` protocol named `FloorPlan`, which is as follows:

```
struct FloorPlan: FloorPlanProtocol {
  var bedRooms = 0
  var utilityRooms = 0
  var bathRooms = 0
  var kitchen = 0
  var livingRooms = 0
}
```

The `FloorPlan` class implements all five properties required from `FloorPlanProtocol` and assigns default values to them. Next, we will create the `House` class, which will represent a house:

```
class House {
publicvar stories = [FloorPlanProtocol]()

  func addStory(floorPlan: FloorPlanProtocol) {
    stories.append(floorPlan)
  }
}
```

Within our `House` class, we have an array of `FloorPlanProtocols` objects, where each floor plan will represent one story of the house. We also have one function named `addStory()`, which accepts an instance of a type that conforms to the `FloorPlanProtocol` protocol. This function will add the floor plan to the array of `FloorPlanProtocols` protocols.

If we think about the logic of this class, there is one problem that we might encounter. The problem is that we are allowed to add as many floor plans as we want, which may lead to houses that are 60 or 70 stories high. This would be great if we were building skyscrapers, but we just want to build basic single-family houses. If we want to limit the number of floor plans without changing the `House` class (either we cannot change it or we simply do not want to), we can implement the proxy pattern. The following example shows how to implement the `HouseProxy` class, where we limit the number of floor plans we can add to the house:

```
class HouseProxy {
 var house = House()

  func addStory(floorPlan: FloorPlanProtocol) -> Bool {
    if house.stories.count < 3 {
      house.addStory(floorPlan: floorPlan)
      return true
    }
    else {
      return false
    }
  }
}
```

We begin the `HouseProxy` class by creating an instance of the `House` class. We then create a method named `addStory()` that lets us add a new floor plan to the house. In the `addStory()` method, we check to see whether the number of stories in the house is fewer than three; if so, we add the floor plan to the house and return `true`. If the number of stories is equal to or greater than three, then we do not add the floor plan to the house and return `false`. Let's see how we would use this proxy:

```
var ourHouse = HouseProxy()

var basement = FloorPlan(bedRooms: 0, utilityRooms: 1, bathRooms:    1,
kitchen: 0, livingRooms: 1)
var firstStory = FloorPlan(bedRooms: 1, utilityRooms: 0,    bathRooms: 2,
kitchen: 1, livingRooms: 1)
var secondStory = FloorPlan(bedRooms: 2, utilityRooms: 0,    bathRooms: 1,
kitchen: 0, livingRooms: 1)
var additionalStory = FloorPlan(bedRooms: 1, utilityRooms: 0,    bathRooms:
```

```
1, kitchen: 1, livingRooms: 1)

print(ourHouse.addStory(floorPlan: basement))
print(ourHouse.addStory(floorPlan: firstStory))
print(ourHouse.addStory(floorPlan: secondStory))
print(ourHouse.addStory(floorPlan: additionalStory))
```

In our example code, we start off by creating an instance of the `HouseProxy` class named `ourHouse`. We then create four instances of the `FloorPlan` class, each with a different number of rooms. Finally, we attempt to add each of the floor plans to the `ourHouse` instance. If we then run the code, we will see that the first three instances of the `floorplans` class were added to the house successfully, but the last one wasn't because we are only allowed to add three floors.

The proxy pattern is very useful when we want to add some additional functionality or error checking to a type but we do not want to change the actual type itself. We can also use it to add a layer of abstraction between a remote or local API.

Now, let's take a look at behavioral design patterns.

Behavioral design patterns

Behavioral design patterns explain how types interact with each other. These patterns describe how different instances of types send messages to each other to make things happen.

There are nine well-known patterns that are part of the behavioral design pattern type. They are as follows:

- **Chain of responsibility**: This is used to process a variety of requests, each of which may be delegated to a different handler.
- **Command**: This creates objects that can encapsulate actions or parameters so that they can be invoked later or by a different component.
- **Iterator**: This allows us to access the elements of an object sequentially without exposing the underlying structure.
- **Mediator**: This is used to reduce coupling between types that communicate with each other.

- **Memento**: This is used to capture the current state of an object and store it in a manner that can be restored later.

- **Observer**: This allows an object to publish changes to its state. Other objects can then subscribe so they can be notified of any changes.
- **State**: This is used to alter the behavior of an object when its internal state changes.
- **Strategy**: This allows one out of a family of algorithms to be chosen at runtime.
- **Visitor**: This is a way of separating an algorithm from an object structure.

In this section, we are going to look at examples of how to use the strategy and command patterns in Swift. Let's start off by looking at the command pattern.

The command design pattern

The command design pattern lets us define actions that we can execute later. This pattern generally encapsulates all the information needed to call or trigger the actions at a later time.

Understanding the problem

There are times in our applications when we need to separate the execution of a command from its invoker. Typically, this is when we have a type that needs to perform one of several actions; however, the choice of which action to use needs to be made at runtime.

Understanding the solution

The command pattern tells us that we should encapsulate the logic for the actions into a type that conforms to a command protocol. We can then provide instances of the command types for use by the invoker. The invoker will use the interface provided by the protocol to invoke the required actions.

Implementing the command pattern

In this section, we will demonstrate how to use the command pattern by creating a `Light` type. In this type, we will define the `lightOnCommand` and `lightOffCommand` commands and will use the `turnOnLight()` and `turnOffLight()` methods to invoke these commands.

We will begin by creating a protocol named `Command` that all of our commands types will conform to. Here is the `Command` protocol:

```
protocol Command {
  func execute()
}
```

This protocol contains a method named `execute`, which will be used to execute the command. Now, let's look at the command types that the `Light` type will use to turn the light on and off. They are as follows:

```
struct RockerSwitchLightOnCommand: Command {
  func execute() {
    print("Rocker Switch:  Turning Light On")
  }
}

struct RockerSwitchLightOffCommand: Command {
  func execute() {
    print("Rocker Switch:  Turning Light Off")
  }
}
struct PullSwitchLightOnCommand: Command {
  func execute() {
    print("Pull Switch:  Turning Light On")
  }
}

struct PullSwitchLightOffCommand: Command {
  func execute() {
    print("Pull Switch:  Turning Light Off")
  }
}
```

The RockerSwitchLightOffCommand, RockerSwitchLightOnCommand, PullSwitchLightOnCommand, and PullSwitchLightOffCommand commands all conform to the Command protocol by implementing the execute() method; therefore, we will be able to use them in our Light type. Now, let's look at how to implement the Light type:

```
class Light {
  var lightOnCommand: Command
  var lightOffCommand: Command

  init(lightOnCommand: Command, lightOffCommand: Command) {
    self.lightOnCommand = lightOnCommand
    self.lightOffCommand = lightOffCommand
  }

  func turnOnLight() {
    self.lightOnCommand.execute()
  }

  func turnOffLight() {
    self.lightOffCommand.execute()
  }
}
```

In the Light type, we start off by creating two variables, named lightOnCommand and lightOffCommand, that will contain instances of types that conform to the Command protocol. We then create an initiator that lets us set both of the commands when we initiate the type. Finally, we create the turnOnLight() and turnOffLight() methods, which we will use to turn the light on and off. In these methods, we call the appropriate command to turn the light on or off.

We can then use the Light type, as shown here:

```
var on = PullSwitchLightOnCommand()
var off = PullSwitchLightOffCommand()
var light = Light(lightOnCommand: on, lightOffCommand: off)

light.turnOnLight()
light.turnOffLight()

light.lightOnCommand = RockerSwitchLightOnCommand()
light.turnOnLight()
```

In this example, we begin by creating an instance of the `PullSwitchLightOnCommand` type, named `on`, and an instance of the `PullSwitchLightOffCommand` type, named `off`. We then create an instance of the `Light` type using the two commands that we just created and call the `turnOnLight()` and `turnOffLight()` methods of the `Light` instance to turn our light on and off. In the last two lines, we change the `lightOnCommand` method, which was originally set to an instance of the `PullSwitchLightOnCommand` class, to an instance of the `RockerSwitchLightOnCommand` type. The `Light` instance will now use the `RockerSwitchLightOnCommand` type whenever we turn the light on. This allows us to change the functionality of the `Light` type during runtime.

There are a number of benefits to using the command pattern. One of the main benefits is that we are able to set which command to invoke at runtime, which also lets us swap the commands with different implementations that conform to the `Command` protocol as needed throughout the life of the application. Another advantage of the command pattern is that we encapsulate the details of the command implementations within the command types themselves rather than in the container type.

Now, let's look at our last design pattern, which is the strategy pattern.

The strategy pattern

The strategy pattern is pretty similar to the command pattern in that they both allow us to decouple implementation details from our calling type and also allow us to switch the implementation out at runtime. The big difference is that the strategy pattern is intended to encapsulate algorithms. By swapping out an algorithm, we are expecting the object to perform the same functionality but in a different way. In the command pattern, when we swap out the commands, we are expecting the object to change the functionality of the object.

Understanding the problem

There are times in our applications when we need to change the backend algorithm used to perform an operation. Typically, this is when we have a type that has several different algorithms that can be used to perform the same task; however, the choice of which algorithm to use needs to be made at runtime.

Understanding the solution

The strategy pattern tells us that we should encapsulate the algorithm in a type that conforms to a strategy protocol. We can then provide instances of the strategy types for use by the invoker. The invoker will use the interface provided by the protocol to invoke the algorithm.

Implementing the strategy pattern

In this section, we will demonstrate the strategy pattern by showing you how we could swap out compression strategies at runtime. Let's begin this example by creating a `CompressionStrategy` protocol that each one of our compression types will conform to. Take a look at the following code:

```
protocol CompressionStrategy {
   func compressFiles(filePaths: [String])
}
```

This protocol defines a method named `compressFiles()` that accepts a single parameter, which is an array of strings that contain the paths to the files we want to compress. We will now create two structures that conform to the `CompressionStrategy` protocol. These are the `ZipCompressionStrategy` and the `RarCompressionStrategy` structures, which are as follows:

```
struct ZipCompressionStrategy: CompressionStrategy {
   func compressFiles(filePaths: [String]) {
     print("Using Zip Compression")
   }
}

struct RarCompressionStrategy: CompressionStrategy {
   func compressFiles(filePaths: [String]) {
     print("Using RAR Compression")
   }
}
```

Both of these structures implement the `CompressionStrategy` protocol by having a method named `compressFiles()`, which accepts an array of strings. Within these methods, we simply print out the name of the compression that we are using. Normally, we would implement the compression logic in these methods.

Now, let's look at our `CompressContent` class, which will be called to compress the files:

```
class CompressContent {
  var strategy: CompressionStrategy

  init(strategy: CompressionStrategy) {
    self.strategy = strategy
  }

  func compressFiles(filePaths: [String]) {
    self.strategy.compressFiles(filePaths: filePaths)
  }
}
```

In this class, we start off by defining a variable-named strategy that will contain an instance of a type that conforms to the `CompressStrategy` protocol. We then create an initiator that will be used to set the compression type when the class is initiated. Finally, we create a method named `compressFiles()`, which accepts an array of strings that contain the paths to the list of files that we wish to compress. In this method, we compress the files using the compression strategy that is set in the strategy variable.

We will use the `CompressContent` class, as follows:

```
var filePaths = ["file1.txt", "file2.txt"]
var zip = ZipCompressionStrategy()
var rar = RarCompressionStrategy()

var compress = CompressContent(strategy: zip)
compress.compressFiles(filePaths:filePaths)

compress.strategy = rar
compress.compressFiles(filePaths: filePaths)
```

We begin by creating an array of strings that contains the files we wish to compress. We also create an instance of both the `ZipCompressionStrategy` and `RarCompressionStrategy` types. We then create an instance of the `CompressContent` class, setting the compression strategy to the `ZipCompressionStrategy` instance, and call the `compressFiles()` method, which will print the `Using zip compression` message to the console. We then set the compression strategy to the `RarCompressionStrategy` instance and call the `compressFiles()` method again, which will print the `Using rar compression` message to the console.

The strategy pattern is really good for setting the algorithms to use at runtime, which also lets us swap the algorithms out with different implementations as needed by the application. Another advantage of the strategy pattern is we encapsulate the details of the algorithm within the strategy types themselves and not in the main implementation type.

This concludes our tour of design patterns in Swift.

Summary

Design patterns are solutions to software design problems that we tend to see over and over again in real-world application design. These patterns are designed to help us create reusable and flexible code. Design patterns can also make our code easier to read and understand for other developers and also for ourselves when we look back at our code months or years later.

If we look at the examples in this chapter carefully, we will notice that one of the backbones of design patterns is the protocol. Almost all design patterns (the singleton design pattern is an exception) use protocols to help us create very flexible and reusable code.

If this was the first time that you really looked at design patterns, you probably noticed some similarities to strategies that you have used in the past in your own code. This is expected when experienced developers are first introduced to design patterns. I would also encourage you to read more about design patterns because they will definitely help you to create more flexible and reusable code.

Index

www.ingramcontent.com/pod-product-compliance
Lightning Source LLC
Chambersburg PA
CBHW062048050326

40690CB00016B/3017